THE LEGACY OF
THE GREAT WAR

THE LEGACY OF
THE GREAT WAR

NINETY YEARS ON

EDITED BY JAY WINTER

UNIVERSITY OF MISSOURI PRESS
COLUMBIA AND LONDON
&
THE NATIONAL WORLD WAR I MUSEUM
KANSAS CITY, MISSOURI

Library of Congress Cataloging-in-Publication Data

The legacy of the Great War : ninety years on / edited by Jay Winter.
    p. cm.
    From public forums sponsored by the National World War I Museum at
Liberty Memorial in Kansas City in 2007 and 2008.
    Includes bibliographical references and index.
    ISBN 978-0-8262-1871-1 (cloth : alk. paper) – ISBN 978-0-8262-1872-8
(pbk. : alk. paper)
    1. World War, 1914-1918–Congresses. I. Winter, J. M. II. National World
War I Museum at Liberty Memorial.
  D504.L44 2009
  940.3–dc22   2009025754

∞™ This paper meets the requirements of the
American National Standard for Permanence of Paper
for Printed Library Materials, Z39.48, 1984.

Design and composition: Jennifer Cropp
Printer and binder: Thomson-Shore, Inc.
Typefaces: Minion and Trajan Pro

The University of Missouri Press offers its grateful acknowledgment to the
National World War I Museum for a generous contribution in support of
the publication of this volume.

CONTENTS

FOREWORD
Sir John Keegan
vii

PREFACE AND ACKNOWLEDGMENTS
Jay Winter
xi

INTRODUCTION
Approaching the History of the Great War: A User's Guide
Jay Winter, Yale University
1

ONE
War Origins
Niall Ferguson, Harvard University
Paul Kennedy, Yale University
33

TWO
Waging Total War: Learning Curve or Bleeding Curve?
Holger Afflerbach, University of Leeds
Gary Sheffield, University of Birmingham
61

THREE
The Soldiers' War: Coercion or Consent?
John Horne, Trinity College, Dublin
Len Smith, Oberlin College
91

FOUR
Ending the Great War: The Peace That Failed?   123
John Milton Cooper, University of Wisconsin at Madison
Margaret MacMillan, St. Antony's College, Oxford

FIVE
The Great War: Midwife to Modern Memory?   159
Jay Winter, Yale University
Robert Wohl, University of California at Los Angeles

EPILOGUE
Hew Strachan, All Souls College, Oxford   185

NOTES   199

SELECT BIBLIOGRAPHY   205

INDEX   213

FOREWORD

Sir John Keegan

The Great War continues to tantalize and fascinate Europeans. Recently too, Americans have begun to take an interest in a conflict that harmed their country little, though their involvement in it inaugurated their involvement in world affairs that now dominates their politics. America's generation-long forgetfulness of the war derives from its involvement in the Second World War, in which it played a larger part than any of the European powers, except Russia, but also from the abiding memory of its Civil War of 1861–1865, with which the Great War so readily bears comparison in terms of scale, intensity, duration and loss of life. Commemoration of family involvement in the Civil War and the Great War is a concern that Americans share with Europeans, greatly aided on the European side of the Atlantic by the work of the Commonwealth War Graves Commission, which builds and maintains the magnificent cemeteries of both world wars. Visiting the cemeteries that lie shoulder-to-shoulder in parts of Belgium and northern France is a familiar experience for the British, not only by those who are searching for the resting place of a family member.

The cemeteries cast a powerful spell on those who visit, as Americans as well as British often do, the effect not only of the events they commemorate and the sheer, almost unimaginable number of deaths commemorated, but also by the manner of commemoration. Because they are the work of three outstanding twentieth-century British artists—Edwin Lutyens, the architect; Gertrude Jekyll, the gardener; and Rudyard Kipling, the poet—they achieve a powerful cultural effect. They are, in fact, unique statements of the national culture, literary and visual. The decisions taken by the original members of the commission—that each of the dead should have a separate grave and headstone, that the headstone should record age, date, and place of death, regiment, and rank, but that ranks should be intermingled at the burial place and that each headstone should allow space for an inscription by the bereaved—ensures that the cemeteries are powerful expressions of both national and personal grief. Even had the official histories not been written the cemeteries would serve as a collective memorialization of the war, from which its chronology and topography could be pieced together. Indeed the cemeteries today are much more visited than the official histories are read.

That reflects both the supremely successful role of the commissioners and the rather less successful role of official historians. The historians decided upon a strictly, indeed coldly impersonal objective top-down treatment of what is described, containing no criticism of commanders, or orders, or management of operations, so that a great national, continental tragedy is narrated entirely emotionlessly. It is not surprising that, as a result, the histories failed to satisfy the urge to know and to understand felt by the war's survivors and that they are left increasingly unread, except by experts and professionals. The deliberate coldness of the Official Histories naturally stimulated an alternative approach, at first of protest and denial by survivors, such as Robert Graves and Siegfried Sassoon, whose work succeeded in giving the Great War an even worse reputation than it deserved, but eventually a growingly imaginative and creative memorialization by a generation of often young historians, who had no personal acquaintance with the reality of the war, often of any war, except through family memory. Such history writing stirred controversy, and perhaps inevitably sides were taken. Schools of opinion formed, particularly among those who objected to the narration of the war in terms of the capability of generals, indeed of their demonization. In the 1950s bitter quarrels arose between denouncers of Douglas Haig, the British commander-in-chief, and the surprising number of his defenders led by John Terraine. There was no outcome to this dispute, except that Haig's attackers were gradually obliged to proceed more cautiously. In time, the argument over the tactics and strategy of the Western Front, for that was the essence of the Haig argument, became less a question of personality and more over collective failings. Why was the British army apparently so much less good than the German at adapting to stalemate? The leadership of the dispute devolved upon Professor Gary Sheffield, who proposed the idea of a "learning curve." Yes, he concluded, the British were slow to adapt but, under close examination, it could be seen that they were adapting and improving to the point where, by 1918, they had become formidable Western Front combatants, highly and profitably skilled in the coordination of infantry and machine guns and their artillery support. The theory of the "learning curve" was persuasive to many, though not to all. I was one who felt that, in circumstances where infantry battalions commonly suffered casualties of between 30 and 50 percent of their strengths in trench-to-trench offensives, it would have been inconceivable for junior officers and their soldiers not to have learned from their mistakes and to seek better ways of implementing orders received from the higher staffs, and that the idea of a "learning curve" was therefore too obvious to be incisive. This difference of opinion has not been resolved and the debate is therefore stuck. It may never be resolved.

Because of the difficulty of dealing with large collective issues—the nature of the war experience, its effect on societies, the attempt made by war leaders, civil and military, to deal with it and control it, we are left with and continually driven back at the reading and analysis of the individual experience, which consistently proves more satisfactory. Thus almost all the best-known and most widely used books about the Great War are personal. That is true even of books that attempt to achieve to capture a collective vision, thus Paul Fussell's *Great War and Modern Memory*, though apparently a cultural history of the war and the generation that fought it, is in practice a categorization and appreciation of dozens of memoirs and works of poetry, in essence the most individualistic literary forms. Paul Fussell, who is a very considerable scholar, wanting to write about the Great War as a European event, decided that he could do so only by meditating on the record of individual experience. There is no dispute about the success of his approach. *The Great War and Modern Memory* is a magnificent book, a triumph of the imagination, which has become and will remain an essential point of entry to all, scholars and laypeople alike, who seek to understand the war.

Other less celebrated but equally creative books also follow the individual and personal theme. One of the panelists discouraged members of the audience from making autobiographical interventions. Historians cannot be so constrained. All who write about war do so ultimately from a personal standpoint. I recognize the autobiographical in my own motivation. My father was a soldier of the Great War, so were his two brothers. Questioning him as I did constantly during the Second World War, about what "the last war," as we called it, had been like, I was answered with carefully sanitized replies. My aunt, the three boys' sister, was more forthcoming. She told me that my grandmother said that, on taking my father, her youngest son, to the railway station to leave for France in 1917, the words "I shall never see you again" were torn from her. Her words proved to be true. All three boys returned intact from the war. But during that winter, she succumbed to a seasonal illness, not the great influenza of the war's last winter, but a simple fever. My grandmother, my aunt said, was so wracked by the anxiety of having three sons together on the Western Front that she had lost all resistance to illness and slipped away. My aunt's disclosure of our humble but dutiful and patriotic family's experience of the Great War, my grandmother's agonized expectation of the worst, my father's compassionately camouflaged account of the reality, proved decisive in forming my historian's outlook. War memories, I decided, were always edited, but it is impossible to edit the raw terror of those who are left behind at home. Somewhere in the no-man's land between the collective record and the personal abides the truth.

Preface and Acknowledgments

This is an unusual book within the historical literature on the First World War. There are entire libraries devoted to the subject, and the avalanche of publications on it shows no sign of abating, now nearly a century after the outbreak of war in 1914. Indeed, it is likely that the pace of publication will pick up in the run-up to the war's centennial.

What makes this book different is its conversational, dialogic character. Instead of focusing, as most books and learned articles do, on the single voice of the historian reporting his or her findings, derived from research in archives and libraries, we offer here a glimpse of how historians operate. Even though few historians say so, it is true that the form of professional reflection about the past we call history is collective in character. That is why we present here conversations; we show historians engaging with one another, probing arguments, disagreeing, moving beyond earlier positions, rethinking interpretations, in effect, learning from one another. Anyone who has practiced history knows that this is the way historians work. They are not hermits, and both through teaching and in professional meetings, operate within a society of scholars and scholarship.

These five scholars' forums on the Great War constitute a glimpse at the way historical writing happens. They bring together eminent historians who have studied the Great War over decades, and who brought to these proceedings much of the excitement and clash of ideas that make this subject one of the most dynamic and attractive in our field.

The choice of subjects to explore in these public meetings was, to a degree, arbitrary. The first considers war origins; the second and third consider the military history of the war first in terms of command and then in terms of the war the soldiers endured. The fourth considers peacemaking in 1919, and the fifth the longer-term cultural consequences of the war.

To be sure, other themes could have been chosen. There is a vast literature on the Great War and women's history; equally rich is the field of imperial history and the war, linked as it must be to the mobilization of manpower and economic resources in every corner of the world for the major combatants on the Western front. The war as a catapult of revolutionary movements has spawned its own varied literature, reaching from the Bolshevik revolutions of 1917, to the origins of the national socialist movement in Germany, the fascist movement in Italy, and the founding of the Chinese Communist Party in 1919. It is clear that at least a dozen scholars' forums could have been organized, without even remotely exhausting the subject or the audience. The subjects we have chosen are essential ones, though, and many students thinking about time-honored questions on the period of the Great War would do well to ponder the words and interpretations presented in this book.

The occasion that precipitated these meetings was the opening of the National World War I Museum at Liberty Memorial, designated by Act of Congress as the American national museum of the 1914–1918 war. Given the fact that American participation in World War I left fewer traces on American life and culture than it did in Europe, the opening of the museum in Kansas City in 2006 presented a unique opportunity to bring to a wide audience the fruits of scholarship on the war written by scholars working on both sides of the Atlantic.

The transnational character of these scholars' outlook is evident: four are British-born; one Canadian; one German; four American. Though raised and educated in Britain, Niall Ferguson and Paul Kennedy work at Harvard and Yale, respectively. John Horne was born in England and raised in Australia. He now teaches at Trinity College, Dublin. Margaret MacMillan was born and educated in Canada and England and now is warden of St. Antony's College, Oxford. Holger Afflerbach was born and raised in Germany and now holds a chair at the University of Leeds. Len Smith teaches at Oberlin College; John Milton Cooper's chair is at the University of Wisconsin at Madison; and Robert Wohl's is at UCLA.

Jay Winter teaches at Yale, to which he returned after thirty-five years of teaching in England and Israel. Each is a recognized authority on the history of the Great War. This is a cosmopolitan set of historians working in a very cosmopolitan field.

The exchanges in this book originated from a series of five public conversations between these ten scholars, who in 2007 and 2008 examined the legacy of the Great War. The series was organized by Jay Winter and George Thompson and delivered at three venues in Missouri: the National World War I Museum at Liberty Memorial in Kansas City; the Kansas City Public Library; and the Harry S. Truman Presidential Library and Museum in Independence. The public conversations were recorded, transcribed, and revised by the scholars and editor. In the first four scholars' forums, Jay Winter served as interlocutor and chaired the sessions; the fifth was chaired by Crosby Kemper. We are grateful to have, in addition to the insights of these scholars, the reflections of Sir John Keegan and Hew Strachan on the legacy of the war and how historians have examined it.

The public conversations and this book could not have been produced without the vision and commitment of many people. From the start the National World War I Museum at Liberty Memorial in Kansas City, Missouri, nurtured this project and brought it to fruition. Their personal and financial support was indispensable; in many ways, this book is their achievement. Utterly essential to the collective effort was the work of George Thompson, who handled the complex logistics and preparations for each and every meeting. I could not have completed my task as interlocutor of the public conversations and as editor of this book without his generous and sturdy assistance. I am grateful, too, for the support of R. Crosby Kemper III, chief executive officer of the Kansas City Public Library, both in providing a congenial second site for the public conversations, but also in providing financial support for the editorial work needed to see the project through. Steve Berkheiser, former executive director of the Liberty Memorial Association; Michael Devine, director of the Harry S. Truman Presidential Library and Museum; and Brian Alexander, president and chief executive officer of the National World War I Museum at Liberty Memorial, went out of their way to help see this unusual project through. My thanks go wholeheartedly to them all.

The staffs of the National World War I Museum at Liberty Memorial, the Kansas City Public Library, and the Harry S. Truman Presidential

Library and Museum deserve much credit for what we have been able to do. In particular we wish to thank these people for their invaluable help in facilitating the public events: at the National World War I Museum at Liberty Memorial: James Barkley, Doran Cart, Mark Cox, Carl DiCapo, Theresa Farris, Denise Rendina, Eli Paul, and David Wilson. We are equally indebted to Mark Adams, of the Harry S. Truman Presidential Library and Museum, and Henry Fortunato, of the Kansas City Public Library, for their generous help in hosting these discussions, and to Erik Bergrud, Park University, for his assistance in promoting and developing the five events.

A project of this scale could not have been possible without the generous financial support of several institutions and foundations. We must record once more our gratitude to the National World War I Museum at Liberty Memorial, for their help, alongside that of the Kansas City Public Library, the Harry S. Truman Presidential Library and Museum, Oppenstein Brothers Foundation, Stanley H. Durwood Foundation, Sosland Foundation, Metropolitan Community College, and Park University. Together they have brought about this experiment in public history, understood as an effort to bring together the academy and the public in the creation of informed citizenship. That sharing of purpose and ideas is what this book is all about.

Jay Winter
New Haven, Connecticut

THE LEGACY OF
THE GREAT WAR

Approaching the History of the Great War:
A User's Guide

Jay Winter, Yale University

Writing history is always a dialogue. When historians put pen to paper, they carry with them the accumulated interpretations their colleagues have developed over time. Frequently, it is against the grain of these interpretations, in opposition to them, in exasperation with them, that historians decide to write. To be sure, there are many occasions when historians concur with their colleagues or draw their attention to previously untapped sources on matters of common interest. But most of the time, historians argue, make objections, and present through their writing a portrait of the past different from those available in print.

This is true both within a generation of historians and between generations. Today's scholars engage with colleagues still at work, and in this book, we can see how they do so dialogically. But the dialogue is also with those historians in the past whose works still inspire reflection, confirmation, elaboration, and on occasion, refutation. We historians are part of a very long engagement with the Great War, an engagement that will continue long after we cease to practice our profession.

The dialogic nature of historical practice therefore makes it necessary to place one generation's thinking about the Great War alongside those of earlier generations. And we are now the fourth generation of historians who have approached the history of the war of 1914–1918. Everyone writing today draws upon or reflects upon earlier publications in this field.

In a nutshell, there have been three earlier generations of writing to which current scholars refer, sometimes explicitly, most times, implicitly.[1] The first was what I will term "the Great War generation." These were scholars, former soldiers, and public officials who had direct knowledge of the war either through their own military service or through alternative service to their country's war effort. They wrote history from the top down, by and large through direct experience of the events they described. The central actor portrayed in these books was the state, either in its *dirigiste* forms at home or at the front. The most voluminous of these efforts was the 133-book effort to write the economic and social history of the war, sponsored by the Carnegie Endowment for International Peace. Most of these tomes were penned by men who helped run the war or who had to deal with its aftershocks.

This first generation was also composed of men whose memoirs went over the ground again for evident purposes of self-justification. This took many forms, from books by generals and cabinet ministers about their contributions to victory, to exculpatory reminiscences about those trying to evade responsibility for defeat. There were also official histories, many of which were written by former soldiers for the benefit of the various national staff colleges, trying one at a time to frame "lessons" for the future. These works were frequently highly technical and so detailed that they took decades to appear. The delay diminished their significance for planning the next war in more efficient ways.

The second generation may be termed the generation "fifty years on." This group of historians wrote in the late 1950s and 1960s, and wrote not only the history of politics and decision making at the top, but also the history of society, defined as the history of social structures and social movements. Of course the two kinds of history, political and social, went together, but they were braided together in different ways than in the interwar years. Many of these scholars had the benefit of sources unknown or unavailable before the Second World War. The "fifty-year rule" enabling scholars to consult state papers meant that all kinds of documents could be exploited by those writing in the 1960s, which threw new light on the history of the war.

In the 1960s, there was much more use of film and visual evidence than in the first generation, though in the interwar years battlefield guides and collections of photographs of devastation and weaponry were produced in abundance. After the Second World War, the age of television history began, and attracted an audience to historical narratives greater than ever before. This became evident in the size of the audience for new and powerful television documentaries of the war. In 1964 the BBC launched its second channel with the monumental twenty-six-part history of the war, exhaustively researched in film archives and vetted by an impressive group of military historians.[2]

Many of the millions of people who saw this series had lived through the war. In 1964, the young men who have fought and survived were mostly above the age of seventy, but what made the series a major cultural event was that the families of the survivors, and of those who did not come back, integrated these war stories into their own family narratives. The Great War thus escaped from the academy into the much more lucrative and populous field of public history, represented by museums, special exhibitions, films, and now television.

By the 1960s, the Imperial War Museum in London had surpassed many other sites as the premier destination of visitors to London. It remains to this day a major attraction in the capital, just as does the Australian War Memorial, an equally impressive museum and site of remembrance in the Australian capital, Canberra.

There was more than a little nostalgia in the celebration by survivors of "fifty years on." By 1964, the European world that went to war in 1914 no longer existed. All the major imperial powers that joined the struggle had been radically transformed. The British Empire was a thing of the past; so was *Algérie française,* and the French *mission civilisatrise* in Africa and South Asia. The German empire was gone, and so were most of its eastern territories, ceded to Poland after 1945. Austria, Hungary, and Yugoslavia were small independent states. And while the Soviet Union resembled Czarist Russia in some respects, these continuities were dwarfed by the massive transformation of Soviet society since 1917.

The nostalgia of 1964 was, therefore, for a world which had fallen apart in the Great War. For many people, the blemishes and ugliness of much of that world were hidden by a kind of sepia-toned reverence for the days before the conflict. "Never such innocence, / Never before or since," wrote Philip Larkin in a poem whose title referred not to 1914, but to the more archaic "MCMXIV." This poem was published in 1964. In much historical writing, as much as in historical documentaries, the dramatic tension derived from juxtaposing this set of prelapsarian images with the devastation and horror of the Western front, and with the sense of decline, a loss of greatness, which marked the post-1945 decades in Britain and beyond. Whatever was wrong with the world seemed to be linked to 1914, to the time when a multitude of decent men went off to fight one war and wound up fighting a much more terrible one.

Decencies were betrayed, some argued, by a blind elite prepared to sacrifice the lives of the masses for vapid generalizations like "glory" or "honor." This populist strain may be detected in much writing about the war in the 1960s, and in the study of social movements which arose out of it. The fiftieth anniversary of the Gallipoli landing provoked a surge of interest in the Great War in Australia and New Zealand, where the loss of the battle was eclipsed by the birth of these two nations. Similarly heroic were narratives of the Bolshevik Revolution, celebrating its fiftieth anniversary in 1967. It is hardly surprising, therefore, that many scholars told us much more about the history of labor, of women, of ordinary people during the conflict than had scholars working in the interwar years.

The third generation may be termed the "Vietnam generation." Its practitioners started writing in the 1970s and 1980s, when a general reaction against military adventures like the war in Vietnam took place in Britain and Europe as well as in the United States. This was also the period in Europe when public opinion turned against the nuclear deterrent, and when the 1973 Middle Eastern war had dangerous effects on the economies of the developed world. The glow of the "just war" of 1939–1945 had faded, and a new generation was more open to a view that war was a catastrophe to both winners and losers alike.

This was the environment in which darker histories of the Great War emerged. There were still scholars who insisted that the Great War was a noble cause, won by those who had right on their side. But there were others who came to portray the Great War as a futile exercise, a tragedy, a stupid, horrendous waste of lives, producing nothing of great value aside from the ordinary decencies and dignities thrown away by blind and arrogant leaders.

The most influential works were written by three very different historians. Paul Fussell, a veteran of the Second World War wounded in combat, produced a classic literary study, *The Great War and Modern Memory* in 1975.[3] He is a professor of literature, who fashioned an interpretation of how soldiers came to understand the war they found in 1914–1918 as an ironic event, one in which anticipation and outcome were wildly different. It was a time when the old romantic language of battle seemed to lose its meaning. Writers twisted older forms to suit the new world of trench warfare, one in which mass death was dominant and where, under artillery and gas bombardment, soldiers lost any sense that war was a glorious thing. Fussell termed this style the "ironic" style and challenged us to see war writing throughout the twentieth century as built upon the foundations laid by the British soldier writers of the Great War.

John (now Sir John) Keegan produced a book a year later which paralleled Fussell's. An instructor in the Royal Military College at Sandhurst, but a man whose childhood infirmities ensured he would never go to war, Keegan asked the disarmingly simple question: "Is battle possible?" The answer, published in *The Face of Battle* in 1976,[4] was yes, perhaps long ago, but now in the twentieth century, battle presented men with terrifying challenges. The men who fought at the Battle of Agincourt in 1415 could run to the next hill to save their lives. Foot soldiers converging on Waterloo four centuries later could arrive a day late. But in 1916, at the Battle of the Somme, there was no escape. Given the industrialization of warfare, the air above the trenches on the Somme was filled with lethal projectiles from which there was no escape. Mass death in that battle, and the other great conflict of 1916 at Verdun, pushed soldiers beyond the limits of human endurance. Nothing like the set battles of the First World War followed in the 1939–1945 war, though Stalingrad came close to replicating the horror of the Somme and Verdun. Here was a military historian's book, but one whose starting point was humane and to a degree psychological. The soldiers' breaking point was Keegan's subject, and with power, subtlety, and technical authority, he opened a new chapter in the study of military history as a humane discipline.

In 1979, Eric Leed, a historian steeped in the literature of anthropology, wrote a similarly pathbreaking book. *No Man's Land: Combat and Identity in World War I*[5] borrowed brilliantly from the work of the anthropologist Victor Turner. He had examined people in a liminal condition, no longer part of an older world from which they had come, and unable to escape from the midpoint, the no-man's land, in which they found themselves. Here is the emotional landscape of the trench soldiers of the Great War. They were men who could never come home again, for whom war was their home, and who re-created it in the years following the Armistice. Here was the world of shell-shocked men, but also that of the *Freikorps,* militarized freebooters of the immediate post-war period, who prepared the ground for the Nazis.

In all three cases, and by reference to very different sources, the subject at hand was the tragedy of the millions of men who went into the trenches and who came out, if at all, permanently marked by the experience. They bore what some observers of the survivors of Hiroshima termed the "death imprint"; the knowledge that their survival was a purely arbitrary accident. Here we may see some traces of the antinuclear movement, putting alongside one another Japanese civilians and Great War soldiers. The moral and political differences between the two cases are evident, but the wreckage of war, so these writers seemed to say, is at the heart of the civilization in which we live.

It is probably not an exaggeration to say that these three books, alongside others of the time, helped create a tragic interpretation of the Great War, one in which victimhood and violence were braided together in such a way as to tell a fully European story of the war, one to which the founders of the European Union clearly reacted. From the 1970s on, European integration was an attempt to move away from the notion of the nation-state as that institution which had the right to go to war, as Raymond Aron put it. The result has been a progressive diminution of the role of the military in the political and social life of most European countries. James Sheehan asked the question in a recent book *Where Have All the Soldiers Gone?*[6] The answer is, they have fled from the landscape of war so devastatingly presented in the works of Fussell, Keegan, Leed, and others.

Now we are in a fourth generation of writing on the Great War. I would like to term it the "transnational generation." The term "global" describes both the tendency to write about the war in more than European terms and the efforts many historians have made to go beyond the history of the war in Britain, or Germany, or France, or elsewhere, to the history of the war as trans-European, trans-Atlantic, and beyond.

Here was the first global war among industrialized countries, reaching the Middle East and Africa, the Falkland Islands and China, drawing soldiers into the epicenter in Europe from Vancouver to Capetown to Bombay and to Adelaide. Here was a war that gave birth to the Turkey of Ataturk and to the Soviet Union of Lenin and Stalin. Decolonization arose from a war that had promised self-determination and had produced very little of the kind. Economic troubles arose directly out of the war, and these were sufficiently serious to undermine the capacity of the older imperial powers to pay for their imperial and quasi-imperial footholds around the world.

The transnational generation has benefited enormously from the work of their predecessors. One reason why I took on the task of acting as "impresario" of these conversations was the wish to show to Americans the richness of the new transnational history of the 1914–1918 conflict. This is not a field very well developed in the United States, but it has a bright future ahead of it.

A word or two may be useful to distinguish the international approach from what I have termed the transnational approach to the history of the Great War. For nearly a century, the Great War was framed in terms of a system of international relations in which the national and imperial levels of conflict and cooperation were taken as given. Transnational history takes multiple levels of historical experience as given, levels which are both below and above the national level. Thus the history of mutiny is transnational, in that it happened in different armies for different reasons, some of which are strikingly similar to the sources of protest and refusal in other armies. The history of commemoration, cited in the discussion on remembrance in chapter 5, also happened on many levels, and the national is not the most significant, not the most enduring. The peace treaties following the Great War, discussed in chapter 4, show the meaning of the transnational in other ways. Now we can see that the war was both the apogee and the beginning of the end of imperial power, spanning and eroding national and imperial boundaries. Erez Manela's work on "the Wilsonian moment" is a case in point. He reconfigures the meaning of the Versailles settlement by exploring its unintended consequences in stimulating movements of national liberation in Egypt, India, Korea, and China. Instead of telling us about the interplay of Great Power politics, he shows how non-Europeans invented their own version of

Wilson in their search for a kind of self-determination that he, alongside Lloyd George, Clemenceau, and Orlando, was unprepared to offer to them. Who could have imagined that the decision these men took to award rights to Shandong Province, formerly held by Germany, not to China but to Japan would lead to major rioting and the formation of the Chinese Communist Party?[7]

Historians of the revolutionary moment in Europe itself between 1917 and 1921 have approached their subject more and more as a transnational phenomenon. After all, both revolutionaries and the forces of order who worked to destroy them were well aware of what may be termed the cultural transfer of revolutionary strategy and tactics. In recent years, these exchanges have been analyzed at the urban and regional levels, helping us to see the complexity of a story somewhat obscured by treating it solely in national terms. Comparative urban history has established the striking parallels between the challenges urban populations faced in different warring states. Now we can answer in the affirmative the question as to whether there is a metropolitan history of warfare. In important respects, the residents of Paris, London, and Berlin shared more with one another than they did with their respective rural compatriots. These experienced communities had a visceral reality somewhat lacking even in the imagined communities of the nation. Here we must be sensitive to the way contemporaries used the language of nation and empire to describe loyalties and affiliations of a much smaller level of aggregation. A journalist asking British troops on the Western front whether they were fighting for the Empire, got a "yes" from one soldier. His mates asked him what he meant. The answer was that he was fighting for the Empire Music Hall in Hackney, a working-class district of London. This attachment to the local and the familiar was utterly transnational.[8]

Another subject now understood more in transnational than in international terms is the history of women in wartime. Here is a theme which we were unable to address within the constraints of this introductory set of conversations. This is clearly an omission which in future we hope to rectify. But even a cursory reading of the historical literature on this subject shows that patriarchy, family formation, and the persistence of gender inequality were transnational realities in the period of the Great War.[9]

Furthermore, the war's massive effects on civilian life precipitated a movement of populations of staggering proportions. Refugees in France, the Netherlands, and Britain from the area occupied by the Western front numbered in the millions. So did those fleeing the fighting in the borderlands spanning the old German, Austro-Hungarian, and Russian empires. One scholar has estimated that perhaps 20 percent of the population of Russia was on the move, heading for safety wherever it could be found during the Great War. And that population current turned into a torrent throughout Eastern Europe during the period of chaos surrounding the Armistice. What made it worse was that the United States closed its gates to such immigrants, ending one of the most extraordinary periods of transcontinental migration in history. Thus population transfer, forced or precipitated by war, transformed the ethnic character of many parts of Greece, Turkey, the Balkans, and the vast tract of land from the Baltic states to the Caucasus. Such movements antedated the war, but they grew exponentially after 1914. This is why it makes sense to see the Great War as having occasioned the emergence of that icon of transnational history in the twentieth century, the refugee, with his or her pitiful belongings slung over shoulders or carts.[10] The photographic evidence of this phenomenon is immense.

The potential embedded in this transnational approach is evident in one institution explicitly committed to escaping from the national confines of the history of the war: the Historial de la Grande Guerre at Péronne, France. The Historial is a museum of the war, designed by historians, alongside museography and written in three languages—English, French, and German, located at the site of German headquarters during the Battle of the Somme, that vast bloodletting in 1916 which the German writer Ernst Jünger termed the birthplace of the twentieth century.[11] Together with four historians of the Great War from France and Germany—Jean-Jacques Becker, Gerd Krumeich, Stéphane Audoin-Rouzeau, and Annette Becker—we reached out across national frontiers to create a new kind of museum, one which treated the Great War as a transnational catastrophe.[12] This blending of different national viewpoints and emphases suited the new Europe of the 1990s, when it became apparent that to understand the integration of Europe at the end of the twentieth century, you had to understand the disintegration of Europe at its beginning. It is this optic which guides the conversations recorded in this book.

It is important to note, though, that these new initiatives in comparative history have built on the work of the three generations of scholars that preceded them. The history of the Great War that has emerged in recent years, in particular in the work of the scholars whose conversations we present here, is additive, cumulative, and multifaceted. No social or cultural historian of any standing ignores the history of the nation; to do so would be absurd. War is such a protean event that it touches every facet of human life. Earlier scholars pointed the way ahead; we who have collectively constructed this book acknowledge their presence among us.

Our modest claim is that these conversations reflect a variety of interests and questions that historians ask today about that foundational moment of the twentieth century, the Great War. For that very reason, it is appropriate that now, nearly a century after the Great War, we take stock of the current state of knowledge in the field. Ours is a rapidly growing community of scholars, and the questions our students ask are unlikely to be precisely the same as the ones we pose. Still, there is a rough consensus that anyone who is seriously interested in the Great War has to confront the five central questions examined here.

The first is that of war origins. Here is a field of study that dates back to the very first days of the war, when each combatant country tried to present its case to the court of public opinion. Historians joined in the pamphlet war and claimed, in every country at war, that its leaders had gone to war reluctantly; that each was forced to fight a defensive war, provoked by adversaries; and that there was no alternative but to enter the conflict.

Right at the end of the war, these assertions were repeated by the victorious powers, which inserted in the peace treaty of 1919 clause 231, known as "the war guilt clause." This is unequivocal in its judgment: "The Allied and Associated Governments affirm and Germany accepts the responsibility of Germany and her allies for causing all the loss and damage to which the Allied and Associated Governments and their nationals have been subjected as a consequence of the war imposed upon them by the aggression of Germany and her allies." The German delegation at Versailles had no choice but to accept this clause and to sign the document, but this verdict was contested at the time and remains controversial today.

The first generation of historians who looked at this matter was parti pris. That is, they by and large justified their country's position on responsibility for the outbreak of the war. It was only in the 1960s that the full documentation emerged to enable alternative views to appear. In the most controversial case, the German historian Fritz Fischer, who was trained as a theologian, found what he considered shocking evidence of German direct responsibility for the outbreak of war, which they saw as a means to gain both European and world mastery. What made this argument so explosive was the implication that Hitler's aggressiveness was not exceptional in German history, but rather a radicalized and more extreme version of what had happened before, during the Great War.

One of the sticking points between Fischer and his critics was how to interpret the September program of war aims, produced by the Chancellor Bethmann-Hollweg. Here was a plan, announced by the chancellor on 9 September 1914 for the annexation of Belgium, the iron and coal provinces of northern France, and the Baltic states, as well as for the establishment of an economic union on the continent under Germany. How do we read this document? Two speakers, Niall Ferguson and Paul Kennedy, do so in different ways. For Ferguson, this document followed the British declaration of war against Germany, and was a reaction against an entirely unnecessary British engagement in the conflict. Without Britain on the Allied side, the French would have been defeated. Imperial Germany would not have collapsed; hence there would have been no space on the political right for the Nazi movement or on the left for the Communists. Perhaps what the European Union is today—a bloc with Germany at its political and economic heart— could have emerged much earlier, and without the tragedy of the Second World War and the Holocaust. Kennedy's views are different, and the framework in which he locates not only this document but German war policy follows his earlier work on the German-British antagonism and on British and German naval policy. Here is a debate that will go on and on. But what sets it apart from earlier discussions is the global reach of the historians who engage with these questions. Grand strategy is their subject, and no part of the world is beyond their reach in piecing together the difficult history of the outbreak of the Great War.

Kennedy[13] and Ferguson[14] are British-born historians of empire. Both started research in German archives, moved to the broader German-British collision in the Great War, and have established preeminent positions as historians of empire, its rise, decline, and reconfiguration. Both command wide audiences for their books among the general public. It was said that Paul Kennedy's *Rise and Fall of the Great Powers* was published in Japanese in two volumes, so that commuters would have an easier time reading it on their bullet trains home after work. Niall Ferguson is a major figure in history beyond the academy, too. His works, like those of Paul Kennedy, are available in numerous translations. Ferguson has entered the field of television history, too, narrating a very popular series on *War of the World* for Channel 4 in Britain. They are both leaders in the study of international history, and add to formidable scholarship the courage to tackle immense subjects and to write beautifully about them. Those who came to their conversation in Kansas City heard what millions of others have read: history with passion; history that matters to any informed citizen.

The second conversation describes the transnational character of current writing on the Great War in another way. Our two participants are military historians. One is a specialist on the German army in the Great War. Holger Afflerbach[15] is a German-born scholar who now has a chair at the University of Leeds. He is representative of the new generation of European historians who live in countries of the European Union in which they were not born nor trained. British university life, and in particular the historical profession, has been enhanced significantly by integrating European-born scholars into its midst. The refugee generation in the Nazi era has been succeeded by a generation of young historians whose outlook is perforce transnational. Welcoming them has been a British-born generation of historians of the Great War, one of whose leading members is Gary Sheffield,[16] who holds a chair in War Studies at the University of Birmingham.

Their field is the history of command and of the waging of war. Here the contrast in approach between the two touches on equally explosive issues surrounding the generalship of the Great War. Afflerbach, who has written the authoritative life of the second commander of the Imperial General Staff in Berlin, Erich von Falkenhayn, has strong opinions about the catastrophic record of German command in the Great War. He even doubts the sanity of Falkenhayn's successor Erich Ludendorff. In contrast, Sheffield, who is one of the leading authorities on General Sir Douglas Haig, offers tempered criticism of the British way of waging the war. He is neither an apologist for Haig, nor one of his many scathing detractors. His balanced view of British warfare leads him to conclude that there was a "learning curve" during the conflict. The ultimate victory of 1918 was prepared through trial and error before it. There were wrong moves; Sheffield does not mince his words concerning the first day of the Battle of the Somme. But even though he admits that that day was not one of victory, he does not see it as an exercise in futility. The decisions taken by Ludendorff are subjected to much more acid analysis by Afflerbach, who detects a certain form of pathology among those who ran the German war effort.

What is intriguing about their exchange is the increasing complexity of the way historians of the Great War treat the question as to why one side won and the other side lost. Military history is a technical subject, and these two historians present the operational and tactical history of the war in a much different light than did earlier generations of scholars. This is a reflection of the way the study of the Great War has brought military history closer into contact with other kinds of history, and of the way in which a broader understanding of military culture has informed the treatment of high command and of the consequences of command decisions.

The third conversation is transnational in other ways. John Horne[17] was born in England, raised in Australia, and trained as a historian back in Britain. He holds a chair of modern European history in Trinity College, Dublin. His partner in this conversation, Leonard Smith,[18] is an American historian of France in the Great War. Both have written about the soldiers' war in pathbreaking ways. John Horne, in collaboration with his South African born colleague in Dublin, Alan Kramer, has changed our understanding of the way the war was waged in 1914. "German atrocities" in Belgium and France inspired headlines and hatred in the Allied camp. The propaganda was so widespread that in the interwar years, these stories were discredited as cheap lies. Horne and Kramer have proved that the stories were true. There were atrocities committed by German soldiers in 1914 against civilians in Belgium and France. They emerged out of the mistaken belief that the German army was facing guerrilla warfare waged by the civilian population against them. That was by and large not at all the case. What had happened was a collective illusion, a belief that what indeed had occurred when the Prussian army fought the French in 1870 was happening again. In their minds, German soldiers in 1914 were still fighting the last war, and the outcome was a record of brutality that all historians now acknowledge as based on indisputable and massive documentation.

It is rare that historians change the furniture of the academic landscape so drastically, but Len Smith has done just about the same thing.

He took one French infantry division and marched with it, so to speak, through the war. He showed that soldiers negotiated with their officers how far they would go in battle and at what cost. Orders were followed when possible, but reinterpreted when impossible. He terms this social contract between officers and men an exchange about proportionality. How much ground for how much blood. This kind of behavior was developed over two years before the outbreak of mutiny in the French army following the failed Nivelle offensive of April 1917. The Fifth Infantry Division was one of those that rebelled against the evidently failed policy of the French high command. They were not pacifists; they were not against winning the war; they were simply against the insane persistence of high command in forcing the issue of a battle in the Chemin des Dames that could not be won.

What both Horne and Smith have done, therefore, is to enter the minds of the soldiers of 1914–1918 in new and penetrating ways. They show that we have to bypass a sterile debate that has been going on in France for some time about whether soldiers fought and stayed the course in the Great War through coercion or through consent. Both Horne and Smith show us how we can go beyond such oversimplifications to see that soldiers were not automatons; they had minds of their own, and they developed strategies of survival and of negotiation that are essential elements now in our understanding of the soldiers' war.

The fourth conversation showed the transnational character of First World War scholarship in other ways. Margaret MacMillan[19] is a Canadian-born scholar who knows the Great War through family history. Her great-grandfather was David Lloyd George, British prime minister from 1916 to 1922. She was educated in Toronto and at St. Antony's College, Oxford, to which she has recently returned as warden. Like Ferguson and Kennedy, she has written on very broad subjects in international history, including the state visit of Richard Nixon to China in 1972.

MacMillan's contribution to Great War scholarship is her distinguished history of the Paris peace conference of 1919, entitled *Paris 1919: Six Months That Changed the World*. Her view of the peacemakers is much more sympathetic than that of earlier writers. In this respect, she is aligned with John Milton Cooper,[20] one of the leading scholars of the history of America in the early twentieth century. His studies of Teddy Roosevelt and Woodrow Wilson are foundational works, and his research on Woodrow Wilson informs his tragic interpretation of Wilson's presidency and the Peace Treaty he helped construct. Like Horne and Smith, MacMillan and Cooper have gotten into the minds of the protagonists, and find them to be flawed but honorable men. As we have all come to see, getting out of war and creating a sustainable peace is an extremely difficult assignment. While perfectly aware of the differences and disputes between and among the peacemakers, these two scholars ask us to understand the huge pressures under which they worked and to avoid a too-hasty condemnation of their efforts.

Cooper is more of an unrepentant Wilsonian than is MacMillan, or indeed other scholars in the field. He considers Wilson's mission to have been noble and his failure as a tragedy. After all, he argues Wilson's principled realism at a time of international chaos meant accepting compromise in the effort to lift the world out of the morass of war and hatred. Yes, the imperial powers fortified their position, but the League of Nations, Wilson believed, had the capacity to transcend the limitations of the balance of power system which had brought about the war in the first place. Cooper's Wilson set the course for the American century, in which regime change in the interest of promoting democracy became part and parcel of American national interest. The echoes of more recent events could be heard here, as they were in every one of this series of historians' conversations about the Great War.

The fifth and final dialogue was between two other transnational scholars. Robert Wohl,[21] who holds a chair at the University of California at Los Angeles, is a twentieth-century cultural historian of Europe. He has written on the origins of French Communism and provided the most profound history of aviation in the Western imagination. His essential contribution to Great War scholarship is his transnational study of a generation—the generation of young men who went to war in 1914. There were dynamic, creative, iconoclastic figures in virtually every European country in the prewar period, and it is their fate that Wohl surveys and mourns. He is less aligned with Paul Fussell's view that "modern memory" came out of the Great War than are other scholars. In Wohl's view, while the war was a profoundly important event in European cultural history, it should not occlude the emergence of disturbing, challenging and, to a degree, revolutionary movements before 1914. Music, painting, sculpture, and literature were all under radical review and reconfiguration by an avant-garde that crossed borders and boundaries with alacrity. James Joyce worked in Trieste, Rome, and Zurich in the period surrounding the Great War. Picasso left Catalonia for Paris, and Kandinsky left Russia for Munich in the prewar decade. Freud was at work demolishing earlier notions of reason as the motive force of human action. It took the whole of the twentieth century to work out the implications of this prewar revolution in ideas. How then can we share Paul Fussell's Anglo-centric view of "modern memory" as a product of the Great War?

His partner in this fifth conversation, the editor of this book,[22] offers one way out of this conundrum. My view is that the overwhelming weight of mass bereavement left a cloud over interwar European cultural life which, to a degree, has never lifted. Where did those in mourning find the symbols and language to help them endure the loss of so many young men? My answer is in older languages in which people had found meaning for centuries. These languages may be grouped under the broad headings of classical, romantic, and religious notation and ritual. Thus the Great War was, in my view, a counterrevolutionary shift in both high and popular culture, a move back into the past to express the sadness and pain that the deaths of nine million men in the Great War had left in its wake.

This view is by definition transnational and narrows the space between the consequences of war among the winners and among the losers. It is comparative history, like that written by Robert Wohl, and it suggests that the catastrophe of the Great War was indeed a defining moment in European cultural life, though not quite in the way Paul Fussell had suggested. Having taught first in Jerusalem and then in Cambridge for many years, I have tried to bring to this set of problems direct experience of societies in which the history of war is family history, the history of young lives truncated, of talent and potential unrealized or foreshortened.

Both Wohl and I are part of a broad community of historians on both sides of the Atlantic who see in cultural history—the history of how people make sense of the world in which they live—evidence of the lasting significance of the Great War. This is the common thread in this book. It is as true in the international history written by Kennedy, Ferguson, MacMillan, and Cooper, as in the military history of Afflerbach and Sheffield, as in the blend of social and cultural history in the work of Horne and Smith. Anyone who wants to understand the world in which we live has to go back now nearly a century and to take account of the foundational upheaval of the world order that Europeans call the Great War. It was "great" not because of its size or its grandeur, but because of its revolutionary effects.

Fortunately, American society did not suffer the consequences of the Great War that virtually all European countries knew. Here the 1914–1918 war has been occluded by the Second World War, and it is to change that optic that we came to Kansas City to honor those who created the Liberty Memorial Museum. Its founders opened the door to a deeper public understanding of the war that launched the twentieth century, and it is to mark and celebrate their efforts that we have created this book. If it helps readers to feel the excitement and the moral seriousness of historical scholarship in this field, something palpable in the five meetings in Kansas City in 2007 and 2008, and if it draws more Americans into considering how their own history is part of this story, then we will have realized much of what we set out to do.

Wilson in London with American soldiers.
Photo courtesy of the National World War I Museum.

Wilson the president. Photo
courtesy of the National World
War I Museum.

Dedication of Liberty Memorial in 1921.
Photo courtesy of the National World War I Museum.

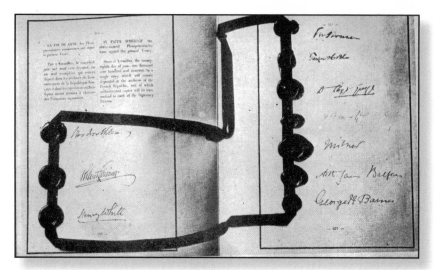

Signed and sealed Treaty of Peace, Versailles, June 28, 1919.
Photo courtesy of the National World War I Museum.

Kaiser Wilhelm, Ludendorff, and Hindenburg.
Photo courtesy of the National World War I Museum.

Hindenburg in the field, second from the left.
Photo courtesy of the National World War I Museum.

Marshal French, third from the right.
Photo courtesy of the National World War I Museum.

Allied High Command: Joffre, Foch, Haig, and Pershing.
Photo courtesy of the National World War I Museum.

Clemenceau and Lloyd George at Versailles.
Photo courtesy of the National World War I Museum.

Harry S. Truman in the Great War.
Photo courtesy of the National World War I Museum.

American soldiers in the front lines.
Photo courtesy of the National World War I Museum.

American patrol in no-man's land.
Photo courtesy of the National World War I Museum.

American rations in the trenches.
Photo courtesy of the National World War I Museum.

German prisoners, November 1918.
Photo courtesy of the National World War I Museum.

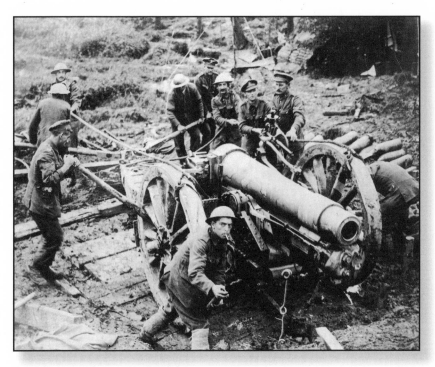

British gun with crew in Flanders.
Photo courtesy of the National World War I Museum.

German 10.5 cm gun with dead crewman.
Photo courtesy of the National World War I Museum.

German prisoners of the French.
Photo courtesy of the National World War I Museum.

ONE

War Origins

Niall Ferguson, Harvard University
Paul Kennedy, Yale University

JAY WINTER: This conversation is the beginning of a unique event. While there has been a mountain of historical writing produced about the First World War, there has never before been a series of conversations among historians who are specialists in the history of the 1914–18 conflict, about what they agree about, what they disagree about, and what they simply have yet to work out. We should not underestimate how lively is the field of historical research on the Great War, as it is called in Europe; historians, who are mostly peaceable people, get very excited at times over questions of interpretation and evidence. This is still a very contested field, for the simple reason that it provides the basis for any interpretation of the history of the last one hundred years. Without a clear view of that war, we are left in the dark over all the major events which followed: the Russian Revolution, the rise of Communism, the Fascist movement, the interwar economic crash, genocide, the cold war, weapons of mass destruction, decolonization, terrorism, the oil crisis, and so on. And because so much rests on an interpretation of the Great War, you the public should anticipate disagreement among the distinguished historians you will meet over the five sessions which are to come.

The shape of these conversations follows the shape of the war. To-day we deal with war origins. Then we turn to war strategy and military thinking, if that is the right word for a war which seemed to get out of anyone's control. Thirdly we consider how soldiers withstood the stress of the kind of war they had to fight; millions had to dig a hole in the ground in order to survive the largest artillery exchanges in history. How did men endure this? How did they continue for fifteen hundred days? This is the third subject we interrogate. Fourthly, we turn to peace-making, to try to work out the kind of peace the politicians created after the conflict came to an end in 1918. And fifthly, and finally, we try to look at how people in the aftermath of the war tried to make sense of it; how they wrote about it, commemorate it, mourned those who fell in it. In effect, this fifth subject is the cultural aftermath of the war.

That is a very long agenda: five conversations about a very long war. And yet, as you will see soon enough, in an hour we can only begin to explore the complexities of this subject. These conversations are meant to draw you, the educated public, in to a world as exciting as any which exists in international scholarship today. What better way is there to celebrate the opening of this, the National World War One Museum here in Kansas City?

For Europeans, the 1914–18 conflict was the Great War, not only because of its dimensions, but because it changed our understanding of what war is. That is why all participant nations, with the exception of Russia, have museums presenting objects, images, and traces of the seventy million men who fought in that war. Museums are, in a way, the cathedrals of the modern world, places where sacred issues are expressed and where people come to reflect on them. A museum is also a kind of a bridge between the academy and the public, a place where people who earn a living in universities can reach a much greater audience than they find in their classrooms. And doing so, I believe, is a public duty. Scholarship, especially about war and peace, is everybody's business. And museums open a window on the work of scholars, just as scholars stimulate museums to change and adapt their representation of the past as historical interpretations change. A museum without contact with scholarship turns sclerotic very fast; and there are one or two in Europe that I can think of that are in danger of doing just that. It's our job, as scholars, to work together with museum designers and curators to create this kind of middle ground between the academy and the concerned public. As one of the historians who has watched the emergence of the Liberty Memorial Museum, I want to take this opportunity to salute the group of people who have created this space of memory.

I use the word "memory" intentionally, because the history of war is not something which has happened once and for all; it is happening now as I speak, and will almost certainly happen again in the next months and years somewhere in the world. Many of the people in this room saw military service; they have direct knowledge of war and immediate memories. We need to hear them, and their voices, and put them alongside other people's voices, voices from nearly a century ago, of the young men who found out what war was.

There is one other reason why history and memory have come together in ways that make museums important. What the First World War did was to bring family history and universal history together. Museums are places where this blending of different stories, large and small, can be visualized, represented, recalled.

The Great War is embedded in family stories and family histories all over the world; the vast character of this war, in which seventy million men served, has become the story of everybody. It is no longer a story of generals and politicians only. It is the story of ordinary men and the families for which they fought. We can see this in all of the war memorials, including the one in which we are meeting today. What matters are the names; all those names in stone, listed outside of this memorial, every single man who died for his country equal to all the others of whatever rank.

This egalitarian sentiment helped bring these vast world events down to a level we can all relate to, and it is that ordinariness of living through extraordinary events which this museum and others like it capture.

Museums tell the story of war, to be sure, but they also tell the story of the return to peace. Families were torn asunder, and then they came together again, at a different time, and in different ways, to be sure, but family life survived the war. That is why we can see the importance of gendering the story of war, of ensuring that there are women's voices heard here; no history of war makes any sense without them.

It should be evident by now that we have a difficult task ahead of us in these five conversations. Our assignment is to try to transmit to you, the public, why this subject matters so much, why it is an exciting area of research, and why we have to engage with it in order to understand the world in which we live today.

I have an advantage here, in that my four decades of work in this field has brought me friendships with some of the finest historians in the world. Two of them are with us today. Together, they constitute what I would call the gold standard of the historical profession. These two men's writings have described a trajectory which is very remarkable, one embedded in the way Britain, Europe, and the United States have developed over the past century. The distinguished work of these two historians shows us that one way to understand the world is to start in Germany, move to Britain, and then come to the United States Charting the interaction of these three great powers helps us understand the devastating transformations in the history of the twentieth century. This trajectory from Germany to Britain to the United States, is after all, first and foremost, the story of the First World War. That's the beginning of the story, but in no sense the end of it. Now, on my right, on your left, Paul Kennedy, my colleague in the History Department at Yale, perhaps best known for his book, *The Rise and Fall of the Great Powers,* is also a historian of sea power. At the same time, Paul has been a historian of the contemporary international system, and of the United Nations, whose early history he has told in moving and powerful ways.

Our second speaker today is Niall Ferguson, who teaches in the History Department at Harvard, an old friend for many years when we were both teaching in England. He is a historian of extraordinary vitality, energy, and gifted in the sense of making history transparent, making it something that you want to read. He writes in a way which persuades you that you are engaged in a conversation with him. One you'd like to carry on with the author, and maybe take up a point or two that you might not agree with. What you see in Niall's work is a depth of knowledge of economics, banking, and military strategy that has brought his books the accolades of colleagues and the general public alike.

Now, one more introductory remark. I hope you appreciate the extent to which what we are doing is to show you the way history happens. It is and has always been a conversation among colleagues. Sometimes the conversations are cordial, sometimes, heated, but they are rarely boring.

Writing history takes time. A long time. My gestation period for a book from the initial idea to holding the volume in my hands is about eight years. Most of it is spent reading and writing, but a lot of it is spent in conversation with other specialists, trying out ideas, objecting to alternative approaches, learning from each other. Yes, we disagree some of the time, but there is usually a body of knowledge we share. We also know what we don't know, and frequently what we can't know because the documentation has been destroyed. And even when we see the same documents, we don't interpret them always in the same way. Now, this collegiality of difference is what I hope to introduce you, the public, to today and in the other four conversations to follow.

Today's theme is the outbreak of the 1914–18 war. We need to turn first to the question of the origins of the war, to its accidental or inevitable arrival, to begin to appreciate the way which in this field historians operate and how historical debate unfolds. It is indeed an honor to ask these two friends and colleagues to open this series.

The stakes are high in this part of our historical work. How we approach war origins may tell us much as to whether the First World War was unique, or part of a European conflict turned into world war that spanned the globe from 1914 to 1945—a second thirty years' war.

My proposal is that, first, Paul Kennedy will offer some remarks to be followed by Niall Ferguson. Afterwards, we will have further exchanges and, at the end of our discussions, we would be delighted to have questions from the audience. The present business is to pass the microphone to Paul Kennedy, on my left.

KENNEDY: Thank you, Jay, and ladies and gentlemen, thank you for coming to join us this afternoon. I'm really honored and pleased to be here. We will find in these five conversations and in the conversation today that we will focus upon some things which look like accidents. After all, to many in 1914, the World War came out of the blue. If Gavrilo Princip, the assassin of Franz Ferdinand, the crown prince of Austria Hungary, hadn't gone around the corner again and again, he wouldn't have had a second chance to bump into the archduke's carriage and shoot him. Contingency matters. What appeared to be the work of a madman or a terrorist assassination really came out of the blue. Things going wrong. And as we try to convey today and as you learn much more about in the next four sessions, there are all sorts of examples of things going wrong—plans which go awry, claims that things will be fixed in a very short time, that you will be able to get in and get out, that violence can be controlled.

What I'm going to do, ladies and gentlemen, for just a few minutes, is to tell you about a number of historical approaches and historical interpretations which go in the other direction. They tend to argue, they do argue, many of them strongly, that this war, this war which was to change all history, was in some respects, inevitable. Now, you have to think to yourself, this is just an example of historians being wise after the fact. But let me just go through a number of the arguments which are made by people we call structural and cultural historians about the coming of the war. A war of this intensity should not have been such a surprise, after all.

Now, first of all, there's the argument often advanced by political scientists like Kenneth Waltz about the anarchic nature of the great power system.[1] Those who adopt this point of view reason/see stability as weathering, aging, fraying over time. Every so often there was bound to be a breakdown in some sort of agreement, in a long peace, and there would come another war. This happened in part because great powers are egoistic; they will not accept that any other great power can tell them what to do; they will not be constrained. These relationships are arrayed in a multipolar system and, from time to time, there are wars, and sometimes big wars. John Mearsheimer, another political scientist in Chicago, wrote a book called *The Tragedy of Great Power Politics*,[2] and its argument is very much along these lines.

Then there is a second kind of deterministic history of the outbreak of the war. Here its exponents place much more stress on economic shifts. These are forms of Marxian or Marxist interpretation, going back to Lenin with his idea of the uneven rate of development, that if some powers' economies are growing year after year and decade after decade, faster than their neighbors, or faster than others, then they will become inherently stronger and they will inherently lay claim to having a bigger position in the world to match their growing economic might and power. Inevitably their neighbors will get fearful of them because of that. And I must admit, there's a great deal of that in my book, *The Rise and Fall of the Great Powers*.[3] And I don't need to urge you to hear echoes in today's debates about the shifts in the global balances towards the Far East, to let you have an insight into the way that argument goes.

Another position of a structural kind has a generational argument at its core. It emerges in the work of people dealing with the nineteenth century, which was formed by their Great War, the Revolutionary and Napoleonic wars from 1793 to 1815. After that upheaval, political leaders and many other people adopted what Paul Schroeder calls a new paradigm.[4] They had decided that the lesson of the Napoleonic War was not to go to war again, to control crises, to keep small whippersnapper states under control, and to come together in concert. That lasted for perhaps two or three generations; but the generation before 1914 had kind of forgotten about it. Its leading members didn't think that perhaps war was such a bad thing. Fortifying this position is another kind of argument. Some cultural historians say that in the late nineteenth century and the early twentieth century there were cultural and ideological twists and shifts which heightened degrees of belligerence, a sort of social atavism, a Darwinian notion of the struggle for survival, not just in the rain forest, but a struggle for survival between the powers.

So, at the time, an awful lot of people wrote about the coming inevitable war. This was particularly true of the Pan-Germans and in Germany, but this inevitableism was there elsewhere too. There was also a certain nihilism: a sense of a shrug—so what if we destroy a lot of things?

And at this point a substantial number of military historians and diplomatic historians will say, the fact that there were these binding military alliances between the central powers on the one hand and France and Russia with the less binding alliance through Great Britain, meant that if a war came, for whatever the reasons, if these wars came, they would not be the very short wars which happened in Europe in the 1860s—the Austro-Prussian war which was just about six weeks in length, and the Franco-Prussian war which was just a season and a half. Every one of the partners in the Alliance, if they were defeated in the field, would then turn to their allies and ask for help. Thus you had an ever broader coalition of support. You couldn't get away with a knockout blow. You could not assume that the side knocked out would sue for peace in short order; it was not going to happen this way. So if it came, it was going to be a big, long war, a slow test of staying power.

There is also an argument that in the early twentieth century there was distinct erosion of civilian control over the European militaries. If you go back to the concert of Europe, you'll see that all of the statesmen there, the political leaders are the ones who call the shots. The argument about 1914 is that the war plans of the military are driving the political leaders to accept things which people like Talleyrand and Castlereagh and others most likely would not have found acceptable. Finally, there's what's called the short war illusion, the belief that you can get this war over very rapidly. You may think I'm pointing to another short war illusion which occurred in this country four years ago. It is probably inevitable that people in power think, if you have the new technology, if you have the most advanced weapons systems, you can move swiftly. This assumption is inherent, in particular, in the Schlieffen Plan, the German plan to knock France out of the war before Russia fully mobilized.

And then there's another set of arguments about tactics and strategy. As the war unfolded into trench warfare and naval blockade warfare, it became apparent that in some respects, defensive weaponry can answer whatever problems offensive weaponry and tactics pose. This is not always true: the offensive had the upper hand in the late thirties and in the German Blitzkrieg thereafter. But the war of 1914–18 turned out to be a period in which the defensive weapons and tactics, of the machine gun, the howitzer, the barbed wire, the naval mine, the torpedo, made a swift and decisive victory, whether on land or at sea, very difficult. We know this now, but it was not as clear at the time. In short, there were many reasons—legitimate reasons—why people thought war was coming, if not in 1905, then in the Agadir crisis of 1911, or if not then, why not in the Balkan Crisis of 1912? And if not then, well soon enough.

FERGUSON: I thought I'd begin by just saying what a brilliant museum I think this is and how much I appreciate the quality of the work undertaken here. I walked around the exhibit, and in the time available, two things struck me. First, how wonderfully well organized it was. When I go into a history museum, I go in looking to be annoyed. That's what professors are like. And I want to find something I can correct. Not this time. And the other thing that struck me was that you all, or the people who were in the exhibits with me, were clearly enjoying it. And that's the most important thing that a museum has to do. It has to engage the enthusiasm of the public, not just of the amateur historians, much less the professional historians, but young people— the kind of people who, when they walk in here, know next to nothing about the First World War. So that's the first item on my agenda. It's been a tremendous achievement and it's a huge honor to be here and to be a part of it.

I went to school in a museum in the sense that the school that I attended in Glasgow, the Glasgow Academy, was dedicated as a war memorial to the fallen in the First World War, almost at the same time as the war memorial here in Kansas City was being built. Every day, as I went to school, I passed a large plaque on which names of former pupils of the Glasgow Academy were inscribed who had fallen in the war. And I'll never forget, as long as I live, the inscription at the top of the Roll of Honor: "Say not that the brave die." Now when I was about eight years old, I have to say that didn't make a great deal of sense to me: say not that the brave die? But they died. Only gradually did I begin to understand what that memorial was telling me—that although they had indeed died, their memory was immortal, as long as I was walking past that memorial and seeing their names.

The First World War was part of my life in an even more immediate way in that my grandfather, John Ferguson, served in the British army in the trenches on the Western front in the Seaforth Highlanders, one of the Scottish regiments that were very much at the sharp end of the British campaign on the Western front. He was gassed, he was shot in the chest, but he survived. He survived with painfully damaged lungs. In my earliest memory of him, not long before he died—I was quite young when he died—was of his wheezing, of his lungs fighting to inhale oxygen, and that stayed with me. By the time I went to university, I was already badly obsessed with the First World War. It was obvious to me that it was the most important event in history, the one you wanted to write your assignments on. But I gradually began to realize that not everybody shared this obsession. It was particularly striking to me when I arrived in the United States for the first time, as a teenager in New York, that the First World War seemed absent from public consciousness in the United States. I do remember one small statue somewhere downtown in Manhattan that caught my attention. I now can't remember whether it was Pershing or whom it commemorated, but what struck me most about it was that it was ignored. Poppy Day came and went. On the eleventh of November in Britain everyone buys a paper pop to contribute to the welfare of ex-servicemen and their families. Not in New York. There seemed no obvious recognition of the significance of this historical event. And I began to wonder if the United States had really participated in the First World War at all, so overshadowed was the war by much less significant conflicts, the Vietnam War and the Korean War, and by, of course, the other World War, the later one. Since those days, in the space of the last twenty years, I think that has slowly begun to change. The First World War has perhaps arrived, in no small part thanks to the efforts of professional historians, particularly those like Jay Winter who dedicated the large part, if not the entirety of their careers, to the study of the war. I sense a change, and let me illustrate what I mean by this. The last place you would expect to hear the First World War mentioned would be in a casino in Las Vegas. I was in a casino in Las Vegas yesterday, not, I hasten to add, to gamble—I'm too much of a Scottish Calvinist to do that. I was at a conference, a conference organized by a group of—let's put it this way—financiers—the partners and managers of hedge funds. And at this conference, a speech was given by probably the most famous economist in the world today, Jeffrey Sachs, of the Earth Institute in New York. And to my amazement, one of the very first things that Sachs mentioned was the First World War, as he was trying to capture the attention of his high-rolling blackberry-checking audience. Sachs said, "We are living through the second age of globalization. The first age came to an end in 1914 with the First World War." And I thought to myself, imagine, in the Wynne Hotel in Las Vegas, I'm hearing a discussion about the First World War. That is something. Then he went on to say something that puzzled me. He said, "This event that ended globalization and plunged the world economy into crisis was inexplicable." And then he corrected himself and said, "Of course, by inexplicable, I don't mean to say we don't have an explanation. As a result of German foreign policy, the age of globalization came to an end." And he carried on and puzzled me even more by arguing that, "Fortunately, as a consequence not only of the First World War, but also of the Second World War, something good happened. And that good thing was that the age of empires had come to an end and only as a result of the breakup of empires, had it been possible for economic revival finally to come to the rest of the world, particularly to Asia." I sat there grinding my teeth. So on the one hand, I was very happy. I was happy to hear an economist acknowledge the importance of history—that happens seldom. And I was especially happy to hear this happen—to hear this statement made in such an unlikely setting. But I was uneasy about the idea that we can't explain the First World War. That it might as well have been an asteroid hitting the earth. Or that if we have to explain it, it's just the Germans who were to blame. The First World War is fascinating because it has echoes in our own time, as Paul Kennedy has already suggested. The war meant the end of globalization—a sudden shattering blow to an apparently remarkable stable and dynamic integrated global economy.

We need to try to understand why that happened. Think only for a moment of the consequences of this catastrophe. Think only of the economic consequences—leave aside the dead—for one second, forget about the nine or ten million people who lost their lives, to say nothing of the subsequent deaths suffered in the Russian Civil War or the associated deaths caused by the great influenza epidemic. Consider the way in which the First World War shattered the entire system of international trade. What could symbolize that better than all those merchant ships being sunk in the Atlantic just off British waters by German submarines? Thousands of tons of shipping at the bottom of the ocean. Submarine cables—what had been the Victorian Internet that had connected the entire world on an electronic system of communication: they were severed by the Royal Navy within days of the outbreak of war. This was a spectacular end to what I think we can legitimately call the First Age of Globalization.

But the trouble is, this kind of earth-shattering crisis is tremendously difficult to understand. One can't, even if one is the best economist in the world, simply come up with a glib explanation. That's where the historians seem to me to have an important part to play.

Sometimes I worry about the way historians are regarded in the United States. There are always echoes of Henry Ford's history as bunk wherever one goes here. Entrepreneurs who impatiently say, "What has this got to do with me? What is this doing for my deal?" My sense is that, if historians can offer some explanation of why the first age of globalization ended with a shattering and unprecedentedly large military conflict, then suddenly they're offering something a little bit more than sophisticated assistance to memory. So what I would like to try and do in the course of our discussion is to address that particular question, the one that seems to me Jeffrey Sachs posed without being able to answer in, of all places, a casino. There's a wonderful essay title in your program which asks whether the First World War was a tragedy or a mistake—that's a classic Oxford or Cambridge examination question, by the way, because it conceals a trap and that trap is, of course, that it's quite possible that it was both a tragedy and a mistake. And I sometimes think that if my grandfather had lived long enough to be here, what would he think? What would he think to see this grandson sitting on a platform in such astonishingly distinguished company in Kansas City in a thronged auditorium trying to explain that historical event, which more than anything else, changed and very nearly ended his life? I think he'd probably say: Yes, it was a mistake made by those people who were running the governments of Europe; but the tragedies—the tragedies befell millions of men just like me.

WINTER: One helpful step forward may be to talk about the differences between the causes of the war of 1914, and the causes of the Great War it unleashed. One of the ways in which we can link these two presentations is to talk about the failure of politicians to control war, once it is declared. There were different levels of causality, some structural, some contingent. And this has been evident from the time of Thucydides on. This is not only a twentieth-century or twenty-first-century matter.

We have to recognize that the war of 1914 became something else—a world war. It changed into something else that no one had ever seen before. This was the first industrial war in the sense of having fully industrialized global powers engaged in it. The American Civil War does anticipate this later development. In 1914, the war that people got is not the one they thought they were going to get. And that was true for Niall Ferguson's grandfather as much as it was for the leaders.

The question I'd like to put to Paul Kennedy is the question of war planning and the responsibility for the unfolding of the war itself in 1914. I think Las Vegas is a perfectly appropriate setting for the view that the leading powers of Europe were engaged in a gigantic game of roulette in which they were risking empires and the lives and fortunes of millions on the basis of having absolutely no idea what they were doing. Keynes liked to distinguish between probability and uncertainty. Uncertainty means you can't predict what will happen: that is the story of 1914. The question of planning leads me to press the matter a bit more sharply, and ask if would you agree, Paul, that there's an element of irresponsibility bordering in some instances on a kind of insanity in the approach some leaders took in the war crisis understood as a rational exercise of decision making?

KENNEDY: Yes, the great German strategist who many of these people studied, but didn't study well enough, Clausewitz, said you can make all the plans you want before a conflict, but after the first day of the conflict, you might as well toss away your plans because the fog of war and a wonderful term—the friction of war—will then cause breakdown; unanticipated things will happen, and they happened very quickly in 1914. I still think that Barbara Tuchman's book, *The Guns of August*,[5] is a wonderful introduction for a general reader wanting to get to know how it unfolds in the first couple of weeks of the war and the number of frictions and the number of things which go wrong. There was a sort of collective lunacy among the military planners. Very few people saw it. Some of the people who saw it thought that it was so unbelievable that people would plan to hurl millions of troops against each other that it wouldn't be carried out. Others, like the Polish-Jewish banker, Ivan Bloch,[6] thought that if it happened, it would be so catastrophic, it would bring down both sides. He was one of the small number of people who actually saw what modern industrialized conflict and war would do. Others, however, of a liberal critical bent like Norman Angell, wrote the best-selling work of the pre-1914 period, *The Great Illusion*,[7] which is about how no rational people would ever think of going into modern industrialized mass warfare. He assumed rationality. Whereas, I think, some of you know, there were other strands which were pushing towards the irrational. But they were reinforced—and this is Jay's point, they were reinforced by the appearance of rational well-planned military operations, drafts, and schemes. The Schlieffen Plan, of which we heard, was one which was drafted about ten or twelve years before the war. It went through modification after modification, but the modifications were, in the views of the planners, just what you do when your motorcycle engine isn't firing very well. You do a modification here, a modification there, to get the machine operating correctly. Very few people understood that, since everybody else was getting their motorcycles prepared, often to go in the opposite direction down the same road, that when the two clashed together, there would be Clausewitz friction on a monumental scale; there would be miscommunications and many things would go astray. My second point is this. It seems to me that very few of these planners had an alternate plan. The German Schlieffen Plan was initially one plan among others. There had existed an alternate for the Prussian general's staff which was to prepare to be on the defensive in the West and to have the great East Front Marching Plan, but it was scrapped in 1913. So this was what Jay is getting at. It's a gamble, and a gamble for everything. It's a high-risk strategy, and the Germans said it quite often: their way of putting it is that you either win the bank or you lose the bank; one or the other. I think when we look at pre–Second World War planning, especially in the U.S. and Great Britain, there's a lot of thought given to learning lessons about the arrogance of the gamblers' assumptions of the leaders of the Great Powers in the First World War.

WINTER: Thank you, Paul. I do agree that one of the purposes of the study of history is to eject a small bit of humility into these discussions. Some politicians appear to be allergic to it. But at the same time, there is a real need to break down levels of responsibility and maybe address a point that Niall has made in his work. He has written that what made the First World War happen was Britain's decision to engage in a continental conflict that had origins first in Serbia and secondly in the conflict between France and Germany. Thus his view is that Britain turned the war of 1914 into the First World War. Niall, do you perhaps still consider that the British decision to go to war on the fourth of August 1914 was one that need not have been made? Do you share Paul Kennedy's point about the failure for Britain to have a second plan, one for staying out of it, the way the United States did for three years, the way Italy did for a year? Was there a real possibility for Britain to remain neutral, and was that chance lost with enormous consequences, not only for the future of Britain, but for the future of the world?

FERGUSON: I certainly made myself notorious ten years ago, arguing that there was an alternative for Britain in 1914—namely, not to intervene and to let the continental war take place, that by that stage was, more or less, inevitable.[8] Incidentally, when technical things go wrong, you are encountering not only the frictions of war, but the frictions of public speaking, which are almost as bad. Historians, as we said earlier, enjoy constructing chains of causation that explain enormous events like the First World War. It's how we operate. This is such an enormous event that it really does need to have commensurately enormous causes, and Paul Kennedy very eloquently listed some of the causes of the First World War that I certainly remember studying as an undergraduate—imperialism, class conflict, great power rivalry, militarism, cultural pessimism, you name it. The danger of this kind of explanation is that you are creating causes with the benefit of 20/20 hindsight with the enormous advantage we have of knowing what came next. Contemporaries didn't. The real challenge for historians is to recapture the uncertainty of the past, particularly for decision makers. And to realize that, while certain things were quite likely—I think a conflict between Germany and Russia was quite likely by 1914—other elements in the collision, in the catastrophe, were quite unlikely. It was quite unlikely that a predominantly Liberal—in fact an overwhelmingly Liberal government in Great Britain which had been opposed to conscription, and which maintained, therefore, a pitifully small army by continental standards—should elect to intervene on the side of France to which no public diplomatic guarantee had ever been given in the event of a continental conflict. *That* was the improbable thing. And on the second of August 1914 when that cabinet met—it was a Sunday—normally they'd all have been fishing or hunting or seeing their mistresses . . .

KENNEDY: Some of them were.

AUDIENCE: Laughter.

FERGUSON: Between meetings.

KENNEDY: The prime minister was . . .

FERGUSON: The prime minister was either seeing his gin bottle or his mistress—sometimes both together. But as they gathered around that table, the probability was that they would not intervene. That was what worried the two members of the cabinet who wanted to intervene. And only two went into the room absolutely sure—possibly three— possibly, they had by that time persuaded us that they wanted to intervene. One was Sir Edward Grey, the foreign secretary, and the other was Winston Churchill, then First Lord of the Admiralty. The rest were, at that point, as they walked into the room, undecided or flatly opposed. For a historian to ignore that and treat Britain's intervention as if it was predetermined from the very moment the Germans began to build a navy in 1897 is completely to ignore the profound uncertainty of the past. To ignore this makes history so boring. You lose all the excitement of the past if you throw out that uncertainty. I can remember when I began to think this way. We professional historians have a fancy word for it—counterfactual history. When I began to think counterfactually, I found that not only was my historical reading accelerated, the teaching I did was better, more successful, undergraduates stayed awake during the lectures, but also I began to understand much, much better the reality of decision making under uncertainty. So I think that counterfactual question, whatever your answer to it is, is absolutely essential. You have to ask yourself, what would have happened if the majority view had prevailed? If Churchill had been forced to resign? The entire government had fallen—if Britain had been plunged into a profound diplomatic or political crisis and the war had unfolded with no British expeditionary force being sent to the assistance of the French? What would the consequences have been? The reason it's worth asking that question is that's the question they had to ask themselves on August the second. And to me, the most fascinating exercise in counterfactual history is to try to see battle tours of future, battle tours of sequences of events that didn't happen. It's only when we contemplate the alternative history, those parallel universes that never came into existence, that we really get a sense of the magnitude of both the tragedy and the mistake. Now in the "Pity of War," I argued that if Britain had stayed out, the war would have been shorter; the Germans would have won. It was quite remarkable that France didn't collapse, even with British support. Anybody who'd any recollection of the events of 1870 would not have expected the French to withstand a catastrophic level of casualties in the opening months of the war. The Germans were extremely good at inflicting casualties throughout the First World War. And never better than in the opening phase when the French suffered the worst casualties of the entire war. Absent the British, it seems to me very hard to imagine the French holding out indefinitely on the Western front. Very hard indeed. As for the Eastern front, the Germans won that war anyway. They would have won it more quickly had there not been substantial support from Britain—financial and economic support to Czarist Russia's already somewhat fragile economy. So we enter an alternative world—a world in which the war is over by say, 1916. In which the Kaiser and his ministers and generals get to achieve the aims that they would have had in 1914 had the British stayed neutral. Now in order to upset my colleagues—and it did upset them—I suggested that this would have been the Kaiser's European Union. Because the September 1914 program that the Germans produced included, among other things, a project for a customs union, the membership of which would have been very much as it was back in 1998. It would have been an early form of the European Union. And I suggested, sticking my neck as far out as far as it's possible to stick a historian's neck, that this would, in fact, have been a better outcome than four years of industrialized slaughter, the ultimate result of which was inconclusive. Germany temporarily, but not permanently, was deterred from bidding for European hegemony. But German hegemony in Europe achieved more cheaply with less loss of life by circa 1916 would have been a better outcome for Britain notably. Not for the world, but from the vantage point of the British empire, that would have been a better result, because by 1918 Britain had, apart from anything else, incurred much heavier losses of manpower than clearly it would have suffered had it not intervened. But also the financial costs of the war were absolutely horrendous.

Today Americans worry about their debt—it's one of these things that periodically dominates political discourse here, as the federal debt gets up above 50 percent of gross domestic product. Britain's debt at the end of the First World War was round about 200 percent of gross domestic product. Britain was crippled by the cost of the First World War. So there's an argument to be made, I think, at least to be advanced, that that silent majority in the British cabinet was right to favor neutrality. That would have been the smart thing to do.

Now let me add a qualification that's come to me with the wisdom of years. There's another way of looking at it. The real point I think I was trying to make was that there was a contradiction between Britain's foreign policy, which, at least in the mind of Grey, was to commit to France in the event of a war, albeit secretly, and Britain's military policy. A consistent policy would have been, yes, we can't let the Germans have hegemony in Europe, we will fight them if they take on the French, therefore, we need a big army. A rational counterfactual would have been the introduction of conscription to support a commitment to France. That seems to me as valid a counterfactual as neutrality. The key point is, you have to be consistent, whether you're Britain in 1914 or the United States in 2003, in the way in which you allocate resources to foreign policy. There's no point embarking on a military adventure without enough trained manpower. That's really the point the "Pity of War" tries to make. Trying to create the manpower after the fact was what led directly to the slaughter at the Battle of the Somme—a barely trained army marching in straight lines towards a much superior German defensive force.

WINTER: That's a very persuasive argument, but I think there are other ways of interpreting the decision that the cabinet took and, indeed, the consequences for staying out of the war. Paul, would you like to offer another point of view on this question?

KENNEDY: Yes, I'll come in, first of all, in support of Niall and then I'll try to saw off the branch on which he is sitting. You know, about fourteen years before the war broke out, there was a big debate within this British cabinet. It was a Conservative cabinet led by Lord Salisbury and a group of his ministers were getting anxious that Britain was in splendid isolation, while other, especially European countries, were coming together in alliances. And so a number of people, especially led by the colonial minister, Joseph Chamberlain, pushed to join one of these alliances and made all the arguments about the perils of isolation. Salisbury, in one of his greatest memoranda, just listed the reasons why we—the British—should not be so frightened and made reference back to the fact that we actually were in isolation for about seventeen years of the Napoleonic and French Revolutionary Wars and it didn't kill us off. You may fast forward to Churchill in 1940 when in his great speech, after taking office and after the fall of France, he says, "We shall fight, we shall fight alone, we shall keep on." He was deterred by the fact that all of Europe was falling so swiftly under Hitler's Panzer Divisions. So you could say, the aberration is there in 1914 and that has been the thrust of a number of Niall's writings. There's also the thrust of a number of people, especially in the U.K. academic circles, the Peterhouse School, so called; Morris Cowling, a number of others who are rather nostalgic about the end of the British empire. To be fair, it's most likely that there would have been a lot of people in Britain who would have said, "Did we have to go in or wasn't there another way?" You couldn't have that debate in France because ninety-eight German divisions were marching in on you. Britain had the insular advantage, perhaps, of a choice; that was what Salisbury and Chamberlain had debated. So the question to ask after listening to Niall saying that there was an alternative, or there were two, is well why did this cabinet behave the way it did? If you go to London, and visit the National Archives, you can see the minutes and discussions of the cabinet. Remember, this is not a presidential system. It's the prime minister who sits with the fourteen other ministers and they have absolutely complete verbatim records of what was said. You have copies of the memoranda which come in from the Home Office or the navy or whatever about why we should do this, why we should do that. You have the cabinet conclusions. So then when a historian comes in and tries to answer this question, you go into the world of the decision makers of that time. And retrospectively, you can say, Grey got too worried. Or Churchill was too combative and too eager. The liberal radicals in the cabinet had just run away from any study of military strategy at all, so they couldn't put an alternative military strategy there.

The idea of Niall's second alternative of national conscription was a hobbyhorse of the neoconservative imperial right. They wanted national service, but nobody else did, and the politicians in the middle thought it would be as unpopular a matter in Britain as the return of the draft would be across much of this country, were it to be proposed seriously in the next presidential election. I mean a full draft, not a selective draft. There were also personal matters which enter here. Apart, I would say from Churchill, who did study war and partake in it, very few of them then could ask the questions about alternative strategies or knew anything about weapons systems. When they were told that the German navy could get across the channel in a day and a half and land in the east of England, there was hardly anybody there who would say, "Well, wait a minute, we have one hundred fifty destroyers and flotillas, we have submarines, we have minefields, and we have a battle fleet twice as big as theirs—I don't think they're gonna get very far." Nobody asked those questions in a practical sense, just as in recent times political leaders have not asked whether there are alternative plans, alternative scenarios. So, it's true that you can say of August 1914, this was a big mistake. But we can't walk away from it at that level of analysis without saying, "How do we get in the mind of those who we think made a mistake," and perhaps we may then discover certain arguments which have merit. For instance, the argument that a German-dominated Europe would not be as benign as Helmut Kohl's or Angela Merkel's European Union. You then see the different levels at which historians go backwards and forwards in their analysis of, in this case, one of the biggest ever historiographical problems of all time.

WINTER: We'll conclude in a few minutes and have time for questions from the audience. I think perhaps Niall should have the last word. One of the questions that I think underpins our conversation is the question as to whether in 1914 anyone could have imagined what war would be. I mean industrialized war, assembly-line killing on a monstrous scale. If war was unimaginable, it was also impossible to imagine bypassing it through a series of logical steps. My difficulty with your counterfactual approach, Niall, is that it's too rational. It's taking war as something that you can predict; that can be discussed in terms of trajectory A going one way and trajectory B going another way. The war you predicted, which is the one without Britain, is one that I would argue is as imaginary as the war that the British cabinet predicted with Britain in it, which would be over by Christmas.

I think the best analogy for war on this scale is the AIDS virus. You think you've got it and it turns into something else and something bigger and more powerful and more devastating, indeed more dynamic than the minds of the people who are trying to contain it. But the question I put to you is, isn't there a fundamental difficulty in arguing that not going into the war would have been better, in that you are assuming that under the pressure of the cabinet deliberations of 1914, the members of that small group of people could have subjected war to consistent, rational analysis? No one had the slightest idea what the battlefield would look like two years or four years down the line. Gas warfare? Aerial warfare? Revolution all over Eastern Europe? The critical point is that they opened Pandora's box.

There is another level of argument to consider, too, one raised by the great British international historian James Joll, who wrote about the "unspoken assumptions" of 1914.[9] One such notion was honor. Every member of the British cabinet had to ask himself: What if we don't go to war? I think a large part of the answer is if Britain hadn't gone to war, then they might as well tear up the notion of honor in the way they approached politics. Honor mattered, then perhaps more than now. To be sure, this may not be a sufficient reason for going to war, but I cannot get into the mind of someone like Sir Edward Grey otherwise. True, he didn't tell the British cabinet what was going on between 1905 and 1914.

They were shocked at the commitment that had been made in their name without the cabinet knowing about it. I'm wondering about that shock, and whether the resort to honor was a way of dealing with it. Joll asked what do people do when they are confronted by massive choices on problems they have never confronted? They go back to simple truths, perhaps learned at school or at home. Honor was one of them. Was it rational? Perhaps not, but then that is one reason why I am not fully persuaded about counterfactuals. They assume we have all the facts, and to be sure the people who took the decision did not. Isn't this what people in economics say when the market doesn't work? That there is imperfect information available to the rational actors?

FERGUSON: Information is always imperfect. You never have it all. We don't really know all the information that the cabinet had at its disposal. There are still intelligence documents that have yet to be declassified in the British archives which would at least tell us what the British knew the Germans had. But there's only one thing as dangerous as underestimating your enemy, and that is overestimating your enemy. And the British made this mistake in both world wars. Paul Kennedy already mentioned the assumption that German naval power was greater than it, in fact, was. In World War II, indeed on the eve of World War II, the British were convinced that London would be leveled within twenty-four hours of the outbreak of war by the Luftwaffe. In both cases, the intelligence was imperfect and exaggerated the threat that Germany posed. The key is always to get your worst-case scenario explicit. The worst-case scenario that haunted the minds of Sir Edward Grey and Winston Churchill was the Napoleonic nightmare where the Germans became as powerful in continental Europe as Napoleon had been at the zenith of his fortunes. And it has always struck me that they did not explore that possibility very deeply.

One of the things few people didn't seem to understand was what was worrying the Germans. One of the most important things that I discovered in my early researches was that the real reason that precipitated the German decision for war was not an ambition to control the Netherlands, establish naval bases in the channel, much less to acquire an empire in Africa, or the like. The principal preoccupation of the Germans in the summer of 1914 was the speed with which the Russian armaments program was proceeding. Now what was fascinating about the

German counterfactual is that it gets you right into the heart of domestic politics as a factor in foreign policy. This is an old argument, but you see, I think a very powerful one. Very often decision makers, particularly those who are in some measure exposed to an elected assembly—a Congress or a Parliament or the Reichstag in the German case—will make decisions of a strategic nature with one eye, or even one and a half eyes, on the domestic political considerations. Why was it that Germany, which as the exhibition in this museum shows, was the most dynamic economy in Europe, felt insecure relative to Russia, which, by comparison, was a third-world emerging market? The answer is that there were politically imposed limits on how much the Germans could spend on their military by 1914. They had really reached the maximum point politically by 1913. The year before the Social Democrats, the left, had become dominant, the biggest party in the Reichstag. And the Germans sat there looking at their military capability and looking at what they thought the Russians were going to have by 1916, and the most compelling argument that was made, the one that won the day in Berlin, was, the sooner the better. If we wait another two years, we simply won't stand a chance. We might as well strike now while we can still, more or less, pass the test. Those were the exact words of the chief of the general staff, Helmut von Moltke—we can more or less pass the test. So what was really motivating the Germans was insecurity vis-à-vis Russia. There was no Napoleonic design in their minds. Their preoccupation—and it's very clear, it seems to me from the German evidence, was just to avoid a situation in which the Russians would be able to dictate terms to them militarily.

So, we move to another realm of counterfactual speculation. What if the Germans had fought differently? Let me conclude with an anecdote that tells you a lot about the difference between the military mentality or the royal mentality, perhaps, and the financial mentality. There was a dinner in 1914 in Hamburg attended by the Kaiser, Wilhelm II. The royal party found themselves sitting near a clever, rather bumptious Jewish banker named Max Warburg, and they had a conversation. And the Kaiser was grumbling about how bad things were looking—Allies all around conspiring against Germany—nobody to be relied upon in Vienna. The Russians were becoming ever more powerful. Warburg looked at them as if he were living in another planet and said words to this effect: "What are you worried about? Germany has everything going for it. Our economy is the one that's growing fastest. 'Made in Germany' is on every second industrial product in England. Why would we want to blow it by going to war?" And I remember when I first read that and started thinking that these comments tell you something. The bankers were not talking to the generals in Berlin in 1914. There was no conversation going on between the military planners and the people who were actually managing, if you want to put it this way, managing globalization.

And that brings me to a final reflection on the dramatic nature, the unexpected nature of the First World War. I want to turn to the minds of the people who ought to have been the best informed in the world—not only the bankers in Germany, but the bankers in New York and in London. If you look at the financial press, look at financial markets in the summer of 1914, the First World War is a complete bolt from the blue. There's no worry whatsoever in financial markets detectable in the bond prices until the twenty-second of July 1914. Long after the Sarajevo assassination. Within less than ten days, there was a financial crisis; all the world's stock markets literally closed their doors, including New York: trading was suspended in New York until the end of 1914. Now, that tells you that, in the minds of the best-informed contemporaries in many important respects, the First World War didn't have deep roots going back to the 1897 German Navy Bill or the annexation of Bosnia by Austria in 1908. It was a complete bolt from the blue. In the summer of 1914, the bankers weren't thinking about the possibility of war at all. The conclusion I want to offer is that the way decisions get taken about war is the key here. In Britain, as Paul said, it was a committee of Oxbridge Public School–educated hand-wringing liberals or combative liberals arguing to and fro about what a German-dominated Europe might look like. In Berlin it was quite different. The general staff had its plan; it was determined to implement it, and finally it was able to impose it, not only on the bankers who were really out of the loop, but ultimately even on the Kaiser himself, who, it's often forgotten, was ready to back down when he saw just how big the war was going to be. When decisions are made in that kind of an environment, when dysfunctional bureaucracies aren't even communicating with one another, when the economic powers are left out of account, that seems to be when the really bad decisions are taken. And remember, ladies and gentlemen, if I'm right and Britain made a mistake, the mistake made by Germany in 1914 was a whole lot bigger. And on that note, I will shut up.

WINTER: Thank you, Niall. I very much like the idea of seeing bankers as pacifists. I'm going to have that as another Oxbridge question to offer in the future. What I'd like to do is to ask you, the audience, to join with me in thanking Niall Ferguson and Paul Kennedy, for coming today and getting this set of conversations off to a scintillating start.

I can say without fear of contradiction that the conversations to follow will be of the same order and I hope the same elegance. Before we conclude today's session, I would like to open the floor for questions or comments. Please direct your questions to either members of the panel and, if we do have time, I would like both of them to have a chance to answer what you have in mind. Please.

QUESTION: Are there lessons that we might learn from World War I and its history that will help us in clarifying the status of the United States' influence—the actual status of our influence in the world today and our role for the next twenty-five years?

WINTER: Paul, would you like to add a word?

KENNEDY: The question, at the beginning, was what lessons can one draw for contemporary thought and reflection from what we've been talking about concerning the First World War. I'd be very brief because we would like to welcome as many questions in a short period. So I would say, lesson one that jumps out at me, particularly after Niall's final remarks, is there may be a lesson about the overestimate or exaggeration of the other side's intentions, and a lesson about the danger of ignoring the enemy's fears, ignorance of the rival's intentions, so that inevitably, governments opt for worst-case scenarios. Clearly, I also think, and I said it in my remarks, it's useful to have a Plan B up your sleeve if you're going into a conflict. Second lesson which strikes me more and more—I'm sure Niall has seen this as well—is that something akin to this mismatch or gap between the bankers and investors on the one side and the planners on the other side is happening right now in this country. When I go talk to people at Bechtel or Boeing or Bankers Association and they talk about China, they just see dollar, dollar, dollar, dollar, and they say do not worry about the massive trade imbalances, because the Chinese economy is bound to us and we are bound to them, so war will never come. When you point out that Britain and Germany were each other's best trading partners in 1914, they don't understand. But if I go to the Naval War College, the bankers are on one planet and the naval planners are on the other planet. This has happened more than once in history. Then surely the biggest thing that we must all be cautious about, if you bump into somebody talking about war or conflict, whether it's in the Middle East or Al Qaida or Far East or whatever, if you know somebody who knows, who absolutely knows what sort of war lies ahead, then, ladies and gentlemen, put your hands on your wallet, because you're about to be hoodwinked or swindled. Anybody who says they know what's going to be happening in the world if we don't do this, something awful will happen, you know it, just really get your hand tight on your wallet.

FERGUSON: In response to the question, let me return to the fact that it's always important to remember how each family's destiny has been shaped by conflict in this country, and of course, in my country. The thing that is sobering, of course, is that the proportions of Americans and indeed of British people who were killed in the world wars was significantly smaller, indeed orders of magnitude smaller than the proportions killed in some other countries, particularly I'm thinking here of Central and Eastern Europe. One of the questions I tried to address in my most recent book, *The War of the World*,[10] is why that conflict we've been talking about, the one that broke out in 1914, just refused to stop. Jay used the phrase "the thirty years' war," which is quite often used by historians to sum up the age of the world wars, but I actually prefer to think of a fifty years' war, that really began as early as 1904 when Russia and Japan clashed over Manchuria and carried on, right the way through with very, very few lulls until the end of the Korean War in 1953. And in that fifty-year period conflict raged, more or less, incessantly, at the two ends of the great Eurasian land mass. The problem was, it was very hard indeed for the English-speaking peoples, for want of a better phrase—for Britain and the United States—to stay out of these conflicts, partly because they had economic interests, partly because ultimately, they feared that their own security would be threatened if one or other tyrannical or totalitarian regime triumphed. The problem in the United States was that, in the first half of the twentieth century—and here I caricature—Americans, for domestic political reasons, were too reluctant to become involved in these Eurasian conflicts. If the United States had been ready to intervene in 1914, I think that might very well have deterred the Germans. If the United States had been ready to intervene in 1939, or indeed in 1938, I think that might very well have deterred the Germans. Part of the point of this museum, it seems to me, and it's a very poetically expressed point, is that more than half the war has passed before the United States becomes involved. That's terribly significant because in the second half of the twentieth century, the United States has tended to err in the opposite direction—becoming involved in conflicts, perhaps, unnecessarily or prematurely as doctrines of preemption have become so important in American strategic thinking. And by the way, that wasn't invented by the Bush administrations. There was a doctrine of preemption at the time of Truman, which was just as important in influencing American decision making in Korea and later Indochina. That's the best answer I can give you. The United States has gone from delayed intervention to often premature intervention, and I think that illustrates how very difficult it is to strike the kind of balance that we armchair strategists are so good at striking. It's easy for us. We're historians. We've never had to make a tougher decision than whether to give someone tenure or not.

AUDIENCE: Laughter.

WINTER: I think we have time for one further question. What I'd like to do, as well is to say that we will carry these conversations on in future meetings which I hope you'll come to. It's after all, one of the critical questions we'll get to, is not so much how to start a war, but how to stop one. And the inordinate difficulty is evidently present in the process of creating and sustaining peace. Creating war, to a degree, has one set of explanations. Creating peace may have an entirely different set of historical problems embedded in it. The last question, please.

QUESTION: Yes, I have a question. Were the men who went to war aware of the dangers of a proletarian revolution they might unleash, or a series of totalitarian reactions if the war got out of hand?

WINTER: Niall?

FERGUSON: There were some people who argued that the best cure for revolutionary tendencies was war. But by 1914, they were by and large seen as being on the fringes. In Germany, for example, it was the kind of argument you might get from the Pan-Germans. But they weren't really terribly close to the center of power at that time. It had actually become apparent to at least some eminent German politicians that a war might have precisely the opposite effect and move Germany and indeed the whole of Europe to the left. And there was plenty of good reason for thinking that. Not only had the recent experience of the Russo-Japanese War produced a revolution in Russia when that war went wrong. But further back, going back to the time of the French Revolutionary Wars, it was clear that unleashing large-scale armies, large mobilizations of young men was the surest way to radicalize society politically. So, I think, by the summer of 1914, very few people had the naïve view that war would actually, as it were, prevent revolution. I think there was a more general understanding that the very opposite might be the case. And that if war was to come on the scale that it came in 1914, a new age of revolutions might not be too far behind.

WINTER: There is a middle point which I think is well worth noting. In some parts of the world, Australia is perhaps a most important instance of the fact that war was a moment when nations were born. And this is not just as a result of the breakup of the empires in 1918. The equivalent of the Fourth of July in Australia is the landing at Gallipoli. In 1915 when they showed that, by the shedding of blood, they were a nation, their ties to Britain began to change irrevocably. New Zealand is a similar case. So is Canada.

But at the same time, it is important to recall that the key players in 1914 were all imperial powers. Every one of these great powers was an imperial power, drawing upon huge resources—in many respects for the last time. The Second World War is totally different. When Britain went to war in 1914, so did Australia. There was no vote in the Australian Parliament; Britain spoke for them. Not so in 1939. Empires both reached their apogee and began to fall apart during the Great War. I congratulate the curators of this museum for showing this imperial side of the war. Paul, would you like to have the last word on this, and on our discussion today?

KENNEDY: I'll build on it, if I may. Niall is quite right to say that while there was a lot of apprehension, say, among French politicians and some German politicians about the growing totalitarianization and urbanization and rise of the second international and early proto-Communist movements, this tended to induce caution. Yes, there were exceptions among right-wing militarists, who argued that we should get rid of the Reichstag and then send everybody off to the war. But they were on the margins. Caution about social solidarity was evident in London, too. In early August 1914, the British cabinet agreed to go into the war and then agreed to the dispatch of a British expeditionary force to Belgium. Then in the midst of that debate some people said, we're not going to send all six divisions we have today over to Belgium and France, we're keeping most of them here until we see whether the organized trade unions will fight with us. And so my final remark, and it's something for you all to reflect on and come back to discuss, is this: what astonished most of the political leaders in 1914 was that those fears were unrealized, that there was this vast up-swelling of patriotic solidarity, people rushing to enlist, insisting that they had to get into the war. That their hopes would be dashed if they didn't get to the recruiting grounds, if they didn't get to the quartermaster, if they didn't lie about their age, and hundreds of thousands of young men lied about their age to get into the fighting. So what was there in the general psyche as well as in the calculations of cabinets that made this war possible, and made it possible for Britain to go to war united? We are still in search of a key to understand this extraordinary moment, the fourth of August 1914, when, with British entry into the war, it became global.

WINTER: Yes, we will return to this question as to whether there is a disconnect between the decency and humanity of the millions who fought the war and the blindness and arrogance of those who directed it. And in the second of our discussions, we will take up that question in terms of military history and military strategy. And I invite you all to come back and continue to hear what historians think about this foundational subject in the history of the twentieth and twenty-first centuries.

TWO

Waging Total War

Learning Curve or Bleeding Curve?

Holger Afflerbach, University of Leeds

Gary Sheffield, University of Birmingham

WINTER: Thank you all for coming to our second historians' conversation about the First World War. When the text of these exchanges will be published in 2009, it will form the only book in our field in which conversation between historians replaces the individual voice. And in my thirty-eight years of teaching, I've come to learn that our profession is a collective; it's less a sum of individuals and more a series of conversations that we have; conversations with colleagues and with students, conversations which are ongoing and filled with both collegiality and difference.

Today we deal with military history, the history of strategy, tactics, operational history. We are in the midst of a long period of important research in this field. Over the last twenty years, there has emerged what some have called "the new military history." It is my privilege to introduce you to two of the people who have been pioneers in this field, Holger Afflerbach of the University of Leeds and Gary Sheffield of the University of Birmingham.

To structure this conversation, I suggest we divide the time we have into five different interrogations. The first focuses on civil-military relations. The question I'd like to pose is this: is it true that in all countries in the First World War, civilians lost control of how war is waged to the military? Is it the case that politicians could not master the generals, the admirals, in the waging of war? This first set of questions seems to me to be one that we can talk about in many different military contexts.

The second one is a question about failure: can we define what constituted failure and by inference what constituted victory on the battlefield of the Great War? And I would like to put to the speakers the proposition that all major offenses in the First World War, except the last one, were failures, in that they did not yield the initial aim or stated objective of the generals who launched them. We'll spend some time on this second facet of the military history of the war.

The third question is this: was there a "learning curve" or was there merely what some scholars have called simply a "bleeding curve" in the First World War? Historians like Robin Prior have argued that there was no serious change in the way the British high command understood the conditions of battle from the beginning to the end of the war. The alternative position, which Gary Sheffield, I think, has established much more solidly than anyone else, is the idea of a learning curve. "Critics failed to acknowledge that the first of July 1916 was not the end of the British army's experience of mass warfare, it was the beginning of it. The Somme marked the beginning of a steep learning curve in command and control as in many other areas." The question as to whether commanders slowly but surely mastered a battlefield that no one had ever seen before is the third matter we should investigate.

The fourth question I would like to put is this: does the term "victory" lose virtually all meaning when casualties reach the one million mark, as in 1916 in the Battle of the Somme and Verdun? Similarly the German March 1918 offensive cost well over a million casualties. Do the staggering costs of these battles constitute more than just a change of degree of bloodshed in battle, but a change in kind, a change in the definition of what battle, indeed what war, is?

The fifth matter for us to ponder today relates to how the war ended, to the strategic decision to end the war while Germany still occupied parts of France and Belgium and while the German army was still intact.

Why didn't the Allies invade Germany and reach a total victory, requiring unconditional surrender, as happened in 1945?

None of these questions is easy, but all are essential to an understanding of the military history of the Great War. To open the conversation, I would like to start with Holger Afflerbach, whose biography of the second man to command the Imperial German army in the Great War, General Falkenhayn, is one of the major achievements in the historiography of the war. Is it the case that the military in Germany ran the war without any political control?

AFFLERBACH: If one looks into any textbook on Imperial Germany, he may find the idea that Germany was run by a kind of military dictatorship, especially in the second half of the war when Hindenburg and Ludendorff took over command. The notion prevails that the two generals could decide everything. But if you look very closely at things as they were in reality, it appears that it was not a military dictatorship; it was rather a kind of chaos. There is a famous quotation from Haldane who said about Imperial Germany that it was a very well organized nation, but if you look at the top level of the state, you find not only confusion, but also chaos. This means that there were too many institutions and individuals who tried to influence politics, and the Kaiser was unable to coordinate them. There is a German saying that "too many cooks spoil the soup," and we can say that there were too many "cooks" in the Imperial kitchen. There was the emperor and his advisers, the chancellor, the Reichstag—the German Parliament—the political parties, the army command, and the naval command, all rivaling for influence. No sufficient cooperation between these different poles of power took place. This got worse during World War I. Ludendorff and Hindenburg really tried hard to control everything but even they were unable to do so. Chaos and lack of coordination on strategic questions prevailed from the first to the last day of the war. For that reason I would not say that Germany was completely controlled by the military. The general staff did try to control the war and it did a lot of harm with its wrong strategies. It was the politicians, though, who bore a very important responsibility for the final outcome of the war, for the defeat.

WINTER: Thank you. Gary, let's turn to the great battles, including the victorious push at the end. Is it the case that the British prime minister, first Asquith and then Lloyd George, lost control of how the war was waged?

SHEFFIELD: Well that again is one of the standard interpretations. I am dubious about that. I think it's not so much that the politicians lost control, as that they did not seek to take control, which is a rather different matter. In the British system, even though Lloyd George affected to believe that General "Wully" Robertson, the chief of the Imperial General Staff, hence the professional head of the British army, was fomenting some kind of a coup in early 1918, this was just complete nonsense. Actually, British generals accepted and understood well the civil-military environment in which they operated, even if they didn't like it very much. Certainly, the generals carried out politicking with a small "p," but even the most highly criticized of all of the British generals, Sir Henry Wilson who was Robertson's successor as chief of the Imperial General Staff in 1918, knew there were some red lines you simply did not cross. So for example, in the spring of 1918, consider this case. Sir Frederick Maurice wrote a letter to *The Times* (which, in the interests of accuracy should not be called the *London Times* or *The Times* of London) saying that Lloyd George was a liar, which of course he was; he had actually lied to Parliament about the strength of the British army on the Western front. Maurice did so in the full knowledge that that was the end of his military career, and everybody including Sir Henry Wilson and Sir Douglas Haig said, well okay, in effect, he might have been right in factual detail, but you simply do not challenge the politicians like that.[1]

WINTER: In public.

SHEFFIELD: In public—you simply do not stand up and do it in public. It's the same today. In the British system, military people do not go on the record attacking the government. When they do—it's actually happened relatively recently in Britain—it is seen as wrong, either a mistake—speaking off the cuff or not knowing who is in the room—or it is seen as a violation of an unwritten rule, something which is simply not done. So, in the First World War, I think we need to divide the war in two halves, from the outbreak of the war in 1914 to fall of the prime minister, H. H. Asquith, at the end of 1916. As prime minister, Asquith was content to allow the military to basically get on with it, and he did not interfere very much. It helped, of course, that the secretary of state for war, Lord Kitchener, was a soldier, albeit wearing a civilian hat, and through him, there was a sense in which the military and civilian control of the army was embodied in one person. Kitchener died in a naval incident in mid-1916. After Asquith falls and Lloyd George comes to power later that year, then you have a rather different situation. Lloyd George is vehemently opposed to Haig, to Robertson, and to the strategy being put forward by them. But Lloyd George fails to do anything about it.

WINTER: Why did he hesitate? He was against the Passchendaele offensive in 1917.

SHEFFIELD: Yes.

WINTER: He had severe doubts. Why did he not speak out? Or indeed fire Haig?

SHEFFIELD: Well I think the second part is easier to answer. I don't think he could actually fire Haig in 1917 because Haig enjoyed the support of Lloyd George's Unionist (that is Conservative Party) allies in the coalition government formed when Lloyd George replaced Asquith in December 1916. Haig also enjoyed the support of the press.

WINTER: And the king.

SHEFFIELD: And the king. After Cambrai in November, early December 1917, Haig loses an awful lot of his support and I believe, as numerous other scholars do as well, that Haig could have been fired had Lloyd George had the courage to do so early in 1918. He doesn't do that. And as far as Passchendaele was concerned, well it's simply not true to say that, as some people have argued, that Haig pursued the preparations for Passchendaele and the battle itself without informing the government or the cabinet. It simply happened. But nobody said, "I don't think this is a good idea, please stop it."[2] And I think within the British system, Haig would either have had to knuckle down or resign, but he was never put in that position.

WINTER: So it's a question of moral courage as well, isn't it?

SHEFFIELD: I think so. And I think Lloyd George simply never plucked up the nerve.

AFFLERBACH: I would say that there's also another reason for this behavior of the politicians—the British as well as the German politicians. This reason is that World War I was definitely a total war in the sense that both sides wanted to achieve victory at all costs. And if you want to win, you are at the mercy of the military because they and only they have to do the job. Let us consider the alternative. Politicians may have concluded that a military decision would be too costly or impossible and that they would have to end the war by agreeing to a compromise peace. In this moment they would have had the upper hand and could have ordered their military to stop fighting. They could have said: "We save what we have; it is not a total victory, but we stop now before it gets worse." This did not happen in World War I—or only at the very end. The politicians wanted to achieve political aims which presupposed full military victory.

Let us now consider the German case. For example in November 1914, Falkenhayn came to Bethmann-Hollweg, the chancellor, and said: "We are finished, we can't continue. The general staff can't guarantee victory anymore. We are in a stalemate. You have to look for political solutions." This happened in November 1914 after only three months of war. Bethmann-Hollweg was extremely reluctant to follow this line of argument because he wanted to achieve political aims which required a military victory.

In everyday language, some historians see the military leaders of World War I as the responsible men and the politicians as the well-intentioned but powerless men who were unable to stop them. In my opinion this is not so. The politicians pushed the military forward. This is the real picture of World War I.

SHEFFIELD: I'd go an awfully long way with that, and certainly it's misleading in a sense to set up Haig and Lloyd George as being polar opposites, because they're not. They both want to pursue total war. It's just that Lloyd George's vision of total war was different from Haig's. And I always thought it strange that Lloyd George, who more than anybody else, I think, remobilized Britain for total war in 1917 and 1918, didn't understand that this remobilization required him to support if not Haig, then Haig's replacement in fighting on the Western front. Now, Lloyd George was not afraid of fighting big and bloody battles, he just didn't want the British to do it. He was quite happy if the Italians made the main military effort. Lloyd George had the brilliant idea in 1917 to transfer the bulk of Allied forces to Italy, which for a variety of reasons was a nonstarter. Similarly, in 1915, he was prepared to support Gallipoli, and what a wonderful decision that was! So what you've got here is actually two variants on total war. Lloyd George is not opposed to it as such.

WINTER: There are contrasts among the combatant countries on this matter. The one case in which civilians remained in firm control of the waging of war was in France. Parliament held the purse strings and used that to review and criticize military matters. To be sure, a substantial part of the French Chamber of Deputies was in uniform. There were people who came back from the front and said, do you really think that you're providing us with sufficient munitions? Why don't you come up with me on Monday and stay for forty-eight hours and see what you think then? But they were not prepared to just sign on the dotted line for any amount of money for the army. They regained control through the fiscal power that they had.[3]

If we can move now to the second fundamental question. Is it true to say that all major offensives, except the last one, in the First World War were failures in that they did not yield the initial aim or objectives as stated at the outset of the battle? And there's a long series of them— the Battle of the Marne was an Allied defensive victory against the German invasion. Gallipoli was Winston Churchill's harebrained idea in 1915 to knock Turkey out of the war by a combined naval and land amphibious operation, which resulted in failure under any stretch of the imagination. The Somme, and one would have to say Verdun, were both failures at astronomical costs in 1916. Then take the Nivelle Offensive on the Chemin des Dames in the spring of 1917: there is no question but that that was a failure. There is some debate about Passchendaele, or the Third Battle of Ypres, but my own view is that it was a monumental failure. And then finally there is the last desperate gamble of Ludendorff in 1918, which failed and, at that moment, produced a counteroffensive that won the war. On this last phase of the war, Gary Sheffield is the leading authority. Is it true to say that all of the major offensives in the war, bar the last one, were failures?

SHEFFIELD: I think we need to define this word failure very, very carefully. You cited some instances on which we can agree. Now, we keep talking about Haig, but there are actually other British generals apart from Haig. If you measure the success of failure of an offensive by the initial objectives, it depends whether you believe some of the things Haig was saying a few weeks or months before the Somme, as in his belief in the possibility of a breakthrough. Or whether you believe what he was saying a few days before the Somme, which is basically the aim is to run down the Germans, relieve pressure on Verdun, inflict attrition on the Germans. Now, Haig may have looked stupid with a big mustache, but actually he wasn't. And just as in politics, it makes eminent sense to downplay expectations. So when what actually happens is less than what you wanted, it still can be talked up as a great success or you can say, well that's what we expected all along. That's something he did. Haig hedges his bets with the Somme. Charteris, his intelligence chief, writes just before the battle, on 30 June 1916: "it is always as well to disclaim great hopes before an attack."[4] So if you consider Haig's statements that he wanted a breakthrough, which certainly Haig was thinking of at various times, then yes the battle is a failure. If you look at the second option, that it was a battle of attrition all along, then no it's not. And I think the Somme, as I've written in one of my books, is not a victory, but it is a success for the Allies, albeit a bloody one.[5] I think the word "victory" as applied to most of the operational history of the First World War is simply inappropriate, if you mean, by that, something like Waterloo or Gettysburg. It doesn't work like that. At least not on the Western front, most of the time. I think Holger has got different views on this, but I think it was a kind of success in inflicting attrition on the German army. And actually, I think it had psychological impact in that, again, I'm open to correction by this, that the Germans at the beginning of 1916 thought they were faced by two major land powers—France and Russia. By the end, they were aware they were up against a third one. Now okay, the British army might be clumsy, it's not as effective as it would like to be, but it's there and actually fighting in very large numbers. So I think against that background, I think you can judge the Somme to be a success. In two years' time, in the hundred days at the end of the war, the final battles of 1918, why does that operation become a success when other ones weren't? I think in very broad strokes, the German army is not what it was. It's had an enormous amount of damage inflicted on it by the Allies in 1916 and 1917 and of course not the least in the spring of 1918, in which the German attack comes moderately close to succeeding, but at huge cost. But also I think on the Allied side—and here I would lump in the French as well as the British—there was a major improvement in everything from high command right the way down to minor tactics, taking in en route logistics and everything else in the meantime.

The conduct of war has changed fundamentally in 1918 because the First World War was basically an aberration in the way that war is normally conducted. There are other periods in history, say for example in parts of the Pacific war in 1941–45, in which you have a temporary stalemate produced by local tactical factors and by technology. But effectively what you had on the Western front was stalemate in place for three and a half years. Well, once those conditions are overcome and then warfare becomes more mobile and, again, then we revert to a more familiar war. We see exactly the same thing happening in later wars as well. If you look at Normandy for two months in mid-1944, it's a stalemate, but then the stalemate is overcome and mobile war begins again. The First World War is different because of the scale and because of the duration of the stalemate.

WINTER: What do you say, Holger? Is this a position you would share?

AFFLERBACH: It is probably better to pose a counterfactual question. Would it have been possible to make a decisive breakthrough during World War I? Probably not. The war was not decided by a breakthrough, actually. It did not happen. We will come back to this when we speak about 1918. On the other side I see that there are several military successes in World War I which definitely changed the face of the war—I will not say the outcome. Let me cite one example. The Germans and the Austrians had a very big success against the Russians at Gorlice Tarnow in May 1915. They achieved a breakthrough. They broke through the enemy lines and threw the Russians out of Poland—Russian Poland. This success enabled the Central Powers to stop the Italians, who entered World War I precisely at that time. We have to consider the strategic implications for the front in Poland and the other in the northeast of Italy. Without the success of Gorlice Tarnow, probably the Central Powers would have had to accept defeat in 1915. For that reason, it seems to me that Gorlice Tarnow was a huge military success. Indeed, it enabled Germany and Austria-Hungary to continue resistance for three subsequent years. Maybe for the worse, because at the end, they lost anyway.

Let us consider the question of what is "military success" from another angle. Strategic analysts in both belligerent and neutral countries had much to say about the reasons for the stalemate of trench warfare. Why did it happen? Was the stalemate structural, in the sense that it reflected a balance of forces and the technology of the time, or was it temporary, reflecting poor command? Most people choose structural explanations. There was little room for mobility on the battlefield and logistical problems of a monumental order. I agree with this argument. I think that there was a balance of forces between the sides which was the decisive element. You, Gary, brought up the example of Normandy in 1944. The final breakthrough of the Allied powers was caused by continuous reinforcements sent over the Channel so that at the end the Germans were numerically and logistically overwhelmed.

Where the balance of forces did not exist, mobile warfare was possible. For example, Gorlice Tarnow or the conquest of Serbia in 1915—within a few weeks the Germans, the Austrians, and the Bulgarians could conquer Serbia. The same happened in Rumania in 1916. The Central Powers conquered around 80 percent of Rumania—in a little more than three months. The German-Austrian breakthrough in Italy in October 1917 at Caporetto, the British breakthrough in Palestine in 1918, and the Allied breakthrough at the bridgehead of Saloniki in September 1918 show too that mobile warfare was feasible. It was possible to make mobile warfare work if the offensive side had the strength and the agility to do so. And I would suggest that this was exactly the case in the famous hundred days of the Allied advance in autumn 1918. The German army could no longer revert to previous practice; that is if a breakthrough of enemy forces seemed imminent, they deployed reserves from less endangered parts of the front towards the decisive sector. Why couldn't they do that any more? Because suddenly there were two million American soldiers in France. The pressure on all parts of the Western front was so severe that the Germans could not deploy reserves effectively. Therefore a breakthrough on the Western front, even under the complex technical conditions of World War I battlefields, seemed to be possible. This breakthrough did not happen, but at least the Allies did push the German army back day by day, and thereby avoid a stalemate.

SHEFFIELD: Again, I'm largely in agreement. But I would put a slightly different emphasis on some of it; simply having very large numbers of troops actually doesn't guarantee success.

WINTER: Think of the Russian army.

SHEFFIELD: Think of the Russians; think of the Americans at the Meuse-Argonne in the beginning of the offensive in 1918 having large numbers of troops who simply were being fed into a mincing machine, and therefore they made very little impact. Only when Pershing was kicked upstairs and they got some better generals in—that's a slightly controversial thing to say, but actually from that point on, the Americans did extremely well.

WINTER: We'll censor that later.

SHEFFIELD: Okay, we'll take that one out. [Laughter] So I would say that I mean Holger was right: having large numbers of troops gave the Allies a distinct advantage, but actually had the trench system still been in place, I don't think this superiority in manpower would have made that much of a difference. Normandy in June 1944, I think is an even better example of this, because what you have here are so many American and British and Canadian soldiers in the sector that they have barely got elbow room to operate. But it's not until a series of things unlocked the tactical deadlock in the *bocage* as far as the Americans are concerned, and around Caen, as far as the British and Canadians are concerned, that actually they were able to make their numerical superiority take effect.

WINTER: Perhaps we can put the point in another way. The German army in 1914–18 may have been one of the most remarkable military institutions ever put together. What was astonishing was how long they held off the forces of the entire world. First, they stopped the French.

Had the first Battle of the Marne, which the German army lost, been fought in nineteenth-century terms, the Germans would have rushed back to Germany, the French would have chased them all the way; there would have been a treaty, and that would have been the end of it. No, this was twentieth-century warfare. After the Marne, the Germans retreated north. They stopped on the River Aisne and dug in. There they stayed, on high ground, on what became the Western front. Then what happened in 1915? The defensive had the ascendency. Take Gallipoli; an attempt to break the deadlock on the Western front. It was a catastrophe. German training of a Turkish force made it very difficult for the Allied invasion force to get to the top of the heights near the beachheads the first day. Or a year later in 1916: after six months in the Battle of the Somme and Verdun, in both cases, the Allies had enormous difficulty in dealing with German defensive strategy. What to me is surprising is not that they were worn down to defeat in 1918, but that they stayed the course so long.

In nearly forty years of working on the First World War, I've only found two documents in British archives that talk explicitly about defeat—they're both naval documents—you probably know them—in 1917 about submarine warfare and food imports and so on. But my guess is, the reason why the British high command and the cabinet believed they would win is not because of superior manpower or command but because they were British.

SHEFFIELD: Well naturally! [Laughter] In fact, there was a deep level of pessimism in 1917. But defeat for Britain meant something rather different than defeat for France or Germany, because given that Germany did not really have the wherewithal to physically land troops in England, defeat for Britain meant actually losing France as an ally and being forced, possibly, to carry out a "Dunkirk" twenty-five years early. And there were some discussions about what would happen in the event of a French defeat, and there is some thought that if the Germans do actually defeat the British and the French in France, there will be a compromise peace, but effectively it would be only a truce. And actually, they were thinking in terms of what they called the Great War, which was the British War against the French, which went on and off for a quarter of a century from 1793 to 1815. So they see that possibly a defeat in continental Europe would mean that Britain would retire for a bit to lick its wounds, but then war will be renewed four, five, six years down the line.[6]

WINTER: This is where we started in this debate between Niall Ferguson and Paul Kennedy some time ago, and which was central to the first conversation in this series. Is it your view, Holger, that the First World War really was fundamentally a struggle between Germany and Britain for control of northwestern Europe? This is, I believe, Paul Kennedy's position.

AFFLERBACH: I don't think that World War I broke out because the Germans wanted to conquer the world. It did not start that way. I think World War I broke out because the German government wanted to aid the Austro-Hungarian Empire to stabilize its position as a great power. The German high command was afraid that an Austrian breakdown would leave them isolated; that they would stand alone without any ally in a Europe of enemies. It was a kind of a defensive attempt to stabilize Germany's political, diplomatic, and military position in Europe. Later, things escalated, partly because new war aims emerged during September 1914. These war aims were not in existence prior to the outbreak of war—they came afterwards and were a brainchild of the first German successes.

I would like to return to the argument that Great Britain was planning on victory. Can we say that Great Britain actually was contemplating only victory in World War I, while Germany was seriously contemplating defeat? I think this is true, indeed, especially in the second half of the war. The German high command knew that defeat was a real possibility. I recently edited the diary and the war letters of General von Lyncker, general adjutant of Wilhelm II and chief of the Military Cabinet.[7] They are an interesting source because they show us how the opinions and expectations of this very well-placed and influential general changed day by day, throughout the entire war. Lyncker in late summer 1916 started to think that a German defeat was a real possibility. I think he was typical, not an exception among the German leaders. Therefore it is understandable that Germany made, in the second half of the war, several peace offers. This series began in December 1916. The Kaiser made a peace offer in December 1916, and the German Reichstag made one in the summer of 1917. The Germans hoped that the Allies would allow Germany to go out of the war with a black eye, as it were, a kind of return to the prewar status quo. The Reichstag in 1917 wanted a peace without annexations. But the Allies would not have accepted such a peace, which they would have seen as a kind of defeat. From the British point of view, a peace which would have returned Europe to the *status quo ante bellum* would have been looked at as a defeat.

WINTER: Well it would have been, I think, politically impossible to sell to the British population, because so many soldiers had already died. Compromise became impossible once the bloodshed had reached a level no one had ever seen before.

SHEFFIELD: I am not persuaded by this argument. From the Allied perspective, the German peace offers never seemed to include the really key bit, which was pulling out of somebody else's territory. Britain goes to war in 1914. It is a balance of power war. They go to war for the same reason that they go to war against the French in 1793, and against Hitler in 1939, and joined NATO in 1949; that is, to stop somebody—and it might be France, it might be Germany, it might be Russia—achieving domination or hegemony over Western Europe. Britain does not want one dominating power. And on another level, Britain doesn't like Belgium being in unfriendly hands because it would threaten British naval supremacy and possibly block commercial traffic going through the English Channel, thereby giving whoever holds Belgium a major hold over Britain's food supply.

From the British point of view, the Germans never really seem to be serious in saying, "okay, we will have a peace which involves evacuating the key points." Whether that's true or not, the perception from the British point of view is that the Germans are never really serious about making the sort of concessions that will lead to a genuine compromise peace.

AFFLERBACH: Yes, I agree on this but for a different reason. Germany was governed by inept leaders during the Great War. Perhaps it is better to say that it was governed by men suffering from multiple delusions. Anyone in doubt of this fact may go to the Liberty Memorial Museum in which the Zimmermann telegram is on display.[8] Let me explain: Arthur Zimmermann, secretary of state in the German Foreign Office, sent in 1917 an unsafely coded offer to the government of Mexico to enter the war on the German side. He promised Mexico the southwest of the United States as a prize. This offer was valid in the event that the United States would declare war on Germany. This is the best example of amateurishness in the way the German government conducted policy. Mexico was powerless and no danger for the U.S. This alliance would have been worthless for both sides, for Germany and for Mexico. But things were even worse: How could Zimmermann have sent a telegram with such a delicate offer to Mexico—on transatlantic cables which were controlled by the British? It was even more foolish to do so in a moment of high tension between Germany and the U.S. As could have been anticipated, the British intercepted and published the telegram. Zimmermann confirmed its authenticity! This affair was one of the reasons which brought the U.S., whose president and public opinion were understandably outraged, into the war.

Now I would like to discuss Gary's point: Why did German diplomats leave out the Belgian question when they were floating various peace balloons? The main argument was that they needed something in their hand, what we call a "Faustpfand," when peace negotiations began, because the British occupied all German colonies. I agree, it was an extremely poor political strategy. The German government made tremendous mistakes, not only on the Belgian question. The list of German mistakes is nearly endless, and I think, at the end, the German empire had to lose this world war because no government could have made so many mistakes and come out as the winner. Such an outcome seems impossible to me.[9]

WINTER: Let me put the opposite case. The opposite case is to divide the war in half and to say that the Russian Revolution of 1917 changed everything. And the war from mid-1917 on after the first Russian Revolution to the end of the war is very different in military terms as well as in political terms from the first half. And the reason why I think this interpretation challenges yours, Holger, is that the German army won the war on the Eastern front.

AFFLERBACH: Yes. That is true, but my claim still stands. I would like to mention only the most blatant idiocy that the German government made in World War I. May I quote from Winston Churchill? He said that the Germans should have waited for only two or three months with their Declaration of Unlimited Submarine Warfare. By then, in March 1917, the Russian Revolution had begun, and it was foreseeable that Russia would drop out of the war. But no, the German government thought that they could not wait. Had the Germans decided to keep the Americans out at all costs, they could have won the war. Then all the learning curves in the world or in the British army would have been insufficient to kick the Germans out of France.

SHEFFIELD: I do agree with that. It's always struck me as bizarre, because we can agree that the German army did indeed win the First World War, part I, by defeating Russia. And rather than cashing in their winnings, and making peace, they went on this ridiculous offensive in March 1918. I mean it strikes me that at the end of 1917, Germany could have said to the Allies, okay, yes you can have everything back in Western Europe; this concession doesn't really matter, because we've conquered this vast empire in the East. But I also want to say that I'm a bit dubious about quoting Churchill's authority, actually. This is the man who brought us Gallipoli after all.

ALL: Laughter.

WINTER: I think we'll draw a veil of discretion over that point. And what I think we should turn to now towards the conclusion of our conversation is the question of the end game. How did the war end militarily? And let me put to both of you this proposition: I would argue that the Allies lost the peace by not invading Germany in November to December 1918 and not forcing a complete capitulation from the old regime that had brought disaster to Germany. Yes, British, French, and American troops were exhausted, not only by battle but by the worst influenza epidemic in history. But still, we cannot avoid concluding that when the guns fell silent, on the eleventh day of the eleventh month of the year, at the eleventh hour, when the Armistice arrived, the German army marched back to Germany intact, thereby setting the stage for the dissemination of the stab in the back legend, the widely shared view that the German army had victory snatched from its jaws by the treachery of Communists, Socialists, and Jews at home. My claim is that the Armistice was not a victory, nor was the peace settlement. What do you say to the view that, by not invading Germany, the Allies actually lost the war and had to fight it again in 1939?

SHEFFIELD: I think it's an overstatement to say they lost the war. Militarily, it was a clear victory, but I think that the Allies did not get the optimum result from the war. There's a very good case to be made that at the end of almost any war, there are disappointments and compromises. Wars which are fought to an absolute standstill with one side being destroyed are very, very rare. They do happen; Germany in the Second World War is an obvious example, but they're very rare. But in most wars, the outcome will be determined by negotiations. And I think the Allies fumbled the ball on this one, in fact. I was very rude about John J. Pershing earlier, but he was absolutely right when he argued that the Allies should have gone on into Germany, and made it clear that actually the Germans had lost the war. Having said that, I'd like to suggest that for Britain, for the Allies, the First World War was a negative victory. And what I mean by that is they ensured that something did not happen, that Germany did not win. But that said, while the world in 1919 was probably a worse place than in 1914, in my humble opinion, it would have been an even worse place in 1919 had Imperial Germany won. Preventing this was a negative victory; what was achieved should not be gainsaid. It strikes me that what happens in 1919 is that an imperfect peace is brought about. This peace, based on commitments that were not honored and restrictions that were not enforced, led to a whole series of events that may or may not have led directly to the Second World War. So what happens in 1918, from the Allied perspective, is a victory—very definitely a victory. But it is a victory which is incomplete. Europe and the world could have evolved in a more peaceful direction. The fact that it doesn't, I think, has more to do with the Great Depression, and the coming of Hitler, rather than any inherent faults in the Treaty of Versailles itself.

AFFLERBACH: I remember a conversation between some American generals who wanted to push forward to Berlin. They were opposed to the Armistice, but some French commander (to my recollection it was probably Foch) replied that continuing the war despite the fact that Germany wanted an Armistice would have been a criminal act. It would have been mass homicide to continue the fighting. Germany was in a very bad military and political situation in autumn 1918. Nevertheless, to continue fighting would have meant to sacrifice additional hundreds of thousands of lives—lives of Allied soldiers as well as German lives. And then perhaps an invasion would have pushed the Germans to a *levee en masse,* to total resistance.[10] The German government could have said to its people: "We tried to stop the war but the enemy rejected our offer and therefore we have to continue to fight." The German leaders would have had a new legitimacy to do so. And what would the Allied governments have said to their soldiers who wanted to go home? And to the parents asking for the reason why their boys were still killed at the front? They would have needed a very good answer to the question: "We could have had peace, but why are we continuing to fight?" I think this counterfactual scenario shows that an Allied invasion of Germany in 1919 was militarily possible but politically very difficult to justify. If something went wrong with World War I, it was that it was too long, not that it was too short.

I have looked into the German archives to find some evidence on this point. The historians in the interwar period analyzed very carefully the options the German army faced in autumn 1918 and tried to find out if it was possible for Germany to continue the fight. The answer was yes, they could have continued, and it would have been possible to stabilize the Western front in the winter of 1918–19. But then what? This would have been the same as Germany stabilizing the front at the end of 1944—and in 1945 there was a total breakdown. During 1919, of course, a total breakdown would have come because of chaos and exhaustion. Continuing the war was, I think, insane from a military point of view.

SHEFFIELD: That's very interesting, but let's consider just a couple of points. Politically, what happens in 1919 is of extreme interest to the British and French because there is little doubt that if the war had carried on, the bulk of the fighting would not have been done by the British army or by the French, but by the United States Army. Haig is warned, actually by Winston Churchill who is in charge of the munitions industry at this time, that his army was going to be halved in 1919. Bayonet strength goes down from sixty-odd divisions to thirty-something divisions. And so concluding that war in 1918 before the Americans come in and, for better or for worse, provide the victorious troops, is a high priority for the British, and though I haven't looked at the archives, I guess for the French as well. Added to that, there is a good deal of conservative thinking that the last thing that the Allies want is for Germany to melt down into Bolshevik Revolution; if so, then where is it going to stop? You know, is it going to be the start of the European Revolution for which Lenin hopes and Haig fears? And finally, there is the fact that British intelligence—which actually is not too bad in 1918, in comparison to some earlier years—breaks down at this crucial moment. And so the British are not very well informed what's actually going on in Germany itself. There are fears and rumors that the Germans are gathering a mass army for a last stand. So Haig, in particular, argues in a cricketing metaphor, that the Allies should—as we would say in England—pull stumps and quit while they were ahead. The Germans are going effectively to surrender. If we push them too far, it might cause Germany to melt down; it might cause Germany to be defended street by street as Holger has just mentioned. And so this is not an attractive option. French generals—I think Foch, in particular, actually says, no, no, let's really put the boot in, let's make sure that we crush the Germans so they're aware that they've been defeated. But in the end, I think it's the British and also the American view which prevails. Which brings us to an interesting view of total war mentalities. The First World War is a total war in so many ways except at the very last, they revert to an almost limited war thinking. This is not at all what happens in the Second World War. The unconditional surrender proclamation in 1943 is looking back to 1918, basically contending that the Allies do not want a repetition of the incomplete victory at the end of the Great War. That is why 1945 is not 1918.

WINTER: There are many documents which show us that for soldiers, the end of the war was a bittersweet moment, one mixing relief on the one hand with exhaustion and bitterness on the other. This may explain something about the strange atmosphere in which the war ended and the peace negotiations began.

But the end of the fighting on 11 November was not the end of the state of belligerency. That required a peace settlement, which came later. I would like to turn to the subject of the blockade of Germany after the Armistice, a blockade which continued until the twenty-eighth of June 1919 when the German delegation signed the peace treaty. Was the continuation of the blockade after the Armistice a war crime? Is it not the case that this was total war against German civilians because the German army had already accepted an Armistice? So the only people who were being punished were women, the elderly, children. It strikes me that the Allies lost a great deal of their moral advantage by engaging in a form of collective punishment, so that German civilians would know the bitterness of war, just as Belgian civilians had done for four years.

AFFLERBACH: Lloyd George was confronted by one of the German delegates to the Versailles Peace Conference, Count Brockdorf-Rantzau, on issues concerning the effects of the blockade. Both Lloyd George and Wilson were well aware of this. On the one hand, there was harshness in the treatment of German people whose Kaiser had fled. The regime that started the war and lost had collapsed. On the other side, after four and a half years of war, of course, many Allied leaders were afraid that the peace negotiations would fail and that Germany would not sign the treaty. The new German government reflected very seriously on not signing the peace treaty because its terms were overly harsh. As a result it made sense for the Allied powers to continue the blockade to control the Germans as long as the treaty was not signed and the war was not formally ended. We know the outcome, but the choices at the time were difficult ones.

The blockade was undoubtedly a very cruel war measure. I believe that Sir Arthur Harris, Bomber Harris, the man who carried out carpet bombing of centers of civilian population in the Second World War, a man vilified by many as a criminal, cited the Allied blockade of World War I as even crueler. Whether the one justifies the other is another matter.

SHEFFIELD: To understand the blockade, we need to understand total war mentalities. I think that in the First World War, at the very end, as in 1942 or the bombing of Hamburg in 1943, what we see is that a democratic civilized people who shared peacetime inhibitions about violence do things which they wouldn't have contemplated before the war and are ashamed of after the war. I think the blockade is of a piece with that. Also, I thoroughly agree with your point about what happens if negotiations break down in early 1919. Don't forget, the British army basically melts away after the Armistice because the average British soldier thinks the war is over.

WINTER: It was over for them.

SHEFFIELD: The people who enlist in 1914 voluntarily or through conscription from 1916 onwards, they think they've got a contract with the government which is that they are in uniform to go and beat the German army. They defeat the German army and they want to go home. And so the British army is in no fit state to take on the Girl Guides in the spring of 1919.

WINTER: That's the Girl Scouts, by the way, for our American friends.

SHEFFIELD: Sorry. The Girl Scouts. In 1919 the British are in no position to engage in an offensive, even if they wished to do so. And I would finally say that lots of British soldiers who are in the Rhineland in occupying forces, they really do not like what they see of the impact of the blockade. They end up sharing their rations with German children. But there was no great outcry at home about it. The election of 1919 in Britain was full of calls to hang the Kaiser, to squeeze Germans till the pips squeak. The population is still in the thrall of a total war mentality.

WINTER: And perhaps a final note. I have been struck in your work, Holger, that you have reached the conclusion that there were one or two leaders in the German military or naval command who were perhaps in need of psychiatric care. One is Ludendorff, the other is Admiral Scheer. This admiral had the idea of taking the German North Seas fleet out to fight a battle they could not win. He wanted to see *Götterdämmerung*, at whatever human cost, to restore their great honor because they never got out of their bases in the Hanseatic ports. Fortunately his sailors mutinied and doused the engines. *Götterdämmerung* never happened. Such an act appears to be close to criminal insanity. Maybe the phrase is a little extreme, but I wonder what your view is. Was there something wrong in German military culture that enabled people like this to reach such conclusions? Ludendorff's vision of the world was very strange, and "extreme" is not nearly the word that we need. Was there something pathological about a military-naval system that put these people in command?

AFFLERBACH: I do not see something pathological in German political culture before 1918. This goes too far, in my opinion. But I admit that the Kaiserrich suffered structurally from very poor personal recruitment for the top echelons in army and administration. This was caused by the rules of the constitution of 1871 and by the role of the emperor and his political and military advisers. Max Weber spoke about a "negative selection" of personnel, and it would be possible to prove this statement with numerous examples. It was indeed not a good sign of the viability of the Kaiserrich that somebody like Ludendorff could come to power. Ludendorff was a gifted soldier, but an extremely unstable personality. If there is something pathological in German military culture, it may be a kind of philosophical concept that willpower is the decisive quality in a soldier. German military culture basically posits that the German soldiers have superior skills to those of the enemies. It was also true that the German army had a very strong belief in itself. They said that due to their qualitative superiority they only needed the reckless, fanatical, and uncompromising will to victory. This is precisely what we see later also in World War II. The German leadership wanted to prevail against all odds to defeat superior numbers. They forgot Napoleon's saying that God is normally on the side of the stronger battalions. The hard-liners in the German high command were convinced that if they had the fanatical willpower, they could do it. Ludendorff was an extreme example of someone with this cast of mind. Maybe others were not so fanatical. Helmuth von Moltke, Erich von Falkenhayn, Kronprinz Rupprecht, or Erich Groener were much more reasonable people; and so was Hindenburg. You know, Ludendorff was only the second in command. He was the dominant thinker, but Hindenburg was also there. Hindenburg was also a more recognizably normal person than Ludendorff. Ludendorff was apparently a lunatic, somebody who turned later on to be a radical anti-Semite, a seemingly disturbed man who, according to Groener, already in 1915 probably belonged in a madhouse. But in terms of our discussion, one thing is interesting. Even this man calls for an end to the war in 1918. His writings show that he was very far from sane, but even he, at the end of the day, urges the Kaiser and the German army to stop fighting. His volte face is breathtaking. After commanding this huge offensive from March 1918 on, at a certain point, Ludendorff said that an Armistice was needed within twenty-four hours. He was fighting for more than four years and then he could not wait ten minutes to get on the phone to try to get Wilson to broker an Armistice. He totally lost his nerve. Perhaps we should be grateful for that, since he did not wind up the way the German army did in 1945. In those days they stopped fighting when the Red Army was in Berlin or rather in what was left of it. Had the German army gone on fighting in 1919, the result would probably have been similar. The only difference would be that hundreds of thousands of lives were spared, at least this time in history.

WINTER: Is it possible to conclude, therefore, that the political culture of a nation, very different in Britain, put some constraints on the way in which high command operated?

SHEFFIELD: Yes, there were and there are still such constraints. In the First World War, Haig was able to continue his strategy, even given the vast scale of casualties which were shocking to a number of people in government. I think it was a very interesting parallel with the Second World War, where the British go into the Second World War, and everybody from prime minister right through the generals, right down to people on the street, accept that we cannot fight that sort of war again. The people will not stand for that level of casualties. Ironically, of course, if you look at individual battles on a percentage basis, it was even more bloody and dangerous in the Second World War for the British soldier than it was in the First World War, but in absolute terms, in Britain fewer soldiers died in 1939–45 than in 1914–18. British troops were in battle for shorter periods of time. But nonetheless, people like Alanbrooke, people like Montgomery, who were themselves Western front veterans as junior officers; they go into the Second World War absolutely aware they cannot tolerate the same level of casualties as Haig did in the First World War.

Let's go back the question of command and insanity. Some people have suggested that Douglas Haig was clinically insane. This is nonsense. In fact, there is a sort of amateurish culture of the British army, then as now, I suspect, which means that you get some wild eccentrics coming to the top of the tree. Yes, that is true, but not the lunatics of the Ludendorff kind. Sir John French, the first commander of the British Expeditionary Force in France, was, I think, pretty wild and unstable in his views, but he certainly wasn't certifiably insane. My favorite character in this sense is General Hunter-Weston. He seems to have had a good brain, but suffered from sunstroke at Gallipoli, and his staff thought that he was never much good after that. This begs the question why is he then put into a position of command on the Western front? But some recent research has suggested that even Hunter-Weston had his uses. He was a sort of grandee, and he entertained lavishly, so that when the king of the Belgians came to visit the British, he was pushed out; it was Hunter-Weston who entertained him at the dinner table. But to take the question more seriously, in both the British army and among the Dominion armies, there was already a meritocracy in place. There were some highly competent commanders: the names of Plumer, Currie, the commander of the Canadian Corps, and Monash, his Australian counterpart, spring to mind. It's interesting to speculate if Douglas Haig had fallen under the proverbial bus, who would have replaced him? By 1918, as Haig himself said, we have a remarkably high number of very competent commanders, and these were people who had come up the hard way by proving themselves on the battlefield.

WINTER: I still find it hard to escape from one simple point. There is still a disconnect between the vision of the political leaders and the military leaders on both sides and the suffering on a scale never before known of the men they led. And that disconnect, I think, has been the central driving force of much of the scholarship which has appeared in the last thirty years.

SHEFFIELD: I think what's new about the First World War is the scale, but if you look at the intensity of the war, it's nothing new. You Americans have seen the same in the Civil War—your civil war, not ours! You see the same in the Napoleonic Wars. The levels of casualties in those battles equal or exceed those in First World War battles. So, I don't actually think there's anything new in that sense. And I do think that British generals knew very, very well what war was actually like. They had done a lot of it after Napoleon's defeat, throughout the world. It is the fact that after 1914 war involves the masses, total populations. That is what made the difference, and that was something that Britain had never experienced; while continental Europeans hadn't really had any experience of this since 1815. Yes, there was the Paris Commune of 1871, but that was an exception. So if war is not absolutely new, what has occurred is its new capacity to reach absolutely everyone and absolutely everywhere.

WINTER: Well, on that point, I think we can turn to the audience after joining me in thanking our participants for such a compelling presentation of their field of research, that of strategy and command in the Great War.

KENNEDY: My name is Ian Kennedy. I wanted to ask about Lloyd George's failing to dismiss Haig after Passchendaele. Do you think he stuck with Haig on the basis, better the devil you know? And also because Lloyd George lacked confidence in handling military men. He wasn't a general manqué like Churchill. And if suppose Lloyd George had nerved himself to get rid of Haig, who do you think he would have chosen and why?

SHEFFIELD: Well, I detect an accent nearer to my home than Kansas City. I think the reason why Lloyd George did not dismiss Haig after Passchendaele, or really after Cambrai, because that's the point at which Haig lost much of his support in government and crucially in the press, remains a mystery, because he got rid of Robertson in February 1918. It could have been the case he thought that getting rid of both of them at one go would be more than the market would bear. It could even be that everybody was aware that the German offensive was brewing; therefore having that sort of change would have been a good thing to do at that point. We simply don't know. I think it wasn't really until the victory at the Battle of Amiens in August 1918 that Haig could truly feel secure in his job. Henry Wilson, who was CIGS (Commander of the Imperial General Staff) by that stage, was no particular friend of Haig, but they formed a sort of rough-and-ready alliance, but I don't think Haig could have been surprised had he been sacked at some point in 1918. Who would have replaced him? Well famously, Smuts and Hankey are sent out to the Western front in early 1918 to, among other things, to look for a potential replacement for Haig. And the name of Claude Jacob, a corps commander, comes into the frame, but he's seen as being far too junior. So in the end, they come back and say, well actually Haig's probably the best we've got. Haig, by that stage, has built up a reputation which is to some extent deserved as a safe pair of hands and all the rest of it—and who do you replace him with? Plumer, who's a perfectly decent general, but possibly lacks the push at the high level? Rawlinson—well, if you think that Haig's devious, you try Rawlinson! Monash has been suggested, but he's an Australian and the fact is that he's a part-time soldier and a Jew. I don't think his being Jewish was as important as the fact that he was an engineer; he was not a professional soldier.

KENNEDY: He's an engineer.

SHEFFIELD: He's an engineer, and there is this sort of trade union idea in the military that you need to have gone through the staff college, and you don't hire anyone from outside. Who do you replace Haig with? Nobody leaps forward as an automatic replacement.

WINTER: Next question, please. Please state your name.

HALE: Yes, my name is John Hale. The German 1918 offensive has basically been stopped but the German army is still a potent force, isn't the Armistice really a result of the coming collapse or the total collapse of the German home economy?

AFFLERBACH: This is pretty much the "chicken or the egg, which comes first" kind of question. In Germany there was really a desperate situation of material shortages—some say of starvation. In 1917 and in 1918, the internal situation of Germany was dire. Industrial production was in a shambles because of food shortages, bottlenecks in transport and raw materials. There was a rampant black market. The mood on the home front was going downhill. That was one of the reasons that Ludendorff tried in his last desperate gamble to win through his last offensive. He thought, and quite rightly, that the German population could not sustain a defensive war for another four or five or six years. Also the military situation was disastrous. I think from summer of 1918 onwards, from the moment that the last German offensive failed and the Allied counteroffensive started, the morale of the German army started to break down. This was what has been termed a hidden military strike.[11] Hundreds of thousands of German soldiers were hanging around at railway stations and pretending to be in search of their units and so on. In these months the fighting power of the German army melted away. And then, last but not least, we have the Balkan front. This has been mostly forgotten, but in September 1918, the Balkan front collapsed. Bulgaria dropped out, Turkey dropped out, Austria-Hungary dropped out. Also these developments were catastrophic from the German point of view. Who could then doubt that the war was also lost militarily?

GLADSTONE: My name is Steven Gladstone and I was wondering, with respect to unlimited submarine warfare, did the German government devalue the importance of keeping the United States out of the war?

AFFLERBACH: Yes. Actually, the decision for unlimited submarine warfare had a quite long buildup. The Germans started unlimited submarine warfare in 1915, though they stopped this in the summer of 1915. The Germans had a body of experts—civilian, diplomatic, and military experts working on that—they had tons of statistics on, for example, food imports to Great Britain and they said we can bring Britain to starvation by submarine warfare in maybe six weeks, eight weeks, three months. There were different estimates. And it was at the end a decision the politicians, the emperor, and the navy and the army made together. They agreed on it—a rare enough event. Some of the decision makers overflowed with joy. But if one looks very carefully one may find out that most of them said the unlimited submarine warfare is a gamble with a most uncertain outcome. They said: "We don't know if we can trust the navy or if the navy is promising too much. The navy promised that no American will ever land in Europe, because they will torpedo all ships and so on. We don't know whether it will work, but the internal situation in Germany during this turnip winter of 1916–17 is very bad. If it continues this way, we will lose anyway. So we have only one last card to play." That is why they all agreed, even Chancellor Bethmann-Hollweg who had previously opposed unrestricted submarine warfare.

WINTER: Did the German army and political elite simply ignore the possibility of America contributing to Allied victory or making a difference on the battlefield?

AFFLERBACH: They thought that America was a malevolent neutral power, delivering war materials to the British and the French. A good part of the artillery shells fired on the Somme had been produced in America. They said: "The Americans have sympathies with the Allied cause; they are delivering war materials and they're aiding our enemies anyway." So they thought probably the Americans would not make much of a difference on the Western front. They would continue to deliver war materials and this would be the same situation as now. Maybe the USA would send some volunteers; it is unclear if the German government considered an American mass mobilization. So the Germans thought that they didn't have much to lose because Americans were anyway a kind of hidden enemy already engaged in the war.

SHEFFIELD: I think we should bear in mind how dangerous the situation was for the British in the spring of 1917. The submarine warfare campaign came, at least from the British perspective, perilously close to actually succeeding. And of course, famously Churchill in the Second World War said the one thing that kept him awake at night was the Battle of the Atlantic. Actually, you see much the same scenario being played out in 1917 as well. At one point, I think Britain was down to a six-week supply of food. But again, to pick up on Holger's earlier point about the German gamble, there's a distinction between a gamble and a risk, a distinction I have heard made in the British army. A risk is something which, if you take, and it goes wrong, you can recover from it. A gamble is something which if it goes wrong, that's it—all your money is on the table. And that strikes me as so typical of German decision making in both world wars—gambling for ever higher stakes until eventually they run out of luck and lives.

AFFLERBACH: I agree. This is what I tried to say previously about German military culture. I see a dangerous tendency to solve very, very difficult political and military problems by gambling. To understand this, we have to understand their obsession with willpower. With sufficient will, they will win. That is why German gamblers—generals as well as politicians—throughout the war put more and more of their resources on the table, and lost them all.

WINTER: Except we are talking about money as metaphor, but the reality was not at all metaphoric. This is what makes me feel that in the Great War, we're dealing with something monstrous. To treat war as a series of gambles, rather than risks, makes me think that the notion that war has a reason behind it, that it is politics by other means, has disappeared. Here we come to the question about the links between the way Germany waged war in 1914–18 and in 1939–45. Perhaps the war efforts were the product of one cast of mind, though two different political orders.

DENTON: My name is Denton and my ancestors came from Lincoln-shire, and they thought that Kansas looked a lot like Lincolnshire.

SHEFFIELD: It does. No barbecue in Lincolnshire, though.

DENTON: No, no. I wanted to see if you saw any links between a per-son from this area who was an enlisted man in World War I, Harry S. Truman. Why do you think he had the gumption to fire MacArthur. Why did he have the gumption to fire the General Haig of our time?

SHEFFIELD: I'm not sure that either MacArthur or Haig would be flattered by being compared to each other. But I absolutely take your general point. And the answer is, Truman understood where the power lay within the American civil-military relationship, and when MacAr-thur stepped over the line, he fired him, and I think we can all be glad he did.

WINTER: The last question. Your name, please.

EVERLY: Steve Everly. And there were some comments made about the equality in forces causing the stalemate. There were instances where lines were breached, but they were not, for various reasons, exploited. I'm just curious if you think that improved tactics or better generalship could have offset that equality of forces you mentioned.

SHEFFIELD: Well, I think you do get improved tactics and better gen-eralship as the war goes on. And in a sense, the idea of a learning curve is evidently true. They had to learn on the job. And they did improve over time. And that's true of the British, it's true of the French, it's true of the Americans, it's true of the Germans. But the balance of forces was still decisive.

AFFLERBACH: If we look to the German army in both world wars, I would say, on the tactical level, their record is excellent. Niall Ferguson has made this point. He calculated how much did it cost the German army to kill one Allied soldier? This means dividing expenditure by casualties inflicted. What about on the other side? How much did it cost the Allies to kill a German soldier? The German army was a very efficient machine on the tactical level. But on the strategic level, there was no learning curve at all. They started with the Schlieffen Plan in 1914, which was a desperate gamble, and they continued to gamble all over the war. I can only say there was no learning curve; if anything, strategic thinking went from bad to worse. And so, I can only repeat, you can't make so many mistakes and expect to win. It's impossible. In World War II we see the same tendencies we have seen in World War I on the German side, only expanded and harnessed to achieve monstrous ends.

WINTER: That, of course, is another story, and one we must leave for another series of lectures on twentieth-century warfare. All that remains is for you to join me in showing our appreciation of the way these two scholars have clarified many complex matters embedded in the military history of the Great War.

THREE

The Soldiers' War

Coercion or Consent?

John Horne, Trinity College, Dublin
Len Smith, Oberlin College

WINTER: Welcome to everyone this evening. Today we turn to the soldiers' war. It may be possible for us to unravel problems about why wars break out—the subject of our first scholars' forum—but it seems to me an even more difficult task to answer the question as to why do men go through battle? In the First World War, why was it not a natural reaction to the terror of battle for a man to drop his gun and turn around and go home? What is it that kept people in uniform? And in the First World War, we're talking about seventy million people in uniform at war for fifty months—fifty months of the most astonishing industrial, assembly-line warfare that had ever been seen on earth. We're dealing with a puzzle that soldiers have faced from the Trojan war portrayed in the *Iliad* to the present, and it will go on troubling people as long as men bear arms.

One reason why I think the study of the First World War is so important for us today is its modernity. It was the first fully industrialized war between countries that had, at their disposal, vast material resources as well as the largest population of young men in the history of the world. This was a democratic war; it touched whole societies. Why those men went to war and why those men stayed at war is the question that we address this evening. In many respects, the questions that we ask are bound to remain open; they cannot be resolved for good. They have to be asked by each generation from its own perspective and with the cadences of its own language.

My colleagues this evening are Len Smith and John Horne. Both are historians of France in the period of the First World War. Both have written important books on the soldiers' war. Leonard Smith has deepened our understanding of how soldiers withstand the terrible strain of combat through applying a notion of what he terms "proportionality." That is to say, soldiers have minds, and they have considered, reasonable objections to the orders that they have to carry out. They frequently don't do so, and in fact if you looked at a military map with an arrow on it, you'll have to conclude that soldiers go in every direction except where the arrow points. How is it that soldiers follow orders? And in what ways do they engage in negotiation with their officers about how much territory is worth how many lives? These are questions which Len Smith has made his own.

John Horne has gone in another direction. His research has enabled us to talk in an informed way about what is in the minds of soldiers when they are in the battlefield, and how they bring with them, among the things they carried, to use Tim O'Brien's phrase, the history of the last war. The last war before 1914 is the Franco-Prussian War of 1870–71, in which soldiers faced guerrilla warfare. In 1914 they and their sons and nephews believed that the same thing was happening. They were wrong about that, but one can understand, thanks to the work of John Horne and his colleague in Dublin, Alan Kramer, their false perception. What the late British historian James Joll termed "unspoken assumptions" in the minds of soldiers about this war can be the tragically misconstrued interpretations of the last one.[1] In both cases, John Horne and Len Smith have entered into the question of what was in the minds of soldiers when they went to war? And is it the case that they consented to carnage?

That question sounds to me like asking someone if he "consents" to bubonic plague. Can a soldier consent to a war in which the greatest concentration of artillery fire in history was arrayed against him?

Ernst Jünger put it this way: standing in a field of battle is like watching a giant swing a hammer and missing your head by a quarter of an inch.[2] How did men endure this? Do they consent to war of this kind or are they coerced into accepting it? Was the key point that there was a line of military police at their rear? Or did soldiers internalize coercion—the fear of humiliation, or loss of the approval of one's mates or one's family?

Let me introduce the subject with a bit more detail on mutinies during the Great War. In 1917, the political character of the war changed. The Bolshevik Revolution in Russia in October brought to power a new regime committed to taking Russia out of the war. They did so in early December, ultimately signing the Treaty of Brest Litovsk with the Germans in March 1918. They also published the contents of the czar's Foreign Ministry, showing to all the world how the Allies intended to carve up Turkey and enhance the imperial power of Britain, France, and Italy. So much for the Allied claim that the war was one for democracy, promoted with great fanfare after the United States entered the war in April 1917. The Allies were forced to reconsider their war aims, and face the fact that Germany had won the war on the Eastern front.

There were, therefore, two phases of the Great War—one from 1914 to 1916, which had produced stalemate, and one from 1917 on, in which both sides had to remobilize and endure further hardship in the increasingly wearying effort to win the war. Now the stakes were not only victory or defeat, but the survival of political regimes or revolution in the case of military disaster.

It is in this second phase of the war that mutinies occurred. One way to understand the Russian Revolution is to see it as the biggest mutiny of the war, an eruption of anger over the war and its seemingly endless character. But our subject today is on a lower order of magnitude than whole nations. It concerns armies, and in various parts of Europe, there were occasions when soldiers said no: we won't continue to fight the war the generals have ordained.

This happened in the French army in the spring of 1917, after a failed offensive to break through German lines in Champagne to the east of Paris. General Nivelle had promised his troops a lightning breakthrough when he launched the attack on 16 April, but nothing of the kind had happened. After massive French casualties, he refused to call off the offensive. It was then that French troops acted. Elements of sixty-eight

French infantry divisions—nearly five hundred thousand men—refused to go back up the line. They started making demands. They wanted better food, more leave time, and above all an end to the offensive. They were not against the war, but against the bankrupt way it was being waged at the top. They were loyal to France, but not to Nivelle, who was replaced by a new commander, Philippe Pétain.

The men went back up the line, but Pétain would have none of the offensive plans of Nivelle. He said he would wait for tanks and the Americans, which is precisely what he did. The mutiny ended; several score soldiers were shot for disobedience, and the war went on.

In September 1917, trouble seemed to be brewing in the British army. About one hundred thousand men rioted in a training camp near Boulogne and went on a drunken rampage. They drank everything in sight, caused lots of damage, and then went back to their bases before further trouble ensued. In October and November on the Italian front, the German and Austrian forces broke through Italian lines at Caporetto, and whole units of the Italian army fled westward in disorder.

In 1918, it was the turn of the German army to reach breaking point. In the failed offensive of March 1918, German soldiers suffered massive casualties—reaching perhaps one million men. They were running out of everything—food, fuel, and perhaps most importantly, belief in victory. In August 1918, the Allies broke through at Amiens on the Somme, and in the ensuing days, perhaps 100,000 German troops surrendered. Some have seen this as a mutiny: a soldiers' strike against an unwinnable war.

Then came the German navy. In the last days of the war the German Admiralty decided it was intolerable that the High Seas Fleet had played such a small part in the war, now a lost cause. So they ordered one last battle, to rescue their reputations, even at the cost of the lives of their men. Sailors would have none of it. They doused their boilers and mutinied, joining forces with revolutionary workers in the North Seas ports. That brought the war to an end and marked the beginning of the German Revolution; the Kaiser abdicated and was unceremoniously pushed over the border to exile in Holland.

Mutiny, therefore, was common to armies on both sides of the line. This we know. The intriguing question is why there were not more such episodes of indiscipline and refusal? One answer is that soldiers were coerced into obedience by military police, by social pressure from home, by a sense of pride in their units which withered when those units were torn apart by huge and ongoing casualties. Another approach is that soldiers were thinking men, who consented to the war, despite everything. They believed in the cause and hated the enemy, who was in the wrong and who had to be defeated. Going on with the war was a form of consent, which was evident even after three bloody years of combat.

In France, in particular, this dispute over coercion or consent has gone on and on and produced a very bitter controversy. Self-styled historians on the political left see repression and brutality as the reason the war went on and on. Their adversaries, who have a range of political affiliations, see soldiers' ongoing commitment to winning the war as a reflection of "war culture" or a set of ideas and images which gave the war its meaning and gave soldiers as well as civilians the grit to stay the course.[3] You would be surprised to see how deep are the animosities which arise from this dispute about coercion or consent, two ways of understanding why soldiers continued to fight this murderous war. We have the privilege of hearing two of the finest younger historians in our field reflect on these disputed matters and on how we might go beyond them.

Len Smith will begin. John Horne will follow. Len, the floor is yours.

SMITH: Jay, first of all, I want to thank you for referring to me as a "young" historian. As someone who turned fifty in 2007, it is a rare distinction to be referred to as a "young" anything. I quite agree with you, however, that historiography and historians have generations, and it has always been a pleasure to learn from previous generations as well as emerging subsequent ones.

I would like to begin by saying a few words about just why coercion versus consent is a controversial issue at all. Doing so helps explain why we need to look beyond received wisdom from the literature and poetry of the Great War, however artistically and morally convincing such artistic expressions might be, in order to understand why millions of soldiers fought each other so ferociously for so long.

One way to introduce the issue of coercion versus consent is to explain how I came to work on soldiers of the Great War as a research subject. My first book, *Between Mutiny and Obedience*, had its origins in my doctoral dissertation.[4] As someone trained in the "local study" tradition of French social history, I investigated closely one infantry division in the French army from 1914 to 1918. This comprised some twelve thousand to fifteen thousand men at any one time and was roughly equivalent to studying a small city. The focal point of the book, and indeed its dramatic high point, were the French army mutinies of 1917, when constituent parts of roughly half the French army refused, point blank, to advance to the front lines and instead held antiwar demonstrations.

As I studied what happened during the mutinies in the Fifth Infantry Division, it became clear to me that the mutinies were not resolved by physical force. Repression *followed* the resolution of the mutinies. The mutinies did not end through coercion, at least not external coercion. In other words, the discontented soldiers decided *themselves* to cease the demonstrations and return to the trenches. They understood that doing so meant accepting repression, including courts-martial, and in the end some particularly morally dubious executions. Thus, it seemed to me that the historian had to look not so much at what the *generals* were doing, which had traditionally been the case in a good deal of military history of the Great War, as at what the *soldiers in the trenches* were doing and were saying. I became convinced that historians had to look at the dynamic of the mutinies themselves in order to understand their resolution. Clearly, there was something going on within the behavior and the rhetoric of the soldiers themselves that compelled them to consent to conventional military authority, when no physical coercion existed to compel them to do so.

The sorts of questions I was posing at the time were part of a much broader shift in historiographical interest in the First World War, pioneered by Jay Winter, John Horne, and others. Historians' attention shifted away from a focus on the origins of the war and the military causes of defeat or victory toward the study of societies and cultures at war.[5] Historians were coming to interpret soldiers not as interchangeable clones who carried out or failed to carry out the commands of their superiors, but as figures of agency closely connected to the societies from which they came. Thinking about soldiers in this way made it possible to study them as part of a general reconsideration of just why European societies consented to pursuing this war long after the point at which people today might see it as "rational" to do so.

As one of the historians attached to this historiographical shift, I have come to think of consent in terms of its own historically specific logic—as a form of commitment that deepened with adversity.

In other words, the worse or more "total" the war became, the more deeply European societies became committed to prevailing in it. Consent could be carried to what we today might see as pathological extremes, yet on its own terms remain "logical." Thought of in this way, consent came to revolve around the internalization on the part of millions of Europeans in and out of uniform of at least some of the values for which they claimed the war had to be fought. Soldiers (and in their own fashion, civilians) fought as hard as they did as long as they did because they identified with the war at the most profound levels of personal and collective identity.

Why, then, might such an understanding of consent be controversial? In the end, most any moral balance sheet of the First World War would be substantially influenced by how he or she evaluates consent as an analytical construct. Historians, particularly in the Anglophone world, have continued to ponder the conflict in moral terms. If the historian believes that, on balance and at some level, the Great War was worth fighting, he or she would be inclined to approve of consent. If, on the other hand, the historian believes that the Great War was a morally indefensible tragedy that accomplished nothing but the ruin of untold millions of lives, he or she is going to think about consent very differently. Indeed, those who hold this point of view are likely to think of consent simply as coercion by another name. More specifically, one would be inclined to think that soldiers were coerced into fighting by fear of the firing squad or by the more subtle means of brainwashing through propaganda.

Of course, the objectives of "scientific" history since the nineteenth century have revolved around steering away from moral balance sheets and trying to understand the past on its own terms. To be sure, these objectives have carried their own ideological baggage over the years. But the issue of whether the Great War was "worth it" or not depends largely on who is asking the question. "Worth it" to whom—national communities, the dead, the survivors, posterity? Many historians of consent today are thus inclined neither to approve nor disapprove of consent as such, and rather to think of it as an ideological or behavioral system. In a word, consent helps explain why millions of people thought fighting this war this way seemed like a good idea at the time.

The dichotomy between consent and coercion has meant different things in different places. It seems fair to say that the fiercest battles over the issue have been fought among historians in France. Strictly speaking, the question is rarely raised there of whether or not the war was "worth it," for a simple reason. From the moment of the German invasion of August 1914, the war was a matter of national survival for France. It had little choice in the matter.

Paradoxically, partisans of consent and partisans of coercion in France share certain common assumptions. There is an old adage that the real victors of the First World War were the schoolmasters of the Third Republic. In the decades before 1914, the regime maintained a fixation on three policy areas—primary education, railroads (a massive, capital-intensive enterprise that helped integrate the nation economically), and conscription (military service being seen since the French Revolution as the exemplary school of citizenship). For good or for ill, the Third Republic by August 1914 had indeed managed to create a national community of citizens that resolved to defend itself in this war or to expire in the attempt.

Partisans of consent among French historians have tended to assume what Great War veteran (and later French president) Charles de Gaulle called *une certaine idée de la France* (a certain idea of France). As applied here, the notion speaks to a seemingly eternal, cohesive Republican community that endured beneath all the turmoil France lived through in the twentieth century—not just the war of 1914–18, but the occupation of 1940–44 and the traumatic wars of decolonization after 1945, notably the war in Algeria. In such a framework, consent in the Great War remained one of the shining moments of French republicanism, and the apotheosis of the Third Republic. This is one reason why the French term *La Grande Guerre* (the Great War) has never been entirely replaced by *La Première Guerre Mondiale* (the First World War).

A fierce critique of consent and the regime that orchestrated it has existed in France ever since the interwar period. Both the revolutionary Left and the Fascist Right understood just how thoroughly the Third Republic had succeeded in constructing a citizenry determined to pursue the war. The revolutionary Left never forgave the regime for blocking the possibility that the war might evolve into an international crusade against injustice, beginning with revolution at home. Likewise, the Fascist Right never forgave the hated democratic regime for surviving the war at all. Fascism in France became obsessed in the interwar period with rewriting victory in France as defeat, because the success of the democratic regime in engineering consent appeared to prove its strength and resilience.

In today's historiography, the critique has emerged that consent is nothing but nationalist coercion under a misleading and even pernicious name. According to this critique, the Third Republic created not so much citizens in the sense of morally autonomous "free" men, but obedient subjects who did what their schoolmasters, bosses, and drill sergeants all told them. In other words, the same forms of social and cultural discipline that made soldiers lambs to the slaughter in the Great War already existed before the war in the agricultural fields, the factories, and the barracks of France. According to this point of view, the war simply brought the pathologies of modern democracy and capitalism to the surface.

A somewhat analogous debate has occurred in Britain, though couched in different terms. As I noted earlier, and as doubtless other speakers in this series have mentioned, an argument persists in Britain to this day as to whether the First World War was "worth it." Simply put, was preventing German hegemony over the European continent worth setting in motion that chain of events that ultimately invoked the decline and fall of Britain as a Great Power? Of course, this question exists only in the realm of counterfactual history and carries with it all the joys and sorrows appertaining to that imaginative field of endeavor.[6]

One way in which British historians have attempted to apply a cost-benefit analysis of the Great War is through conventional military history, directed toward an explanation of why battles and wars are won or lost. British military historians have long excelled at this kind of history, through an unsurpassed depth of research and attention to detail.[7] Debate as to whether the Great War was "worth it" has centered on the quality of the British high command. In a word, historians have argued over whether, as the German general Eric Ludendorff unforgettably put it, the British soldiers were "lions led by donkeys."

Historians do not dispute that the common British soldier was a lion. The debate, rather, has been about the "donkeys." This connects a very specific British debate to the question of consent and coercion. If the generals were donkeys, the issue was coercion. If they were not, the issue was consent. For historians of the former opinion, the generals and the politicians who back them merit condemnation for provoking the downfall of Britain as a global power. Historians of the latter opinion can tell a story of national persistence and survival through consent parallel to that of France.

There are still more national inflections on the debate between coercion and consent. In Italy, a debate has simmered for many years around the relationship between the war effort and the Italian state.[8] A vigorous left-wing historiographical tradition, inspired by Karl Marx and particularly Italian Marxist Antonio Gramsci, has seen the liberal (or quasi-liberal) state of prewar and wartime Italy as inherently coercive and hence the soldier as the *ipso facto* victim of coercion. In other countries, the debate between consent and coercion has not really taken place as such at all. One such country is the United States, where historians have tended to assume that American soldiers willingly took up arms for their nation in both world wars, a vocal though rather marginal pacifist movement notwithstanding. Consent is taken as a given.

This being said, I would argue in this context that a distinction might be made between *assent,* the initial acquiescence to war, and *consent,* the continuing social and cultural decision to continue in increasingly dire circumstances. One could argue, therefore, that the United States was simply not in the Great War long enough for consent as construed here to emerge.

While I am less familiar with the literature, it seems that coercion versus consent is also not such a particularly vexed historiographical issue in the Habsburg Monarchy (or rather the successor states following the breakup of the monarchy in 1918), Germany, and Russia. All three, of course, were authoritarian regimes defeated in the Great War. In Central Europe outside Austria and Hungary proper, it has been tempting (though not entirely accurate) to assume that soldiers fought only because of the repressive apparatus of the dying monarchy. Likewise, in Germany and Russia, the defeat and overthrow of the wartime autocratic regimes has, perhaps, contributed to an assumption that coercion precluded consent, at least before the revolutions of 1917 in Russia and 1918 in Germany.

Soldiers themselves could write about their experience in the Great War very differently at different times. The images that have emerged from these writings have had considerable political significance. Historians often talk about a paradigmatic shift, a "literary turn" in historical analysis beginning in the 1980s. They began to look to literature rather than the social sciences for analytical models, and to textual analysis rather than behavioral modeling to investigate the past. But one could argue that a "literary turn" in the study of the First World War actually began several decades earlier, in the 1920s and 1930s, and was initiated by soldiers themselves through their published testimony.[9] During the years between the two world wars, a single literary form, tragedy, became the presumed analytical structure for understanding experience in the trenches. The soldier played the role of the tragic victim, a figure of great integrity, but flawed by an innocence bordering on gullibility. He simply understood the tragic nature of the war too late, whether he survived it or not.

In Britain, literature has played a role in the debate about "lions led by donkeys," which I have argued here is a reformulation of the debate about coercion versus consent. The most ardent and conservative defenders of the British war effort as it was waged (that is, the defenders of the generals) have sometimes disparaged accounts of tragedy and victimization as self-pitying whining.[10] One intentionally insulting term to describe such authors is the "Boo Hoo Brigade." While such a term unnecessarily derides what most critics agree is some of the finest British literature of the twentieth century, it is worth noting that what has been most celebrated subsequently was not necessarily most celebrated at the time of the war. While Wilfred Owen remains by far the most popular British war poet today, he was overshadowed even in the interwar years by the heroic poetry of Rupert Brooke, best known for his famous line of August 1914: "Now God be thanked who has matched us with His hour."

To be sure, the searing antiwar poetry of Owen and the patriotic, romantic elegies of Brooke make clear that the two were writing about very different kinds of experience in the Great War. Yet it is possible to see the authors as two sides of the same coin. Brooke saw little fighting, having died of a blood infection en route to the Dardanelles in 1915. For his part, Owen, who certainly saw more than his share of combat in the trenches of the Western front, "did his duty" until he was killed in the last days of the war. His unforgettable denunciation of "war" in the abstract never, it seems, interfered with his willingness to continue his personal fight. "War" as an affliction of the human condition and "his" personal war as he experienced it proved different things. The romantic hero and the bitter stoic determined to see it through to the end have walked hand in hand in the construction of memory of the Great War in Britain ever since.

Germany has had its version of the soldier as victim. The two most famous literary figures in Germany were Paul Bäumer, the hero of Erich Marie Remarque's *All Quiet on the Western Front* (1929) and the auto-biographical figure presented in the works of Ernst Jünger, especially in the *Storm of Steel* (1920).[11] Paul, the naïve boy seduced into joining the army by the selfish nationalism of his schoolmaster, experienced the annihilation of his very soul well before he was killed on a day described in official dispatches as "all quiet on the Western front." Jünger became the soldier who became the war. He identified with the war to the point of embracing its violence and its brutality as something that led to the recasting of a new kind of virile man. It could be argued that these two apparently different figures are two sides of the same coin—victimized men whose humanity, in one way or another, was stolen from them by the war. Neither Paul Baümer nor Ernst Jünger would prove very promising citizens of the German experiment in democracy in the Weimar Republic. The Paul Baümers who survived did so too morally impaired to resist Fascism. The Ernst Jüngers did not wish to resist it.

I am by no means arguing here that tragedy and victimization are "wrong" or "incorrect" ways of thinking about experience on the World War I battlefield. Rather, I am arguing that the "literary turn" that began in the interwar period in thinking about experience at the front explains only part of the story.

A vast paper trail exists telling all sorts of stories of consent, coercion, and much else in between. In *The Embattled Self,* I argued that testimony to experience in the trenches does not tell a single story, and that moreover it remains an exercise in futility to expect it to do so.[12] Much more "experience" exists in the published paper trail of letters, trench newspapers, memoirs, diaries than can be accounted for in a simple narrative of tragedy and victimization. These emerged only at the end of a very involved history of testimony that began during the war and continued through the interwar period in which soldiers employed any number of narrative strategies in order to understand their experience. So tragedy and victimization were where the story of testimony of experience ends up, not where it was all along. As a national community reading that literature and constructing a national memory of the war, France could consent to the war at one point in its history and radically reject it at another. It drew very different morals from the story of the Great War across the twentieth century.

WINTER: Thank you very much, Len. Now to have a second point of view on the question of consent and coercion, I turn to John Horne.

HORNE: Like Len, I thank you for the introduction, Jay, and for the flattering misattribution of youth; and I'd also like to thank the Truman Library and the Liberty Memorial World War I Museum for hosting this event. It's a privilege and a pleasure to be here. Although I don't necessarily want to agree with Len all evening, I support him on this, that the historian of the soldier's experience has constantly to deconstruct the soldier's own postwar accounts of that experience. I do say deconstruct—not discount—because the processes that you refer to, Len, are extremely important in their own right. If we discuss the question of memory we may want to come back to the soldiers' postwar narratives, and to what you, Jay, have called the moral witnessing of that experience.[13] But we can't take those retrospective statements as testimony of what combat in World War I was like at the time. For the view from hindsight rarely reproduces the open-endedness of the original experience, its provisional nature, or its daily emotional range. So what I would like to talk about is how we as historians can reconstruct that experience. In particular, I'd like to try and enlarge the conceptual toolbox available to us for doing so.

Let me start with two preliminary observations. In a way they're obvious, but I think it's important to be reminded of them. The first has to do with the type of warfare that World War I entailed. Jay, you've already referred to this as the unprecedented experience of industrialized, mechanized warfare, and I think that's exactly right. I'm always intrigued by the degree to which the American Civil War prefigures the type of warfare that we find in World War I. But Europeans, the German General Staff apart, didn't really pay very much attention to that conflict. The kind of siege warfare that one finds lasting for four years between Washington and Richmond, Virginia, is something that doesn't stick in the European mind between 1865 and 1914.

The European experience of warfare in that period, whether it was continental or colonial, is very different. It's one of attack, movement, and resolution—of war still seen as an instrument of policy that will achieve calculated aims without changing the world making the calculations. So when World War I breaks out, the realities of industrialized warfare come as a deep military shock. But more than that, we're also

talking about a particular configuration of military technology that results in the defensive being hugely advantaged. This is what produces
the stalemate of trench warfare on virtually all fronts. Given the precon-
ceptions of combat based on movement, attack, and rapid victory, that
industrialized deadlock means that World War I also comes as a profound cultural shock to European societies.

The central military conundrum of the war was how to restore the
offensive or to find some alternative means to defeat the enemy, whether by attrition, economic warfare, or some other means. And that conundrum, which had no immediate answer, preoccupied the generals
throughout the conflict. The beginnings of a solution appeared by 1918,
when we see the future of warfare—tanks, aircraft, combined arms operations—being mapped out, but in my view it was still the warfare of
attrition that defeated the Central Powers. The importance of this for
our discussion is that it also shaped the soldiers' war. How to survive
the industrial killing-fields where, unlike in World War II, costly battles
rarely had a decisive outcome: here is the fundamental issue. I don't
know if anybody's ever done a direct comparison of the two battles of
the Somme and Stalingrad. They were both terrible, terrible battles, but
the difference, it seems to me, is that after four months of bloody conflict, Stalingrad produced a decisive resolution and both sides knew that
to be the case. The Somme didn't. I'm not saying that at the time no
meaning could be attributed to the Somme; but the way in which it affected the war was indirect and longer term. So a particular experience
of defensive industrial warfare was the soldier's lot in 1914–18.

My second preliminary observation is that the basic political unit
fighting the war was the nation-state, the exception of course being
multinational empires, notably Austria-Hungary and Russia, which precisely resisted nation states and nationalism. The nation implied a sense
of community, something that had developed strongly in the fifty years
before the war. It's interesting that, whatever we might conclude about
the real causes of the war, all sides in 1914 felt it to be defensive and
thus a struggle for existential survival on the part of the communities
involved. Now, the nation in arms was the ideal expression of this community at war. And it was this that produced the mass armies based on
the universal obligation to military service—not just the standing conscript army but also the reservists up to the age of fifty who were called
up in 1914. Because mass national armies faced the military deadlock

and everything that stemmed from it—trial and error on the part of the high command, soaring military losses—the political and social contracts that underwrote the nation were turned into claims of entitlement on the part of subjects and citizens, and reciprocal obligations on the part of the state, in recognition of the sacrifice that ordinary soldiers had made. This was a central dynamic of the war and its legacy.

Of course, high commands were hardly rights-based organizations. They had an authoritarian approach, especially with respect to conscripts and reservists. But how high commands and national armies together managed to deal with the military deadlock seems to me to be a vital issue—as Len has indicated in the case of the French mutinies. It was through the soldiers' experience that the modern state encountered industrial war, and this makes the soldiers' experience central to understanding the war as a whole.

Now let me come to my principal contention for this discussion. Len has laid out very clearly for us what the debate on consent and coercion has done, why it's been fruitful in some ways and something of a diversion in others. But I question whether the binary formula of coercion and consent is adequate for addressing the soldiers' experience. I wonder if it isn't better to use two sets of terms to address two different aspects of the question, and I want very briefly to indicate what I see those as being.

First, it seems to me that the real opposite of coercion isn't consent but persuasion, because consent is a property of the soldier's own response to the war, whereas coercion and persuasion are the opposite ends of a gamut of pressures that are brought to bear on the soldier in order to induce him to place his life on the line. I don't mean to suggest that coercion and persuasion remain purely external. As you've already suggested, Jay, soldiers internalize disciplinary codes and many soldiers also believed that to fight in the war was the right thing to do. But the sources of coercion remained outside the soldiers in the legal obligations of military service and the penal codes of the armies concerned. And the sources of persuasion were likewise external, in codes of masculinity, fear of disapproval by family and community, and the mobilization of values behind the war, including the argument that the national community was under threat. All this constituted a powerful moral and cultural environment making it difficult for the soldier to refuse his "duty."

This being so, soldiers operated within a force field of coercion and persuasion, and the question of how this evolved in different societies across the war becomes a major subject. It's also one of which contemporaries were acutely aware. The professional military, as I've just suggested, was often wary of the mass influx of citizen soldiers into the army, whether they were volunteers as in the British case, or the reservists and territorial formations that dwarfed the peacetime conscript armies in the case of continental Europe. Some high commands responded by reinforcing harsh codes of military justice. This was the case in Russia and especially in Italy under General Cadorna down to the disaster at Caporetto. But if they were going to deploy mass national armies in the particularly difficult battle conditions of World War I, coercion wasn't enough. Motivation and therefore persuasion were both vital, including acknowledging the soldier's own self-persuasion to fight the war. Hence, an important social and cultural phenomenon is the growing recognition across the war in most armies of the importance of the soldiers' morale. The concept was older, but it developed rapidly during the war. There was a growing emphasis on reinforcing morale, with entertainment, better leave, and the political instruction programs that were instituted by nearly every army in the final years of the conflict.

Persuasion and coercion aren't necessarily alternatives—they usually work in tandem with each other. Nor can one simply see a kind of linear development in which persuasion gradually replaces coercion in the twentieth century. The *Wehrmacht* and the Red Army in the Second World War each knew degrees of both—coercion and persuasion—that dwarf anything seen in the First World War. As soldiers' morale fell, both coercion and persuasion might intensify, and arguably that is what happens in response to the French mutinies in 1917. But my provisional conclusion on this first issue, the force field in which soldiers operate, is that whatever we say about the level of coercion, persuasion in most armies increased across the war in line with the emphasis on morale and the realization that these were armies of citizen-soldiers. Failure to achieve this became one of the causes of defeat.

However, a second set of terms is required to reconstruct the subjectivity of the soldiers' experience as it existed in between the force field of coercion and persuasion and the realities of industrialized siege warfare. That "in between" might sound like a purely passive place, leaving the soldiers with little room for maneuver. But they remained agents of their own destiny to a far greater extent than victims of genocide or other extreme situations in twentieth-century history. Many other elements featured in the world of siege warfare, for all its attendant difficulty in producing a coherent plan for winning and the constant exposure of soldiers to death, mutilation, and the loss of comrades. These other elements include loyalty to the fighting unit, officer-soldier relations, links with home and loved ones, attitudes to the enemy that range from hatred to complicity, and the desire for the high command not to waste lives—the proportionality that you've written so well about, Len. They include, too, the importance of logistics (the feeling that you're backed up by a military administration that can deliver the stuff you need to fight and survive on the battlefield), belief or disbelief in victory, and the possibility of going home.

Rather than the binary terminology of "consent" and "coercion," with its implied simple alternatives of "for" or "against," the soldiers' experience might better be explored with a three-way distinction between acceptance, endurance, and refusal. Acceptance is the soldier's version of society's consent to the war, which we see on such a massive scale at the beginning of the conflict. But as time went on, the soldier's acceptance wasn't expressed in the language used by the press or propaganda on the home front. His sense of the nation might be rather different to that of the civilians, one expressed in terms of the threat to his own community or family. Crude home front caricatures of the foe might be replaced with a more nuanced view of the qualities of the enemy dug in only a few hundred meters away.

However, endurance is the central term, in every sense. For it articulates how soldiers, and especially combat troops, focused on the business of surviving while attempting to achieve the goals set by their commanders. It overlaps with acceptance, since it usually doesn't query the purpose of the conflict. But it might contain elements of refusal—for example, the avoidance of matters that seem unfair or counterproductive or even a protest against them. Endurance draws on the resources of the society from which the men came, from popular culture to family links, and was laced with humor, irony, solidarity, and resignation. It also bathes in the social life of the front—from officers and buddies to the cohesion of the military unit. It was the medium in which the soldiers lived most of the time.

Finally, refusal runs from the individual level—desertion, self-mutilation—to the collective level of mutiny, revolt, and revolution. But of course, refusal might overlap with endurance and even with kinds of acceptance. Once again, the French mutinies of 1917 are a case in point. For as you and others have demonstrated, Len, the soldiers accepted the need to defend the *patrie* and to prevent the Germans advancing any farther (just as they had at Verdun the year before). But they refused to sacrifice themselves on the altar of the high command's inability to come up with a workable offensive plan.

Where does this leave the subject of our debate? Firstly, it seems to me that breaking apart the binary opposition and using this threefold approach—acceptance, endurance, and refusal—helps restore a sense of agency to these millions of soldiers of the Great War, to deconstruct the myths that we find in the postwar narratives. Even when they were pinned down under shellfire, these men weren't simply or always victims. Many felt involved in the war and at least sometimes had some options in how they responded. The evidence is that they did so in multiple ways.

Moreover, the distinctions enable us to reconstruct the soldiers' experience on a differentiated national basis. For example, accepting that the war was one in defense of the nation meant something quite concrete for French soldiers, whose country was invaded and some of whose wives and children remained under German occupation. It provided a rather more metaphoric understanding for the Germans, who believed they were defending the homeland on the Somme to avoid having to do so on the Rhine. Acceptance of the war in these terms was still more abstract for the British or Irish soldier—never mind the Australians, Canadians, or Americans.

Secondly, I think that the terminology allows us to establish a variable relationship between the soldier's own experience and what I call the force field of coercion and persuasion. For example, mobilization in 1914 was a key moment. At one level, it was highly coercive because outside the United Kingdom and British Empire, men were responding to the legal obligation to turn up and fight. But we know that this was accompanied by deep acceptance, that even in Russia and Austria-Hungary, initially at least, the levels of noncompliance were far lower than the high commands feared. But refusal might come at points of low coercion, and arguably the Russian mutinies of 1917 occur at precisely the point where coercion has virtually disappeared after the February revolution.

Thirdly, I think that "endurance" enables us to get at a major problem encountered by the consensus school, if I can put it that way, in dealing with soldiers. The notion that there was a "war culture" in 1914 works very well.[14] There was a qualitative shift in the cultures of societies going to war, and soldiers were part of that. But one of the problems is to explain how this "war culture," even if we use the term in the plural, worked on the fighting front when the soldiers were caught in the deadlock of the Great War in a way that civilians weren't. How was their "war culture," if you like, different? I think that the notion of "endurance," which allows acceptance to be combined with elements of refusal, begins to provide a key for understanding that.

Finally, it seems to me that the notion of "refusal" provides us with a particularly interesting category. It allows us to look at certain acts that have not been much studied—flight, desertion, self-mutilation, and suicide—as a spectrum of individual responses of rising gravity. It also allows us to imagine a comparative study of collective refusal, and perhaps allows me (at last!) to take issue with you, Len.

You seem to hint that consent (in your sense) may have been more important than usually allowed in the cases of Italy, Germany, Austria-Hungary, or Russia, all of which experienced defeat, revolt, and revolution, though you rightly point out that the debate has not had the same prominence in the historiography of these cases. I think this may be a "Western front" illusion, and that as we move from west to east, we have much higher levels of refusal than the "consent" school has often assumed, although the nature of the refusal varied considerably among soldiers and between armies. So the mutinies that we find in revolutionary Russia in 1917 are rather different from the mass surrender by Italian soldiers that occurs at Caporetto in October 1917, and this is different again from the disintegration of the Austrian army from the spring of 1918 on, when the subordinate nationalities start melting away. This differs, too, from what German military historians have labeled the "hidden military strike," in which German soldiers simply start voting with their feet from mid-1918 on, if not before, a phenomenon that also includes mass surrender. World War I was at least as much about revolution and rupture as it was about survival and continuity, and the range and nature of "refusal" by the soldiers is crucial to understanding that.

In the end, it seems to me that the challenge is to devise a comparative cultural history of experience that might allow us to set aside the post-war myths and really examine the soldiers in the war. I hope that this is something our debate tonight will help us to do.

WINTER: Thank you, John. Let me see if I can raise two issues that might provide some further exploration of the subjects and evidence we are considering. The first is the invention of the category of post-traumatic stress disorder in the First World War. It's called shell shock. In 1980, it gets into the medical handbook as a legitimate syndrome, which meant doctors treated it and would certify that those who suffered from it deserved a pension. The term "shell shock" is invented in the First World War, and the number of soldiers who suffered from this disability is itself a matter of uncertainty. At least we can be sure that a substantial number of those who went through artillery barrages and trench warfare experienced something like it at some point. What's amazing to me, is not that so many suffered, but that so many others had the stamina to fight, to endure, and to come out of the war as recognizably sane human beings. I've studied the First World War for forty years—it's a story of carnage, but it's also a story of how ordinary people—Harry Truman perhaps among them—came out of the artillery war without damage to mind and body. However, a substantial minority of those who weren't so fortunate bore the traces of that experience for life, giving birth to a condition—shell shock—which has left its mark on our language and our sense of what war does to people. This condition was called "combat fatigue" in the Second World War; the term was "soldier's heart" in the American Civil War. And now we use the term "post-traumatic stress disorder." If I'm right that roughly 20 percent of the medical casualties had some element of post-traumatic stress disorder in the First World War, then the theory of consent is in need of revision. I put to you, Len, that it's impossible to square the argument that you've advanced with the medical evidence of psychiatric and physical casualties. Yes, as you rightly say, experience is multiple and difficult to classify. We all know, from our own private and family lives, that sane people know moments of insanity alongside moments of emotional calm and clarity. But the idea of consent in the First World War requires us to consider circumstances in which thousands—I would say perhaps hundreds of thousands—of men were pushed beyond the limits of human endurance.

This happened because they faced weaponry that basically gave them no chance of heroism or of courage or even of military skill because the artillery weapons that caused 60 percent of all casualties were miles away from the battlefield. For that reason, and that reason alone, it strikes me that the concept of victimization is valid as part of the story and maybe even as an essential part of the story—not the only one, by any means.

What the First World War did was to mobilize men to fight one war, and then force them to fight another, more horrible, war, one that no one had ever seen before. We know what the men of 1914 were like. Most were decent, loyal men, proud of their country, men who wanted to defend their homeland. They went off to fight a war and wound up living in an altogether different wartime world. If they consented to national defense, it is difficult to say they consented to fight the industrialized assembly-line murderous war that followed from Christmas 1914 on. I would even suggest that the word "endurance" gets changed in the course of the war, as well, John.

And that leads me to my second point. I wonder whether the term "endurance" also needs to be reconsidered. Yes, soldiers used the term. To them endurance meant putting up with hardship in order to break through the enemy lines and achieve victory. Trench warfare was always seen as a prelude to breakout. To a different kind of war, a war of movement. The problem was that for three years, each attempt at breakthrough brought about nothing of the kind. A war that is supposed to have a beginning, a middle, and an end, had a middle and a middle, and then another middle, and then another year and another battle and another last push, and a middle that went on and on and on.

This kind of war pushed men beyond the limits of endurance. Many withdrew from this intolerable reality into their own minds; shell shock in this sense was a kind of mutiny against the war men were forced to fight. Post-traumatic stress disorder incorporates many kinds of injury, but among them is the notion that the war the soldiers lived had escaped from human control. That's why I wonder whether the concept of "consent" is one in need of revision, when set in the context of a revolutionary kind of warfare.

SMITH: I'd like to make my point in another way. Perhaps one of the reasons that the coercion versus consent debate ran into a blind alley revolved around a kind of positivist history of consent, one based on the romantic view of a brave and unshakeable national community (notably the French one) emerging bloodied but victorious and unbowed. This, of course, implied an image of a very specific kind of soldier—patriotic, loyal, and very attuned to his own political identity. Such an image approaches that of wartime propaganda, and of course squares poorly with the victims of shell shock or other less clinically specific forms of wartime trauma. But I have always argued for a nuanced and decidedly nonpositivist view of consent. I began thinking about the French army mutinies in the context of the history of Republican citizenship in France. Much more so than democratic citizenship in the United States, Britain, or other Western democracies, French notions of citizenship drew from the work of Jean-Jacques Rousseau, specifically his assertion of a general will of the collective citizenry greater than the sum of its parts.[15] For the soldier obeying commands of the general will (in this case military authority as an instrument of the French state, itself the incarnation of the general will) meant obeying one's self. In effect, this hard-wired a construction of obedience into the deepest forms of political identity of the individual soldier. So I don't think I ever saw consent in these old-fashioned romantic terms. I've always found it a bit unfortunate that the debate between coercion and consent, particularly in France, has tended to veer in reductionist directions: either one or the other existed exclusively. We cannot accept that kind of claim. And at the risk of heading back toward the zone of excessive agreement, I'm quite supportive of John Horne's idea of a richer terminology, because I think it helps lead us out of this blind alley.

WINTER: But how do you handle the issue of mental breakdown? The doctors who treated these people were coercive. They used electroconvulsive shock treatment. Nobody's going to tell me that that involves consent. In fact there's a famous French case in which a military doctor said, "Yes, you are going to get this." The enlisted man said, "No, I'm not." "Yes you are, I'm your officer, I give you an order." Then the exchange continued. "No." "Yes." "No." "Yes." The doctor came to put the electrodes on his forehead and the enlisted man knocked him out. He went before a court-martial. He was found guilty and fined one franc, and then was dismissed from the army. Mind you, he never got his war pension, which was what this was all about anyway.[16] My question to you, Len, is how do we integrate into the discussion of soldiers' "consent" those who come back from war as shattered men?

HORNE: I think it's a very interesting angle of approach to the debate, Jay, but the first thing I would come back to is the proportion of soldiers involved. The issue is significant; but we're talking about a minority of soldiers who suffered "shell shock." As such, it fits into the spectrum of individual refusal. Shell shock is an involuntary refusal of the psyche transmitted to the body. Moreover, the treatment of shell shock also matches what I attempted to identity as a field of force that contained both coercion and persuasion. If we look at the representation that Pat Barker gives of mental breakdown in her *Regeneration Trilogy* of novels on World War I, which is closely based on historical evidence, we clearly have coercion in the form of electroshock therapy, but we also have persuasion through psychotherapy, often for officers.[17] We have both. I think it's also interesting that within what I've called endurance, mental breakdown becomes understood as part of the "landscape of war," as you called it. Early on, there was a tendency, especially on the part of traditional officers, to dismiss shell shock as the behavior of malingerers and cowards. But after about 1916, it became impossible to do so because there was just too much evidence of men who behaved very bravely in certain circumstances but who cracked in others. So I don't think that post-traumatic stress syndrome can be used to portray all soldiers as victims.

SMITH: Not everyone recognized shell shock. You could still think that they were malingerers, if you were George Patton in the Second World War. To be sure, he got into a good bit of trouble because of it. But Patton believed that a man in a hospital bed suffering from shell shock, post-traumatic stress disorder, or whatever clinical term psychiatrists wish to apply, was a coward.

HORNE: But I'm not sure that was a universal view amongst general staffs or officers during the war.

SMITH: That's why you have to present a more varied picture, in which some officers were sympathetic to psychological injuries, and others were not.

HORNE: Can I just add one further point on this issue, which is related directly to the question of narrative? I doubt if the First World War brought about an end of conceiving of war in older narrative forms. You referred in opening this evening to the *Iliad*, and one of the reasons I believe that the *Iliad* is such a foundational text is precisely because it's a narrative of warfare that contains heroism, of course, but also antiheroism, cowardice, jealousy, and much else. At the deepest level, I think, a capacity to tell stories, to construct narratives about what we go through, is fundamental to our ability to function through time as human beings. There is no doubt that the First World War was a huge challenge to that ability, but I'm not convinced that it destroyed it. That is the point about the creative (and maybe therapeutic) capacity of the literary soldiers' postwar accounts. You show in your new book, Len, that the narratives after the war are very different from the narratives during the war, but the point is that both existed. I would like to give a brief example of the ways narrative worked to overcome trauma for ordinary men. This is drawn from the French postal control (the service that opened soldiers' letters in order to monitor morale) and concerns the Seventy-first Division, which comes out of Verdun in mid-July 1916. The men are shattered, and the first postal control report twenty-four hours later says these men cannot write home, they can't construct a coherent account of what happened, they're deeply demoralized. In fact, it's a portrait of shell shock of the kind to which you, Jay, were referring. The army was so worried that a week later it asked for a new report and, interestingly, the postal controller says, "Well, amazingly, the men have started to put together stories." They say: "you know, okay we were beaten back at this point, but we rescued our commander who'd been seized by the Germans and we survived and we did it and we've managed to hold on," and they now see their experience as part of a broader national effort at Verdun.[18] In a very basic way, they've constructed a narrative and this, it seems to me, promises endurance and possibly survival.

WINTER: Resilience may be part of endurance. I'm sure that's true. But at the same time, there is a fundamental issue of how did soldiers deal with a war that at least some of their officers didn't understand? No one fully understood it. And when the American army came to fight in 1917, they had to learn and relearn lessons that had been learned bitterly, bloodily in the previous three years by the Allies.

The relationship between authority in the military force and en-listed men went through a crucible during the war. Len, your scholar-ship has illuminated that subject. But to me what emerges from that crucible itself is far from consent. It's a negotiation that you yourself have maintained allows for soldiers to obey orders and then to disobey them when to carry on meant certain death. This is your point, I be-lieve, John. It is to present soldiers as saying, "yes, we will not allow the German army to break through our lines. No, we are not sheep going to the slaughter, and we are not going to go commit suicide for that fool who's running the show." That sense of multiple facets to soldiers' thinking about battle is, I think, one of the fruits of recent research on the war.

And yet this conclusion leaves open many questions about what con-stitutes valid evidence about the soldiers' war. In other words, whose story do we listen to? There are stories which have all the force of eye-witness testimony, and yet the authors weren't there. Ernest Hemingway wrote the greatest account of Caporetto, the major Italian defeat of late 1917, even though he wasn't there at the time. He had no idea what the Battle of Caporetto was like. And yet he wrote the most remarkable nar-rative about it.[19]

SMITH: Tolstoy wasn't at Borodino, either.

WINTER: But he was a soldier.

SMITH: And he had fought in the Crimea, nearly four decades after 1812.

WINTER: Yes, Tolstoy was a soldier, that's certainly true. There are other instances where we can find people who have the genius of imagi-nation to recount a battle in which they have not fought. But for your interpretation of narrative, Len, whose story counts? I think this may be a matter of political choices. We choose the narratives with which we agree, or those which move us. Perhaps this is one of the reasons why this subject is so powerfully contested by historians whose political out-looks differ.

Let's consider for a moment the case of mutiny in Russia. The Russian Revolution was the outcome of the greatest antiwar movement in history.

It broke out in 1917 following the refusal of millions of peasant soldiers to fight a war that to them seemed stupid and meaningless. They wanted to go home and take land for their own benefit. How does this major set of events fit in to the story of consent and coercion?

SMITH: It strikes me that we should think about the Russian Revolution in terms not of refusing the war, but of transforming it. The Russians (and non-ethnic Russians in the newborn Soviet Union) fought a long bloody civil war *after* the Bolshevik seizure of power. Millions of people on both sides still had quite a bit of fight left in them. The same could be said for others, such as the soldiers of the Czech Legion and those who fought for and against Béla Kun in Hungary.

WINTER: No one would accuse Lenin of being a pacifist, that's for sure. But the point is that in Russia as much as in France, the war the soldiers got was not the war to which they consented. The war they got was much, much worse, and that may be true in almost every war. I am afraid I still subscribe to the notion of soldiers as victims: not all and not always, but wars create victims, and among them are the soldiers who endure them. I'm one of the "Boo Hoo" school, I think . . . [Laughter]. One of those who accused me of this crime, Corelli Barnett, threatened to punch me in the nose if he ever met me on the street, after the BBC television series I did on the Great War.[20] Haven't met him yet, I'm still as you see me. . . . [Laughter]

The fundamental point here is that we are dealing with questions of political choice. You may wind up choosing an author whose evidence corresponds to the view you want to find in the first place. And that is against the ethos of our profession. We should try to escape from it. In France, you can't escape from the political coloration of historical interpretations. People disagree on the subject because they're talking about what France is, not what the First World War was. In this country and in Britain, I might add, the political debates are further removed from the historical debates—not entirely, but they are further removed from contemporary ideological conflicts. John lives in that wonderfully apolitical country, Ireland . . .

HORNE: And it seems we disagree on everything.

WINTER: John, would you agree that we do have to face the fundamental question of what constitutes representative evidence about the soldiers' war?

HORNE: Can I just say that there are important technical issues here to do with the availability of evidence? One of the corollaries of what we've been saying about national armies and the role of the schoolmasters not just in the French Third Republic but also in Russia, for example, where we now know the level of literacy to have been higher than previously thought amongst the soldiers mobilized in 1914, is that ordinary soldiers wrote letters on an unprecedented scale. In other words, in the conditions of trench warfare, these men who were literate as never before, wrote as never before. Here is a parallel with the literacy of the veterans of the American Civil War.

Thus the evidence about the soldiers' war is potentially vast. Now, there are certain technical questions—the postal control, as it existed in the French army, left huge records and they do, I think, provide us with the basis of saying something reasonably balanced (for all the difficulties of working with the sources) on what French soldiers felt, though it doesn't exist for 1914–15. We have to find ways of compensating for that gap. In the British case, the same source, which did exist, has more or less disappeared: it was destroyed in the interwar period. So there are questions of imbalance in source materials, but I would say we have a plethora rather than a dearth of sources.

WINTER: To add one additional element before concluding, it seems to me one of the most misleading sources about consent or coercion in the First World War is commercial or documentary film. We simply cannot assume that the war shown on the silver screen was the war the soldiers knew. The battlefield was too chaotic for the motion picture camera, which drew a proscenium arch around its vanishing point. Documentary film was staged virtually all the time and presented sanitized images of the fighting. To a degree, then, the soldiers' war is one we still see only through a glass darkly.

This is where I think we have to leave it. We historians have an enormous task ahead, which is to do justice to the soldiers of the Great War, to go beyond the politicized categories of heroism versus cowardice, masculinity versus impotence, and we're just beginning the task at hand. Now may I thank, on your behalf, John Horne, Len Smith for enlightening us this evening. [Applause]

And on democratic grounds that Harry Truman would have approved, I would like to hear if there are questions from the floor.

QUESTION: I'm Pam Smith and I'm from Florida. I teach a lot of military students, and I see in their writings an understanding of acceptance, endurance, and refusal. How do you use these terms in teaching?

HORNE: I think perhaps the Russian case during the First World War would be a good example of how to use these terms. One sees an acceptance gradually giving way to a kind of dogged endurance in which there are still elements of acceptance. And then what's so interesting is individual acts of refusal gradually coalesce into a collective refusal. But on the other hand, it doesn't necessarily work out in a chronological sequence like that, so that one might also find situations in which one sticks at endurance and elements of refusal are contained. I think that's really what characterizes France in the Great War. In other situations, one ends up with refusal, but the refusal is of totally different kinds, which I think would characterize, say, Germany, Austria-Hungary, and Russia at the end of the war. Refusal to go on with a war that could not be won was a commonplace outlook, an understandable one.

WINTER: One way forward is to make the distinction between those three possibilities at different stages of the war.

HORNE: Yes.

WINTER: Because right at the outset, you'll get all three anyway. But there is a moment of reinvestment in the war, as you say, John, at a certain time when people think they're going to win. I don't want to get into the Iraq question, but if the surge were to work in such a way as to stabilize a government, I think you might find a very different response to the conflict among Iraqi and American soldiers. The key point is that these three categories shift over time in a war of any length at all.

SMITH: Since we're now talking about the present situation in Iraq, let me observe that this war is being fought by volunteers who are their own kind of *self-motivated agents*. A recent article in *The Economist* quoted an unnamed senior military figure as saying the *nation* is not at war, the *military* is at war. So the nation is not really suffering attrition to speak of, at least not in ways directly attributable to the war—the stock market is doing what it does, gas prices rise and fall, et cetera. But few doubt that the *military* certainly is suffering attrition. And I think it's interesting to think about what soldiers, as we speak, are writing home about Iraq in that context, from within a military society in ways troublingly separate from the civilian polity that it serves. As a citizen, I find this upsetting—the kind of gulf that appears to exist between the people over there and the people over here. And it would be interesting to see how that expresses itself in the kinds of the categories—consent, coercion, endurance, refusal—we have been talking about today.

WINTER: Other questions, please.

QUESTION: About ten years ago there was a movement in England to sort of say sorry to the people who refused to continue fighting in the war. There were maybe three hundred or so who were . . .

HORNE: Shot for cowardice.

QUESTION: Shot for cowardice. The British government refused. I don't know what came of it.

WINTER: They've been pardoned posthumously.

SMITH: One of former Prime Minister Tony Blair's last acts.

WINTER: One reason why these men were pardoned is that there's a doubt as to how many were shell-shocked and were convicted of cowardice or desertion when they were really insane. There's a real doubt as to how many of them came to a decision: "This is wrong, I can't do it anymore." The French Parliament set up a special tribunal in 1932 to reexamine many of the cases, and a number of those who had been executed were subsequently pardoned, some on the grounds that although citizens, they had originally been denied the right of appeal. Millions of British soldiers were subjects of the crown in the First World War, but they didn't have the vote. French soldiers had the vote, and therefore, they could appeal to their representatives to secure fair treatment by the courts. Being denied an appeal was patently unfair. In the British case, too, there were doubts, though not on the same grounds.

HORNE: Can I just add that in the French case there was a terrible period at the beginning of the war when there were many summary executions. This is a perfect example of what happened when the official and professional military were fearful of the effect of desertions on the rest of the men who had been mobilized at the beginning of the war. Joffre, the French commander-in-chief, felt that if the offensive didn't proceed, and people were "allowed" to act as "cowards," then this would contaminate the rest of the mobilized army, made up of millions of reservists. So a number of people were shot in a summary fashion. And as Jay says, there were campaigns to exonerate them. Eventually many were pardoned by parliamentary act. Later on in the war, every capital sentence had to be approved by the president of the Republic.

But I think your question also raises a very interesting matter of memory and law. Is it appropriate for us, eighty or ninety years after the event, to reverse legal decisions of the time rather than engaging in acts of purely historical—not judicial—recognition? Is that an appropriate way to handle something that was the product of a society very different from ours and with very different assumptions?

SMITH: I'm not sure just what a pardon does. Does a pardon reverse the judgment? Or is it simply an official act of forgiveness on the part of the sovereign, be that sovereign the monarch or the people? I believe it is the latter.

WINTER: The other possible answer to your question, Len, is that pardon gives some peace to the families of the men who were shot. They then have the right to put their names on the local war memorial, to put their family history together with that of their neighbors', to bring closure to a traumatic past, on perhaps the most important level of all, the one we live in our homes, with our loved ones.

QUESTION: I would like to ask about consent and coercion in revolutionary Russia. In 1919 there were Americans in Russia. They didn't know whose side they were on. There were military units there from other countries, too, like Czechoslovakia. We have talked about "consent" on the Western front, but what about Russia in the period when the First World War elided into civil war?

WINTER: You're raising something I think we haven't really dealt with and will deal with in our discussion of Versailles. That is, what do the words "consent" and "coercion" mean when the Great War turned into a revolutionary and counterrevolutionary war? We were talking about the war that began in 1914. But after 1917, the political character of the war changed radically. Something happened in Russia which was perhaps even more significant than the war fought over the previous three years. Once you inject the issue of revolutionary or counterrevolutionary history, you get, I think, into an area which is very remote from the motivation of soldiers in the trenches of the Western front.

One of the points on which we historians agree is that soldiers' morale was largely a function of the ties between front and home front. The people in uniform were fighting for people at home. Fast forward to 1919 or 1920. What are the soldiers sent by the Western powers doing in Vladivostok? What are Americans doing up in Murmansk? Are they fighting for Kansas City? What is most striking after the Bolshevik Revolution is the translation of the First World War into a civil war over the fate of the revolution. This new political landscape was one in which issues of coercion, persuasion, and acceptance took on an entirely different set of meanings for the men who did the fighting.

SMITH: Certainly, sending American troops to Siberia was a doubtful decision that poisoned relations with the Soviet Union from its birth. Woodrow Wilson was himself very divided on the issue from the beginning, and I believe swiftly regretted sending soldiers. So I think quite profound confusion existed at the highest levels of the American war effort.

HORNE: And perhaps it's just worth stating that the American army, of course, ends up as an army of occupation after the First World War. American troops, along with British and French troops, go into the

Rhineland in Germany as occupiers. That's a precarious coda to the war in which the American experience becomes something very different to what it's been on the Western front.

WINTER: There is another dimension of the issue of morale that we haven't been able to deal with yet. That is the issue of the morale of African American soldiers in the American army.

HORNE: And Africans in the French army.

WINTER: Were soldiers fighting to achieve rights they did not have before the outbreak of war? Did they believe that the societies for which they fought "owed" them a degree of dignity denied them before the conflict? Simply to raise this question is to show the importance of avoiding homogenizing these vast armies. They were made up of very different populations, with very different political agendas. Here we historians have much work to do, but at least we have started in the right direction, especially so with respect to this important tapestry of consent, acceptance, resistance, and revolt we have been weaving today. Many thanks to our speakers and to the audience here in the Harry Truman Presidential Library and Museum.

FOUR

Ending the Great War
The Peace That Failed?

John Milton Cooper, University of Wisconsin at Madison
Margaret MacMillan, St. Antony's College, Oxford

WINTER: This series of conversations enables us to appreciate how extraordinarily active, alive, effervescent, is the study of the First World War in many parts of the world today. I welcome John Cooper, an old friend, and Margaret MacMillan, a new friend, because they have contributed in fundamental ways to our understanding of both war and peace. The two form a double helix, circling around each other. Indeed, it seems clear that the only way to define peace is by defining war. Every imagining of peace has as its mirror image an imagining of war. This was especially true at the end of the First World War. When we turn to the subject of peacemaking in 1919, we are dealing with one of the foundational moments of international history. In a sense we are here to consider how that event—those "Six Months That Changed the World," in Margaret MacMillan's subtitle of her book—how those six months shaped our lives today. That is one of the issues I'd like to explore today.

I'd like to start it off by asking a question that may sound self-evident, but one which has hidden ambiguities in it that will help frame our discussion of peacemaking. The question, Margaret, I'd like to put to you is, when did the war end?

MACMILLAN: That is a difficult one, I think. Some people would say it didn't end until France fell in 1940; that the First World War was the first part of the "thirty years' war" in Europe, and you could argue that because, in a way, what happened in 1940 was unfinished business from the First World War. You could also say that it didn't really end on November the eleventh, 1918, because there were a whole lot of small wars after that, in Winston Churchill's phrase, "the wars of the pygmies have now started, the wars of the giants have ended." And so you had wars between, for example, Romania and Hungary, Poland and Czechoslovakia, and a major war between Poland and Russia which ended up in a treaty in 1921. You had a whole series of small wars all around what was the collapse of a Russian empire. And so peace, probably, you could argue, didn't really come until about 1924. But the big war, the catastrophic war, the Great War, ended on November 11.

WINTER: John, from an American point of view, is the eleventh of November really the end of the war?

COOPER: Jay, although this is a harsh thing to say, I think, psychologically, for Americans it was a war that ended too soon. Militarily, the AEF was going to take over the major burden of the war, because the British and French simply were exhausted in their manpower. The plans were for an invasion of Germany in 1919. Also, psychologically, Americans were geared up for the war. They had been very much geared up, partly because a certain amount of war hysteria had been deliberately fomented. In some cases, it was also because they fomented it themselves. And John Higham—the late historian of Johns Hopkins University—once wrote that you can't understand the passions afterwards, such as the Red scare at home, except in some terms of unspent emotion from the war. So that there was a sudden ending. Of course, people were grateful for this and very glad, but on the other hand, there was a lot that was left over. So for Americans, it was an unsatisfactory ending to the war.

WINTER: That leaves us with the question as to what were the expectations of peacemaking when Woodrow Wilson became the first sitting president to leave the country during his term of office. What was in his mind? We can broaden the question in a moment, but you as a scholar of Wilson and of America and the war would be well placed to tell us more about him.

COOPER: Wilson has a reputation, of course, as being an idealist. That's pretty much the first synonym that's attached to him, and he would have welcomed that, but only to a point. The other thing about him was that his great political mentor and influence was Edmund Burke. So he very much, very early on rejected grand designs in trying to put some kind of pattern on the world. He was an idealist, but a very, very practical, cautious one. He was trying to create a new process, a new process to maintain world order. That's what he really wanted from the League of Nations—not so much a finished set of institutions that were going to just put everything into concrete, not at all. He saw this very much as a process, an organic process. On the *George Washington,* sailing to France, he had two different encounters. He had his group of experts, you know, he had the Inquiry, including people like Walter Lippmann, Charles Seymour, and others. And there was a moment when he called them together on the *George Washington* and said, "Tell me what's right and I'll fight for it." But then, afterward, he talked to George Creel, who'd been propagandist-in-chief during the war. And Wilson said to him, "It is a great thing that you have done, but I'm wondering if you have not unconsciously spun a net for me from which there is no escape. It is to America that the whole world turns today, not only with its wrongs, but with its hopes and grievances. The hungry expect us to feed them, the ruthless look to us for shelter, the sick of heart and body depend upon us for cure. All of these expectations have in them a quality of terrible urgency. There must be no delay. It has always been, so always people will endure their tyrants for years, but they will tear up their deliverers to pieces if a millennium is not created immediately. Yet you know and I know that these ancient wrongs, these present unhappinesses are not to be remedied in a day or with the wave of a hand. What I seem to see, with all my heart I hope that I am wrong, is a tragedy of disappointment."[1] So in other words, here he saw this. He saw it coming.

WINTER: I'd like to broaden the question, Margaret, and put it perhaps in an international perspective. When the nations, the victorious nations came together, they were joined by those who hoped for great things from the deliberations dealing with dependencies, colonies, those deserving, perhaps, of self-determination, in Wilson's phrase. What was the environment in December 1918 and in January 1919—what were the expectations in public opinion as opposed to the leaders?

MACMILLAN: There were a whole lot of expectations and, I think, that's what was going to make it so difficult to make peace. I think, first of all, there was a feeling that the war had been so catastrophic and so costly that something—first of all, someone—must pay. It must be someone's fault—and that's a very natural human reaction. Someone made this happen and someone should pay; someone should pay for the damage done and someone should pay for all the lives that have been lost. Someone should pay for the whole catastrophe. I think there was also a feeling that the war had been so long and so costly, both in terms of human lives and other costs, to economies and societies and in the amount of destruction done to Europe and to European civilization, that something better must come out of it. Otherwise all that tremendous waste would be for nothing, and so I think there were these, in some ways, contradictory expectations, first that someone should pay and someone should be punished. Yet there was also this feeling that, having done all this to the world and to ourselves, and Europeans felt this particularly strongly, we must build something better. And added to all of that, there was a sense that the world was in a state of flux. One of the many interesting things about the First World War is that it left so much that was undecided. It wasn't like the Second World War, where it was quite clear who the defeated were and quite clear victors and the thing was definitely over. And it really wasn't like the end of the Napoleonic Wars, although the great model they had in their minds when they met at Paris in 1919 was the Congress of Vienna which tried to deal with Europe after those long wars of the French Revolution and then the Napoleonic Wars. The circumstances when the Congress of Vienna met in 1814 and 1815 were quite different. By that point, Europe was sick of war. In 1918 and 1919 by contrast there was a sense that it wasn't all over and there was a sense that things had not settled down. In fact, things were wide open, because what had happened as a result of the

First World War is four great empires had collapsed. Germany, which had ruled over a number of people who weren't German, the Poles in particular, had collapsed. Its state collapsed, and it appeared to have collapsed completely, destroying its empire. Russia too was in a state of disintegration. All those people around the borders of Russia from the Baltic peoples to those in Central Asia were trying to claim their independence again. Austria-Hungary, which had controlled so much of the center of Europe, had vanished. The Ottoman Empire, which still controlled parts of Europe and a great deal of the Middle East, was clearly about to vanish, and more than that, there was a general sense that political and economic and social institutions were under threat. And so in those circumstances, you have the desire for revenge beside the desire for a better world. You have a whole lot of people saying, finally now is our chance to build a better world, whether they followed the Bolsheviks in Russia or whether they were nationalist groups who said at last we have a chance to have our own state. There was a widespread feeling that a lot was possible and, of course, all the powers that came to Paris were democracies and so they had to take account of public opinion. That put tremendous pressure on the statesmen. They were under pressure from their own populations and it's a very brave politician who will say to his or her own population, sorry, what you want is totally impossible—that doesn't usually happen because politicians are always thinking of the next election. The statesmen were also under tremendous pressure from petitioners—all those people who thought here finally we can get what we want. Over the course of the peace conference, literally dozens of peoples came to Paris to say, we want our own state, or we want rights for women, we want rights for African Americans, and we want our colonies to be independent. They were trying to operate in Paris under this tremendous pressure. Wilson was right. There was no way that all those conflicting expectations, in some cases totally impossible expectations, could be met. With all the different national groups: Wilson said later on that he had not realized how many there were. "I never," he said, "would have uttered those words, self-determination." Some were in the process of forming because once you're told you have a chance to become a nation, then that spurs you on. And in Europe, they all claimed territory, but of course, the claims overlapped because European history was so long. When national groups looked back into their own history, they didn't say, "Let's have a nice neat little country like Switzerland." They went back to, usually, the extent of their greatest borders, which meant that you often got different nations demanding the same bits of territory.

WINTER: The question of what constitutes a nation is something that I've always found puzzling. The word "self-determination" begs the question, who was the self and who does the determining? Who has the right to say that a nation has a self that requires a state? The former Yugoslavia is an example of how that goes wrong. What did Wilson mean, John, about self-determination? Was it something for Europeans alone? Was it for the Africans and Asians someday later down the line? What did self-determination mean to him?

COOPER: Wilson would not claim pride of authorship for that term; it was Lord George who coined the term "self-determination." I always ask where is self-determination in the fourteen points? It's not there. I think he saw it primarily in the short term for Europeans, but not even fully there. In the fourteen points, for example, he does not talk about breaking up the Austrian-Hungarian Empire. He doesn't talk about an independent Czech nation or anything like that. He favored autonomy at the time. So self-determination can mean a lot of things. It doesn't necessarily mean a separate nation. Now, as far as getting beyond the European world, the white world, that gets more complicated. Wilson's record on race in this country is not good, and that's putting it mildly. So it is probable that he was somewhat embarrassed about the question as to whether self-determination applied to the nonwhite world. Erez Manela has just written an excellent book about the unintended consequences of Wilson raising this dream of nationhood in Korea, in China, in India, in Egypt.[2] As Margaret was saying, there were many petitioners in Paris in 1919. One was a young Vietnamese who was supporting himself as a waiter and a cook in Paris who rented a suit to go try to be heard by the peacemakers. I forget what his Vietnamese name was then, but it was later Ho Chi Minh. W. E. B. DuBois was there. And all of these different petitioners were clamoring for self-determination. And Wilson, in many ways, was having to damp down these hopes. And then later, Henry Cabot Lodge, the chairman of the Foreign Relations Committee, had a field day with the hearings on the peace treaty. Every group that had a grievance against the Versailles settlement came in there and clamored for self-determination—Koreans, Egyptians. And Chinese spokesmen were also up in arms, because Wilson had made a compromise which was to allow the Japanese to stay in Shandung, rather than to return this territory, previously a German concession, to the Chinese. Wilson chose not to challenge that because the Japanese were threatening to boycott the League of Nations; they wouldn't join up. So he admitted it was a bad deal, he didn't like doing it, but it was one of those things that emerged from difficult negotiations. Wilson wanted to institute a process of change. Self-determination was going to come at different paces for different peoples. He was not entirely indifferent to the rise of the colonial peoples. And unlike some, I think, the mandate system was an intelligent way of trying to square that circle. In other words, the former German colonies were not ceded outright to the other powers that conquered them. In other words, Australia didn't get Papua New Guinea outright. South Africa didn't get Southwest Africa outright; they became mandates of the League of Nations. Now, some people said, oh that's just a fig leaf to cover up what's really a colony. Yes and no. Because there was inspection by the League of Nations, there was a promise on the part of the mandatory power of eventual independence—this is something the Europeans had not done for any of their colonies and, as a matter of fact, the United States had not done it for its colony, the Philippines, either. So these are inconsistencies and prejudices in Wilson's approach to these questions. The person, I think, who recognized that best was W. E. B. DuBois, who was in Paris in the spring of 1919 attending a Pan-African Congress.

WINTER: Let us consider another controversial matter. Was this peace a Carthaginian peace? Did this treaty prepare the ground for Hitler by persuading people of all political views that the peace settlement was unjust? Was it not absurd to believe that an earthquake like the war of 1914–1918 could be the responsibility of one single person or nation?[3] What is your response to that, Margaret?

MACMILLAN: When I started to write my book on the peace conference, the standard view which I think a lot of people still share is that the treaties made—and the Treaty of Versailles was the one that is generally singled out, but there were others—the treaties made were collectively a very bad thing. The criticism is that it was a very harsh peace.

It was unfair, and Germany in particular, but the other nations, too, were right to complain. As a result, so the critics say, we got another war twenty years later. As I started to do more work, I just thought, oh this is too simple, to say that the peace settlements led to war twenty years later. What after all were people, leaders for example, doing in those twenty years? In the 1920s, there were very real attempts made to make the system work. The international order was beginning to reestablish itself. We can come to this later but it would have made a real difference if the United States had joined the League of Nations—I really do believe that. Then a number of things happened, some of them human decisions. You had the Great Depression of 1929, which turned nations inwards and made them become more protective and helped to really damage the system. And you had Hitler rising in Germany. Don't think any of this was a foregone conclusion. But it did happen and that led to real strains on the system. When I looked at the Treaty of Versailles with Germany, of course the Germans hated it, but anyone who loses a war or anyone who loses a legal case, never likes the decision. You don't get people saying, "You know, that judge was absolutely fair to award damages against me." The Germans did not like losing. They lost on the battlefield, although very soon in Germany this myth grew that Germany had been stabbed in the back at home, that Germany had never really been defeated. The Germans also felt, in a sense, they'd wiped the slate clean because they had got rid of the Kaiser and had become a Republic. So, they argued, it was a different Germany and why should it be punished for the failures of the old one? The Germans also assumed, and John will know more about this than I do, that Wilson had promised them a just peace based on the fourteen points. In Germany such views and assumptions were shared across the general political spectrum. They were also very sedulously and very aggressively fostered by the German high command and by the German foreign office. A special department in the foreign office was set up to present Germany's part in the outbreak in the First World War, and it very selectively released documents which seemed to show that the outbreak of the war was really an accident and Germany was no more responsible than anyone else. You got a sense in Germany that the peace treaty was very unfair. If you look at the Treaty of Versailles, it was certainly niggling and irritating in many ways. Yes, Germany did lose territory, but virtually all the territory it lost was not occupied by Germans but by other peoples such as Poles. Yes, Germany did have to pay reparations, but every Allied statesman knew that Germany was never going to pay the reparations bill that was set. The Allied leaders had to say something to their own people. Again we have the issue of public expectations. The French prime minister, Georges Clemenceau, could not tell his public, "Look, sorry, the war was fought on French soil and a great deal of damage was done to France, yet Germany is virtually unscathed by the war—sorry, we're not going to be able to get any money out of Germany to repair the mess." He couldn't say it. And so the figure was set, which everybody knew was way too high and they knew they were never going to collect, and in the end they never collected all that much. By one estimate, Germany paid less than France paid Germany after the Franco-Prussian War of 1870–71. What is so important in human affairs, whether domestic or international political affairs, is what people think is the case. And the belief in Germany, which was shared, not in France so much, but certainly shared in the English-speaking countries, was that Germany had been very unfairly treated.

COOPER: I agree with Margaret. I think she's hit the nail on the head. In some ways I have often thought that that peace conference, and especially the terms of that treaty, had been, perhaps, one of the most over-studied events in recent human history; overstudied in the sense that if only we can find out more about these few things that they did wrong, then we can make it right. That wasn't the problem. As you've pointed out, Germany's problem was they'd lost the war. The treaty may have rubbed a little bit of salt in the wound, but the wound was already there. What was wrong with that peace settlement? It was that very soon after, the victors lost the will to maintain it. The vanquished had never been made to submit—John Dowers's phrase for Japan after World War II is "embracing the defeat."[4] The Germans had never been made to embrace their defeat. But in turn, starting with the United States, we began to show that we did not have the will or the interest to maintain this settlement, that it wasn't going to be made to stick.

WINTER: Let me try to lower the level of generalization a bit. Let us separate the indictment of the peace treaties in plural, from the way that settlement created the mess we live with in the Middle East. I have trouble squaring blatant imperial agreements to divide the Middle East between French and British spheres of interest with the structure or framework or process or organic development that you are emphasizing in Wilson's thinking about self-determination. And the second indictment of the peace settlement is that the Soviet Union, more precisely Revolutionary Russia, isn't there. What is a new international order when the Soviet Union is quarantined, and when the Great Powers including the United States send troops to Russia to overthrow the new regime?

MACMILLAN: I'm going to disagree with you a little bit. Not on your first point that many of the boundaries in the Middle East were drawn, at Paris and in the conferences immediately afterwards, for imperialist reasons. The British and the French looked at the Middle East and they said, "We want it." The British said to themselves, "We don't want the French to get very much." And the French said to themselves, "We don't want the British to get very much." Their old imperial rivalry. On the other hand, I think there was a real problem in the Middle East and that is, with the collapse of the Ottoman Empire, there were a lot of mainly Arab but also Kurdish-speaking territories which had not ruled themselves and which did not yet have strongly based national movements. Egypt was a different case: it already had its own national movement and established borders. There were Arab national movements in the big cities like Damascus and what is today Syria and in Baghdad, but otherwise, Arab societies still had very traditional structures—tribal you could call them. What do you do with those territories? Are they yet capable of ruling themselves? Nor was there yet a Kurdish national movement although there certainly is one today. So, if you are the Great Powers, do you just leave those territories to themselves and say let's see what happens? There was a power vacuum in the Middle East and maybe the mandate system was a way of dealing with it. But I agree there are all sorts of problems with the settlement in the Middle East, but we have to remember that the facts on the ground were difficult. The second—what was the second?

WINTER: Russia.

MACMILLAN: On the indictment that Russia was not at the peace conference, that is a tricky one because it's not clear the Bolsheviks wanted to be there. Lenin and Trotsky assumed that the world was going to have a worldwide revolution. In Lenin's phrase the Bolshevik Revolution was the spark that will start a prairie fire. And when the Bolshevik leaders looked out from Moscow, that's what they seemed to be seeing because there were demonstrations, often very violent demonstrations, and strikes in Germany, in Italy, in Britain, even in Winnipeg in Canada. And there were attempts made to set up councils of workers and soldiers which were called Soviets. So initially at least, the Bolshevik view was that the revolution was going to spread through the world, so why should they bother to talk to the capitalists anyway? In the early spring of 1919 there was an aborted attempt to have some sort of Russian representation in Paris and it failed. Clemenceau, the French prime minister, didn't want any Bolsheviks in Paris because he thought his own middle classes would have a fit, which they would have done because they'd lost a lot of money in Russia. For their part the Bolsheviks didn't want to come. I don't think it was ever as straightforward as the Bolsheviks being excluded because I'm not sure they wanted to come.

WINTER: But we do have to deal with the question of Western intervention in attempting to overthrow the Soviet regime. How serious were the peacemakers in making war on the new regime?

MACMILLAN: I don't think they were all that serious. And John may want to add to this. Western troops were in there initially to help keep the Russians in the war and protect the ports and the routes through which Western supplies were coming in. It's a bit like American troops being in China during the Second World War to support the Nationalists against Japan and then ending up supporting the Nationalists or the Guomindang, to give them their Chinese name, against their enemies, the Chinese Communists. The foreign troops—and there were Canadian troops there so for the Canadians this is important—the foreign troops came to support the Russian war effort and ended up more or less supporting the White Russians who were fighting the Bolsheviks. There were American troops in Siberia, but they were more there to keep an eye on the Japanese, really, than to do anything else. The Allied effort was really half-hearted, and by the spring again of 1919, the Canadian prime minister went to Lord George and said, "I'm pulling Canadian troops out. We don't want to be there." There was a wonderful meeting of the Council of Four—the big four statesmen—in Paris and they said, you know, we must intervene. And Churchill was pushing for it. And Lloyd George said, "With what?" You know, they didn't have the troops. Basically, the Western intervention was half-hearted and it was wound down pretty quickly. But Allied intervention became a very important part of Bolshevik mythology—that the Western powers had tried to strangle the revolution in its cradle, and they will always try to destroy the Soviet Union.

COOPER: I taught in Moscow for a semester in 1987, and I came to that part. I was teaching the history of Korea from 1900 to 1940, and I just said, "Sorry, the United States did not try to smother the Bolshevik Revolution." I said, "If we had, we didn't have nearly enough troops, we didn't put them in, we didn't make any such effort," and I was met with stony silence because I was, of course, contradicting one of their founding myths. Wilson, in fact, had had his baptism by fire with revolution already with Mexico and had fumbled around and done very badly with it. He learned his lesson.He said at one point in 1916 to try to push back the Mexican Revolution would be as serious an error as the great powers made in the 1790s to try to push back the French Revolution, a revolution as profound. So, Wilson didn't believe in trying to smother revolutions. He just didn't believe in it. He thought if we put a few thousand troops in, we might help stabilize the situation, but as Margaret said, the main American force was in Siberia and was there to counter the Japanese.

WINTER: You can imagine a few thousand Russian troops in, let's say, Germany in 1919, it might not have been seen as so trivial an intervention. The notion of the worst of both worlds is what I'm getting at, both regressive and progressive. In other words, I am struck by the contradiction between the way the peace was structured to keep as much of the old imperial order intact as to satisfy Britain and France and the commitment to create a new structure which might be able to develop in the opposite direction. And I wonder what you would say about this, John, that basically if you try to create contradictory processes, one imperialist and one moving in another direction, then failure is inevitable.

COOPER: No, Wilson's answer to that would be that you have to work with where you are. You have to do it. You can't—you simply can't—overturn imperialism in one fell swoop. He wasn't a revolutionary, to be sure. You know, you could argue, the whole system is rotten and revolution was the only answer. I don't particularly accept that. But you have to work from where you are. You have to try to reform the system with what you've got. And yes, he had no illusions about the designs of the British and the French, and especially the Italians. I mean his worst fights over these matters were with the Italians. So he did know what he was dealing with. He'd never made common—wholehearted, shoulder-to-shoulder—common cause with the Allies. Now remember, the United States was an associated power, not an ally. That was a very important distinction for Wilson. So his view was you've got to start with where you are. Granted, of course, there's contradiction built in there, but on the other hand, for Wilson, as a good Burkian, contradiction was the nature of politics.

WINTER: Let me ask both of you. You've both had a good, hard look at Woodrow Wilson in the course of these months. Did he have a stroke? Did he change because of medical problems that turned what might have been a flexible politician into an inflexible one?

COOPER: You mean the small stroke at Paris . . .

WINTER: Before the great stroke that ended the whistle-stop campaign later on. I'm talking about Paris itself. There are two Wilsons. The Wilson who is a man of political sophistication, and then there's the Wilson who thinks that the French chambermaid is a spy for Clemenceau. Yes, sometimes paranoid people are right, they really are being spied on by their chambermaids. But in this case, there is a real question about biography in the midst of this, and both of you are biographers of distinction. And I wonder whether you read Wilson as a man who begins to break down in the middle of the Versailles settlement?

MACMILLAN: It's such an interesting question in great historical events—how much the individuals matter. And I do think there are times when it does matter when individuals are making very important decisions, so yes, I think Wilson is important. I would have two questions about Wilson. First the question of his health. There's a very thorough study that Princeton did of his medical condition in Paris and they had doctors look at all the evidence who concluded that he probably did have a small stroke. According to the Princeton study, what often happens, apparently, when you have a stroke, is that your existing characteristics get exaggerated. I also have a question about Wilson's own character. How flexible was he before his illness? John will know much more than I do, but he had his tremendous self-righteousness and the conviction that he spoke for the masses and that he understood the masses in a way that nobody else did. This, of course, infuriated the European statesmen who were also democratically elected. Having said that, he did negotiate and he did compromise in Paris. He compromised with the Italians whom he couldn't stand. When the Italian prime minister Vittorio Orlando burst into tears because he wasn't getting the territory he wanted, Wilson was the first man to take out his handkerchief and give it to him. So he did try and keep talking to people he didn't like. He certainly compromised with the British and the French on the reparations issue. He compromised on borders. And so I think he did help to make the best of the difficult job of making peace. And I think what John was saying earlier was so right. I mean Wilson thought the settlement in Paris was the beginning and he thought the League of Nations was the beginning and he said, if we haven't done it correctly, the League can do it. It was to be an ongoing process, just like democratic politics which are a constant process of compromise and trying to get things better.

COOPER: On Wilson and his health at Paris. He did have this serious illness early in April 1919, after he made that quick trip back to the U.S. to deliver the State of the Union address to Congress. He then came back, and he did have this fairly serious illness. He was out of commission for four or five days there. And that's when the question arose, did he have a small stroke? On this medical authorities disagree. Weinstein, who studied it most closely, concluded later that he didn't; he had some strain of the flu that was pretty bad and that he came back from that.[5] There are elements in Wilson's character that are in conflict or imbalanced. One is he did have a tendency towards self-righteousness. His friends back at Princeton used to say, "We've got to get to Tommy before he makes up his mind because it's all over then." On the other hand, he also knew this, and deliberately tried to find a balance, without trying to commit himself too much too soon on things. And I see this weakness, frankly, part of it as age and fatigue. Especially, he had never worked under such conditions as he did in Paris. And before, as president, he'd been very well able to regulate his time and to shepherd it and to get rest and recreation, too. He actually had a very short working day as president. On the other hand, he had tremendous concentration and got a heck of a lot of work done. And in Paris in 1919, it's different. He is under severe pressure. He has a constant stream of people to meet all the time, and it wore on him. So I see that pressure as more decisive in explaining his behavior in Paris, not so much a dramatic intervention like a small stroke.

Before I published the last book I wrote about the fight over the League of Nations,[6] I sought the advice of the chairman of the neurology department at the University of Wisconsin. He read the materials I gave him about Wilson's medical condition. And he said, "You really should put some more uncertainty into this." And he said, "We don't know. We can't read back from the massive stroke that Wilson suffered while he was trying to build up public support for the League of Nations." The neurologist said, "You know, for people who suffer these kinds of strokes can be like the lightbulb that burns brightest just before it goes out. They can be entirely functional." As Margaret said, in Paris after his illness, Wilson is negotiating nonstop. The same is true after his return to the United States at the end of June 1919. He spent two months negotiating with the senators, first individually then meeting with the foreign relations committee before he then went out and went on his whirlwind speaking tour—more concentrated speaking than he'd ever done in his life, even during his presidential campaigns. So this is a man who's still operating at a very high level.

If we return to Wilson in Paris in 1919, he was certainly depleting his reserves. From some point fairly early in the peace conference, Wilson is not operating at his best. I think you can see a gradual decline of his powers.

WINTER: I put to you that those who rejected Wilson's position on the League of Nations had good Constitutional arguments for doing so. Would you agree that this is an argument about the American Constitution being incompatible with the Covenant of the League of Nations?

COOPER: Wilson didn't think so. He thought it was possible to do it within it. Now he did have a very latitudinarian view of the Constitution. He called it a living document, not a straitjacket. He believed that there were enough safeguards in there, that Congress retains the power to declare war, that Congress has the power of the purse, so that any obligations, any financial obligations were entirely subject to congressional authority. Yes. We were compromising sovereignty. And his critics were quite right on that, but he believed that this was the price to pay to prevent another world war.

WINTER: Is that your view, too, Margaret?

MACMILLAN: Yes, I think he felt that—I agree he felt that there were enough safeguards and it was also that special clause saying the Monroe Doctrine would not be affected by the League of Nations. But I think he was someone who believed, as John said, in institutions developing over time. I think he saw that the world was a different place than it had been when the American Constitution was written and that the capacity of nations and peoples to do damage to themselves and to the world was that much greater and that we simply could not go on in the same way. I think it was the same impulse that was behind the United Nations at the end of the Second World War: that we live in a world in which we cannot afford to have nations settling their differences through resorting to war because the consequences for us all are so dreadful. And I think he was also a great believer in the whole process of compromise and consultation in democratic politics and I think he saw the League as something that would do that. Nations would operate a bit like elected representatives and would work out together ways in which they could find common ground. And I think he saw it as something that would keep on evolving.

WINTER: Let me ask you now whether Wilson misjudged the other Great Powers and their capacity to frustrate his project for a League of Nations? If we consider the British prime minister, Lloyd George, is it justified to say that Lloyd George simply let Wilson have his League as long as Britain's imperial interests were secured?

MACMILLAN: I think Lloyd George was sympathetic with many of the goals of the League—I mean he came out of a liberal tradition and certainly the idea of some sort of international way of settling disputes, for example, was not new in the world. Europeans and North Americans have been talking about it for much of the nineteenth century. The whole idea of the League received tremendous support in Europe including in Great Britain. Lloyd George was, of course, also concerned to protect Britain's interest, and that was natural. It's like a politician who comes from a state like Kansas or Missouri who can think in national terms, but also thinks in local terms. That's their job, to do both. And Lloyd George was, yes, very concerned to protect Britain's interests. The Europeans also understood that Woodrow Wilson was very keen on the League and that he was going to insist on it and that they could not afford to break with him over that. But I think Lloyd George was sympathetic to the idea of the League. Clemenceau, the French prime minister, was less so. Clemenceau said, "I like the idea of the League, but I don't believe in it." And I think that was probably his attitude.

Lloyd George, of course, was in a fairly good position because Britain had really got everything it wanted—or pretty well everything it wanted—before the peace conference started. What it wanted was German colonies and it had those, or its own colonies had them. What it wanted was an end to Germany's naval challenge and it had that already because the German fleet was interned in British ports or sunk. If Lloyd George was not as fervent about the League as Wilson was, he certainly saw its advantages. His own dominions, and Canada among them, were pushing for it. The Canadians were very strong in support of the League and more of the British were having to listen to their own empire.

WINTER: Let me turn now to one of the hardest questions that Wilson himself posed. We've heard earlier in this series of conversations among historians of the 1914–18 conflict that the sweep of the war had created casualties the world had never seen before. When you put the peace treaty against the cost, doesn't it look, to a degree, that there is some lack of fit between this enormous effort and this modest outcome? Wilson was very sensitive to the issue of what we owe the dead. I wonder whether you would comment on that, John.

COOPER: I will. I would like to refer to one of the paintings in the Imperial War Museum in London. On one wall is displayed perhaps their greatest painting, I think in quality and in size, by far in size. It is John Singer Sergeant's painting, "Gassed," which is this painting of these British soldiers who've been blinded by mustard gas with bandages over their eyes, each one has got his hand on the shoulder of the one ahead, waiting to be treated. It is a huge painting. Below it are two paintings of the peace conference done by Sir William Orpen, who was the official British artist for the peace conference. One is of the Council of Eleven meeting and the other is of the signing ceremony on 28 June 1919. Now, when I visited the museum, I'd only seen reproductions of these paintings and I'd assumed these were very large paintings. They're not. They're modest-sized paintings. What you've got is this gigantic Sergeant painting of the wounded soldiers, and then you have these two paintings of the peace conference, and the way that Orpen has painted them, by the way, is they're both in their ornate settings. The council is meeting in the French Foreign Ministry, and the peace treaty signing, of course, is in the Hall of Mirrors at the Palace at Versailles. The human actors in the diplomatic world are in the two paintings, which are dwarfed by Singer's canvas. That should illustrate the point you were making, Jay, about the tremendous sacrifice and carnage and destruction that had gone on and the stature of these pygmies who were trying to patch it up.

I think, of all of them, and no disgrace to Lloyd George or Clemenceau or any of the rest of them, but I think Wilson was the man who really bore this burden, who knew how much suffering the war had caused. When he went on his speaking tour on behalf of the League of Nations, he kept saying that if we don't get it right this time, if we don't create some new structure to keep the peace, it's going to happen again and it is going to be so much worse. And he talks about the different kinds of destruction.

Once more I return to the point I made earlier that perhaps the war ended too soon. If that war had gone on for about a year longer, it would have begun to look a lot more like World War II. Tanks were being developed. The British had finally gotten their act together to have functional tanks. They had also gotten airplanes with a much longer flying range and the capacity to carry heavier bombs. So you were going to get bombing and the war of movement that we associate with World War II. This was going to happen in World War I. It was there, just around the corner, the kind of accelerated carnage that we associated with World War II was about to happen. And Wilson also had inklings about the kinds of lurid ideologies of nationalism emerging at the time. Bolshevism frightened him. He was, I think, less viscerally perhaps opposed to it than were some of the others around him, but on the other hand, he could see that this was bad, this was something very, very bad, the worst of Jacobinism and beyond that. And if you're going to save the world from this, if you're going to rebuild some kind of peaceful decent world, this is the last chance. So yes indeed, he's got that great sense of a mission to repair the human and political damage the war had caused.

WINTER: Then, would you agree that there's a disconnect? Even though Wilson may have done what was possible, it still was incommensurate with the destruction that had preceded it?

COOPER: But Jay, what's the alternative? Some claim that Wilson was trying to re-create a nineteenth-century order, that he's not sensitive enough to the pluralism of the world, and all the rest of that. I listen to that and say, okay, first of all, where's he supposed to get his values from anyway? We're all creatures of where we come from. And second, where's the alternative? Just to let revolution sweep the continent and bring about a new order? What kind of order would that have been? Yes, the outcome of peace negotiations was incommensurate with the suffering which preceded it, but Wilson seems to me to have been the only one absolutely dedicated to preventing the return of war and all its ravages to the world.

WINTER: Is that your view, too, Margaret?

MACMILLAN: More or less, but I don't think he's the only one trying.

COOPER: Agreed.

MACMILLAN: I know that one of the many debates and disputes over the Paris Peace Conference concerns how Wilson was perceived in Paris. Were the Europeans just these mental and moral pygmies who didn't appreciate his ideas? I think that's wrong. A lot of the Europeans understood very well what they'd just done to themselves and how they didn't want to do it again. But I agree with you that the peacemakers couldn't say, let it rip. Things were already bad enough. People were starving in some of the most prosperous cities in Europe. The Red Cross was feeding people in Vienna and this in one of the biggest cities and most prosperous cities in Europe. Things were dreadful. The flu epidemic was killing off people. Diseases like typhus, which hadn't been seen in Europe for two or three generations, were suddenly reappearing again. The peacemakers did feel that they had to try and do something. There were other problems, too, which made the situation different from the ending of the Second World War. In 1919 Germany didn't feel it had been defeated. Perhaps the Allies should have occupied it, but the Europeans didn't want to invade Germany and occupy it, partly because they didn't want to lose any more lives and partly because, quite frankly, they didn't want the Americans to be too strong and that was a very important consideration. And so what you were left with was, a German question, which had been there right from the time Germany became a country in 1871 and that is what do you do about this great big powerful nation sitting at the heart of Europe? Germany is a destabilizing force if it's not brought into the European community—as it has been now and we must all hope and pray for good. So there was a German question and how to deal with it. In some ways Germany was in a stronger position—odd though it seems—after the end of the First World War than it had been before. It no longer had Austria-Hungary to worry about. It no longer had a common border with Russia, something which used to give the German Supreme Command absolute nightmares when they thought of all those Russians coming in uniforms across the borders. Sadly, Germany wasn't brought fully into the international system in the interwar years. Another problem in Europe were all those nationalisms which had been brewing away through the nineteenth century. My own view of nationalism is it's one of the most destructive forces in recent history. The sort of nationalism that wants its own state, which will stop at nothing to achieve that, is immensely destructive. That force was not something the peacemakers had created, but there it was. Then there was Bolshevism, and I agree with you that few people—Churchill was an exception—quite realized how dangerous it was going to be. Bolshevism was very destabilizing to existing structures. You also had a situation when the United States for various reasons decided not to stay involved in Europe's affairs. It almost could have made the same decision after the Second World War. When there were problems in Europe, there were a lot of Americans who said, "We've done our bit, let's go home." And I think it was only the presence of a really strong Soviet Union that kept them in. There wasn't that challenge at the end of the First World War. Altogether the circumstances in 1919 and in the years immediately afterwards were not all that propitious for a lasting peace. The peace settlements in my view weren't all that bad, and a lot of very decent and very well-meaning and very hard-working people tried to make the peace work. We tend to see the 1920s as only the calm before the storm, before you get into the 1930s when it all goes downhill from that point on. In fact, when you look at the 1920s, there were some very promising signs. In Germany you have a statesman, Gustav Stresemann, who does try and bring Germany back into a normal relationship with the other powers. You get the Soviet Union calming down a bit and beginning to establish relations with other nations. You begin to get the reestablishment of the old trade patterns, you begin to get prosperity growing again, and so I think there was a possibility of a lasting peace. As historians we know how the story ended, but what we always have to do is look at the choices that faced decision makers at the time.

COOPER: Could I just add something to what Margaret said? The United States did not entirely retreat into isolationism in the twenties. In fact, isolationism, per se, active, conscious, deliberate, passionate isolationism is really a phenomenon of the thirties. One point that seems to me to be important to emphasize is how weak the isolationists were at the end. I mean you've got this coterie of very interesting colorful characters; you've got Senator Reed, who was right here in Kansas City; you've got Bob La Follette, Hiram Johnson, William E. Borah. They are powerful and eloquent men who argued that, but these isolationists were only fourteen senators. Some were willing to be in the League of Nations with enough reservation and safeguards, which meant really neutering it completely, but not all of them meant that. And when you look at all our surveys, imperfect as they are, of public opinion at that time, there is some sense shared by millions of people that we have some obligation to build a better peace, an enduring one.

WINTER: Let me press you on another facet of the peace treaty, John. Why is it that there were two versions of the peace treaty ending the Ottoman Empire, the first with American responsibility for Armenia and the second with none? Why did the United States not live up to a widely shared view that a tragedy had occurred at Anatolia? Why did the United States not accept a mandate for Armenia?

COOPER: Because the Senate wouldn't accept it. It was as simple as that. Wilson, in fact, proposed such a mandate. This happened after he suffered his stroke and after the second defeat of the treaty. He came right out and proposed a mandate for Armenia. And such people as Henry Cabot Lodge, who of course had been great spokesmen for the cause of the Armenians, a great friend of James Bryce and all the rest of that, somehow, he now reversed his position and said no, can't do it, sorry. And they just tossed it aside. Now that is retreat. I agree with you. Wilson was not at all anxious to have the United States involved in the Near East. And it is important to bear in mind that we never went to war with Turkey. He did not want American intervention there. On the other hand, he did try, as best he could at the conference, to prevent any further carving up of Turkey because, the victors had claims on pieces of Turkey, a part for France, a part for Britain.

WINTER: Italy, too . . .

COOPER: Italy was going to have a slice. Everybody was going to have a slice of Turkey. And he was able to block that. But he was not anxious to be in there.

WINTER: Let's deal with the other side of the Middle East. Is there any possible way of squaring the Balfour Declaration with Arab visions of the future of the Middle East? Were these two completely contradictory commitments or was there a way in which Lloyd George or others could see that they could be squared?

MACMILLAN: Initially I think perhaps they could have been. The Balfour Declaration promised a homeland for the Jewish people in Palestine, which was, in those days, a province of the Turkish empire. And at the same time, Britain's chief representative in Cairo was having discussions with the Arab leader Faisal and his father, the sharif of Mecca, in which the British seemed to be promising the Arabs' independence if they fought against Turkey. In fact, I think that could have been squared because the Arabs were prepared at that time—Faisal certainly was—to compromise with the Zionists who wanted a Jewish homeland in Palestine. Faisal actually had talks with Chaim Weizmann, who was a leading Zionist in Britain and who really was responsible for getting the Balfour

Declaration done. There is actually a picture of the two of them standing outside of Faisal's tent, both wearing Arab headdress. The Arabs might have been prepared to accept a Jewish presence in Palestine as long as they had an independent Arab state somewhere else. "The Arabs," in fact, is a misleading term. There was not a unified Arab public opinion. Faisal who fought in the desert with Lawrence represented a family, the Hashemite family, which was trying to further its own interests. There were various other Arab national groups, but as yet, no broadly based Arab national movements outside Egypt. In retrospect perhaps there was no real hope of a compromise between Arabs and Jews. The British were certainly promising this, that, and everything to anyone. After all, they were in the middle of a war and they were prepared to promise whatever it took to win the war. And they were also quietly doing these deals in the Sykes-Picot Agreement to divide up the Middle East between them and the French. But I think when the Arabs—again, it's looking back—when you get people saying the Arabs were promised a huge or several Arab states—independent states all over the Middle East and you actually look at the wording, they're not promised that. They're promised an Arab state and what that would mean was up for negotiation. And it really, I think, depended also on how strong the Arabs were.

COOPER: Wasn't there a notion of the caliphate being revived and modernized, a caliphate with all sorts of different peoples within it? If so, then there was room for a Jewish enclave in Palestine.

MACMILLAN: Yes and it was really only when the Palestinian Arabs began to react to the growing presence of the Jews in Palestine that you began to get other Arabs taking it up as a cause, and there were other reasons why they took it up as a cause. Ink in the long run. What I think really was going to hurt Israel was that it came to be perceived as Western imperialism. Yet again, the West was doing what it wanted and not what the locals did.

WINTER: This reaction, Palestinian reaction, happens right at the time in 1919. There are riots in Jerusalem over the question of continued European domination. There were riots in Cairo, as you were saying. There were riots in Seoul, in Korea; there were riots in Beijing, leading to the formation of the Chinese Communist Party, all at the same time as the peace treaty is being concluded. The signs are not good for the stability of the postwar order.

Perhaps, in conclusion, we ought to remind our audience about the huge element of uncertainty at the moment. Standing in Paris on the twenty-eighth of June 1919, let me conjure up the image of both of you having press passes to the signing ceremony of the peace treaty. You are there, the door opens, and the German delegates, like guilty schoolchildren, are marched in past the French wounded veterans, the *"Gueules Cassées"*—the men with the broken faces—people who have no jaws, no teeth, no nose, no eyes. And you see the German delegates humiliated, filmed in their humiliation, forced to sign a treaty that they obviously feel is repugnant. You are there at the moment when it looks as if the world's on fire in many different places. What prospects do you see for the world, putting yourself there—not what we know now, not what we knew in 1929 or '39. But at that moment in 1919.

MACMILLAN: Wilson himself thought it was hopeful. He said to his wife as they left Paris that night, "We've done the best we can." If John and I had been there, how we saw the peace would have depended on whether we were pessimists or optimists by nature. If we were pessimists, we would have said, "It's ghastly, you know, nothing is going to put the pieces back together again." If we were optimists, we'd say, "Well, that's done. At least we've got that treaty, let's move on."

WINTER: Which are you?

MACMILLAN: I think I would have been an optimist. I think I would have said, we've dealt with that, let's see what happens. A qualified optimist.

WINTER: John?

COOPER: Henry Cabot Lodge said, "I can only be an American." I'm only an American. There were very few Americans at that time who said, oh, the world's gone to hell, let's retreat and then let it burn itself out. Even the isolationists thought otherwise. Their argument was that this peace was neo-imperialist; indeed the imperialists had won and we should not have any part of this bad bargain; we should be careful not to have overcommitments so that we can be the bright shiny beacon, that the only way we're ever going to help the world is by setting a righteous example. Most Americans are thinking, the world has been through a terrible ordeal, things don't look so good now, but they're better than they were. At least we don't have this huge war going on, and let's see what we can do with it. The disagreement then comes as to how much we should be doing. Yes, as you said, Jay, how much we should compromise our sovereignty. And I don't think it was beyond human wit to come up with some way to bring Wilson and Lodge together. There were ways around their differences. I guess I am an optimist; unless a situation looks absolutely hopeless, you try to do the best you can. That is my view of Wilson.

WINTER: Right. It's very rare, I think, in my experience, the forty years in the practice of history, to meet two optimists at the same time.

AUDIENCE: Laughter.

WINTER: And two optimists who write about the First World War at the same time, which is not the most propitious circumstances for optimism. But it is a testimony, I think, to the good scholarship and good feeling that my colleagues have offered us today to allow us to take a look at the Versailles settlement in a new way. And I'm quite persuaded that this conversation is simply one among many which will continue, since whenever people in this country consider how to get out of war, they go back to the Great War and to the Versailles settlement. Indeed there are those who believe that George Bush is a Wilsonian, and see in Wilson the man who created certain principles of building democracies in defeated countries, principles that he subscribes to. Now he may be engaged in creative misinterpretation, but at the same time . . .

AUDIENCE: Laughter.

WINTER: At the same time, the notion of regime change was at the heart of Wilson's absolute refusal to negotiate with the representatives of the Kaiser's regime. He insisted that that regime fall, and a new one be put in its place before he would help bring about an Armistice. These matters were very well known at the Paris Peace Conference of 1919.

I'm not at all being critical of Bush on this issue to say that he took from Wilson's behavior in 1918–19 a series of lessons that we can dispute.

COOPER: No, no, no. Wilson was the original multilateralist. Yes, Wilson tried regime change in Mexico and got burnt badly. He learned his lesson there. No, David Kennedy, I believe, calls George Bush Woodrow Wilson on steroids.

AUDIENCE: Laughter.

WINTER: The last question I want to put to you is this—if we look at Versailles and then remove ourselves back to where we are in a country that is trying to find a way out of war, one way or another, what lesson do you think you could draw from Versailles that could help point the way forward?

MACMILLAN: Oh, I want to say I'm a Canadian and I shouldn't interfere in American politics.

COOPER: Oh come on, Margaret.

MACMILLAN: That one's hard. The thing about Versailles is it was possible to actually do it because the war was over. How you extricate yourselves from a war that is going on, it seems to me is another issue. The arguments I'm really struck by that seem to be going on in the United States at the moment involve to begin with, the question of, if we leave, what does it mean for the people in Iraq, which is, I should think, sheer horror, judging by what's going on at the moment. And also, secondly, and this is really, I think, the question for Americans, is what does it mean to the United States? What does it mean to the capacity of the United States to influence affairs in the world? What does it mean for the stability of the Middle East, which is very important for the United States. And so I think, bad as it is in Iraq now, if the occupation forces pull out, there will be no peace to be made because there is no one with whom to make it. I think the costs of pulling out at this stage may be worse than the costs of staying in and I never thought I would have said that a few years ago.

WINTER: Is that your view, John?

COOPER: No, I draw a different conclusion. I do agree with Margaret. Except for looking at how people behave diplomatically, we cannot conclude that the Paris Peace Conference has much direct relevance to the situation today. Then, as Margaret said, the war was over. They were dealing with a war that was over. Granted, there were still plenty of smaller conflicts going on, but I think the things that they ought to be studying in the White House right now relate to past disengagements from defeats, for example, how the French got out of Algeria or how we got out of Vietnam.

WINTER: I have a different viewpoint, John. I do think that Versailles is a lesson in the limits of American power. And it's also a lesson in the different approaches to the concept of sovereignty as between the United States and other countries who have very different notions of what international engagement may mean. So the way I read Versailles and Wilson's contribution to it is as a high-minded liberal interventionist effort to change the international system fundamentally, and it's an effort that failed. My view is that it was bound to fail, but that Wilson did what he could to make it workable. I do think the current discussions about where American power starts and stops would benefit substantially from having a look at how statesmanship constructed the question of how to fit together American interests and aspirations with the interests and needs of other powers at the beginning of the twentieth century.

COOPER: I'm not sure we disagree that much. Where I would see it a bit differently is how to interpret Wilson's multilateralism. One of the questions he returned to on his speaking tour in 1919 was the one saying that with the League, we're going to have to intervene in faraway awful places like the Near East, like the Balkans. Why then should Americans be killed, American blood be shed there? And he said—at one point he's in Utah, he said, "If you've got a fire in Utah, you don't send to Oklahoma for the fire brigade." In other words, the future international order would be regional in character. In his view, we weren't going to be intervening all over the world. It was going to be the Europeans who would handle the problem. Yes, we would contribute some money, maybe we'd send some ships over, but the people who are closest on the line would be doing it and, again, it was going to have to be multilateral. He did not believe that the United States was a colossus leading the way. That's more Theodore Roosevelt and that's more a recent thing.

WINTER: I welcome questions from those of you in the audience who wish to raise them, but first, can I ask you to thank my colleagues in the usual manner?

WINTER: First question.

QUESTION: I heard you talk about the Franco-Prussian War but I didn't hear anything about the Treaty of Brest-Litovsk, and since the Germans came so close to winning the war in the spring of 1918, how could they even not give them reparations?

MACMILLAN: Sorry. How could the Germans not give reparations to the Allies?

QUESTION: The Treaty of Brest-Litovsk was so harsh; in light of what the Germans forced the Russians to accept there, how could anybody show any mercy to the Germans at the end of the war?

MACMILLAN: It's a very good question, and indeed Brest-Litovsk was a very harsh and punitive treaty which took whatever gold, basically, that could be squeezed out of Russia and also, of course, took a huge swath of Russian territory and extended German and Austrian influence over even more. And it's a treaty that's often forgotten today. It's a treaty that Lenin signed to get Russia out of the war and he was prepared to sacrifice a lot. And it did affect the peacemakers' views at Paris of Germany. It also does give some idea of what would have happened if Germany would have won the war. But of course, that's not an argument for saying, just because Germany behaved badly, it should be treated badly in turn. And I think the reparations issue hinged on whether Germany was responsible for starting the war, which people thought at the time, it should pay damages. Interestingly enough, a number of historians are coming back to that point of view now, that even if Germany did not technically start the war, it was responsible for creating the circumstances in which the war broke out. The view at the time on the winning side was that Germany should pay because it had done damage to other peoples, it had invaded and attacked France, and it had invaded and occupied Belgium. And so I think there was a perfectly justified expectation that Germany would pay reparations and this was not something new. Payments were something that happened after the end of most European wars. And it was going to happen again after the end of the Second World War. There is a feeling even now in international relations, if you start a war and you lose it, you pay. And I think the problem from the German point of view was, as I said earlier, they felt they shouldn't have to pay and it became a widespread feeling and they, in the end, didn't pay that much. But no, I think there was ample justification both in practice and in Germany's own behavior for expecting that Germany would pay reparations. The other question, of course, was whether it was sensible? John Maynard Keynes said, no it wasn't. He said, instead of worrying about transferring resources, both in kind and in cash, out of Germany, it would be much more sensible to try and get the European economy going again. And that's where the United States might have made a difference. There was this curious situation that the United States had become the lender to Britain, which was, in turn, the lender to its other allies, and the United States and the individual American banks were putting pressure quite reasonably, in a way, on the British to pay up. But what that meant was the British, then, needed reparations and they needed to put pressure on the French to pay up. The French in turn needed reparations very badly from Germany. And of course, as you may know, what happened in the end in the 1920s—and this goes back to John's point about the Americans remaining involved—American private lenders—lent money to Germany which then paid its reparations to France, which then paid the British back, who then paid back their debt to the United States. And this caused a lot of friction and bad feeling all the way around. Keynes's idea was that all the inter-allied debts should be canceled and then there would be no need, or less need, to get reparations out of Germany and the other defeated nations. The Americans wouldn't go for it. As they said, a debt's a debt. You know, we've lent you the money, now pay us back.

QUESTION: I'd like to ask the question, if I may, what implications or repercussions from this peace treaty might have led to the war in Asia in World II, the rise of Japan, and militarism in Japan? Are there any repercussions from that conference that would have led to Japan rising militarily in the subsequent decades?

MACMILLAN: I think individuals and peoples use history and grievances become something around which you can mobilize or use to justify and to make claims for the future and for the present. World War I was in fact a world war—not in the same way that World War II was, but there was fighting in Africa, there was fighting in the Middle East, and there was fighting in Asia. And so it did affect a number of nations around the globe. It had, I think, very significant repercussions in Asia. First of all the Japanese, of course, were an ally in the First World War, but felt aggrieved by the treaty because they had wanted recognition—really what they wanted was recognition that they were seen as equals of British men, Frenchmen, and Americans. And there was a lot of sensitivity on this issue because there were various racial exclusion laws, including here in the United States and in Canada which discriminated against Asians and in Australia, of course. And so I think what the Japanese wanted out of the peace conference was a recognition that they were not just allies, but really equals, and they wanted a clause in the covenant of the League of Nations which was called, for shorthand, the Racial Equality Clause. There was a clause which said there should be no discrimination on the basis of religion and I think a couple of other things, and the Japanese wanted to include race—which in those days, people used as a term, really, for nation or ethnicity; it was disallowed. Wilson was afraid that he'd lose votes in the U.S. Billy Hughes, the Australian prime minister, made a huge fuss and said, "We will walk out of the peace conference. We will never accept this sort of thing." When the Japanese delegates went back to Japan, the reaction was Japan has given away too much. The Japanese also wanted the German concessions in China in Shandong Province, which they had conquered in the very first months of the First World War, and they got those, but with an understanding that they talk to the Chinese about giving them back. The nationalist reaction in Japan was that we tried to play the game, we tried to go along with the great powers and look how they treat us—they really will always exclude us. And that fed into, then, Japanese nationalist feeling in the thirties. It was part of the general bill of complaints against the West. In the case of China, China was also an ally. And the Chinese, in fact, did a lot—both China and Japan did a lot to help the Allied victory in the First World War. The

Chinese provided labor, which freed up soldiers from digging trenches and transporting goods, and there are war graves with Chinese characters on them in France, for the Chinese who died there. And China wanted its own territory back. Woodrow Wilson had talked about the rights of people to govern themselves and how peoples must not be handed over to other peoples to be ruled without their consent. And so the Chinese assumed that they would get what had been German possessions, or concessions as they were called, in Shandong Province back. And at the peace conference, the powers looked at Japan, which was strong, and looked at China, which was in a mess, and I think quite cynically for reasons of the great-power politics, thought we better keep Japan happy and not China, so they gave the German concessions in China to Japan, and this caused fury in China. When the news got to China—it arrived on the morning of May the fourth, 1919—there were huge demonstrations in Beijing, which spread across the country to other cities. In fact the whole period became to be known as the May 4 movement and out of it came a decision by some Chinese to form a Communist Party. They turned against the West. As a Chinese student said on May 4, 1919, Woodrow Wilson and the others say all these wonderful things, but I've come to the conclusion they're all great liars. That decision at the peace conference was a very important factor in turning, at least, some radical Chinese nationalists in a different direction. So I think the peace conference did have repercussions for both China and Japan. It became part of the feeling they had against the West.

COOPER: I've asked several historians of Japan whether they thought the Japanese were serious about the Racial Equality Clause, or whether this was just a very shrewd negotiating ploy to soften the Westerners up for Shandong. And they don't know. I think it was both. I think the Japanese diplomats would have been absolutely delighted to get that Racial Equality Clause, but certainly they were playing a very shrewd game. The other point on which I concur, though, is what Margaret said about the twenties and how things really improved in Europe and there was actually a wonderful springtime—we usually associate that with Locarno. That happened in Japan, too. Moderate governments came to power in Japan in the 1920s and they did get out of Shandong. They got out of Siberia. Who knows what might have happened in Germany if the Depression hadn't come along, or again, with Japan, whether the militarists and expansionists really would have gained as much power as soon as they did. So there are a lot of contingencies in there.

WINTER: Another question.

QUESTION: When Margaret MacMillan gave a lecture here last year about Versailles, she made the point that the delegates at the conference didn't pace the conference properly. They didn't give themselves enough time to deal with specifically German problems. And I wondered if you would just say a little about that.

MACMILLAN: Yes, I think they never really had anything like this before. If you look back at the Congress of Vienna at the end of the Napoleonic Wars, it was actually so much easier. The delegates then didn't have to worry about opinion and they didn't have to worry about getting reelected because they were mostly from undemocratic countries. At the Paris Peace Conference, the Allies thought they would have a brief preliminary conference to draw up the terms for Germany and then they thought they would sit down with Germany and the other defeated nations, including Ottoman Turkey, and do the old style negotiations and do a bit of horse trading. That's what the Germans expected and the fact that there never were those sorts of negotiations became yet another thing that the Germans got really irritated about. The Allies found drawing up the peace terms so complicated and that new problems kept coming in.

As John was saying earlier, the pressures on people like Wilson were enormous. He had people from nine o'clock in the morning until evening. The peacemakers were not just dealing with the aftermath of the war, they were also dealing with a new range of problems and all these little wars that were breaking out. So by the time they finally cobbled the terms they were going to offer Germany—and those were the most difficult ones to do—and they finally got the League of Nations Covenant drawn up, it was April and they thought, we cannot actually sit down with the Germans and now have a full-scale debate again because the whole thing will begin to fall to pieces and it had been so difficult to get those terms cobbled together. The Italians had walked out with a very great deal of fanfare. The Chinese were threatening to walk out, the Japanese were threatening to walk out, the Belgians were threatening to walk out, and they faced the prospect of not having enough nations left in Paris to make peace. And so what they did, which in retrospect was foolish, was they summoned the Germans to Paris in May, and said, "Here are the terms. Take it or leave it. And you can submit comments in writing, but we're not having any face-to-face negotiations." The Allies felt that time was running out and the other thing that was happening was their own power was diminishing day by day. They couldn't keep those huge civilian armies in uniform. The treasuries wouldn't allow it. Their finance departments wouldn't allow it, and the soldiers themselves wanted to go home. And in fact were saying so. Canadian soldiers for example rioted in Britain and caused all sorts of damage. The longer the Allies put off signing the peace treaty with Germany, the more difficult it was going to be. There was a big question mark about whether Germany would accept the terms. And in fact, it was only at the last minute that the German government decided to accept them. Up to that point, the Allies, very reluctantly, were planning to invade Germany. And the Supreme Allied commander, Marshal Foch, said, "yes of course, I'll obey orders, but I must tell you that it may be very difficult if not impossible to do so."

QUESTION: Isn't there another view of Wilson and the ratification that it could have been ratified and that Lloyd George and Balfour and others would have accepted reservations?

COOPER: In the end, indeed, Wilson is the roadblock. He refuses to compromise, after he had his stroke. I have been accused of laying too much emphasis on that, that that's supposedly a way of letting Wilson off the hook. I'm not interested in letting Wilson off the hook. But to me, if someone suffers a massive stroke like that, how could it not have huge consequences? Wilson's intellect, that is his cognition, was not affected and in some ways, he's still himself. But the emotional balance—those things that go into judgment and into political leadership—were very badly compromised. In terms of his negotiating with the senators, he kept negotiating. He spent the entire month of July meeting individually with them. Then he did what only two other presidents have ever done. He allowed himself to be grilled by a congressional committee. Lincoln did it once during the Civil War. Ford did it once in the post-Watergate times. Presidents have to be very careful about this, and most of the time they draw the line; there is the separation of powers, we will not do it. Wilson invited them to the White House rather than he himself going up to Capitol Hill to do it. But basically, for three hours he submitted to a grilling from the senators. And Hiram Johnson was furious at the whole thing. He said, "We didn't handle ourselves at all well. He wrapped us around his little finger," and that kind of thing. So, Wilson did it. Then what happened was, the Foreign Relations Committee then voted through a package of amendments. That's not just reservations; these were amendments. We're going to go in there, we're going to change the text of the treaty; we're going to do this, this, and this. We're going to throw out Shandong, we're going to throw out Article 10; we're going to do all of these things. And that's the point at which Wilson decided, I had better take my case to the people. Not to end negotiations with the Senate, but to improve his negotiating position, which he did, as a matter of fact. In the meeting with the Foreign Relations Committee, Wilson said that the American people won't stand for these changes, and Senator Brandegee replied, "Well, there's no way that the people can vote on it. The Senate will." And they did.

WINTER: Can we have one more—perhaps just one more question?

QUESTION: Thank you. I just wanted to know, talking about the view of Lenin and Trotsky about this revolution that's going to spread throughout the world—how did the participants understand this phenomenon?

MACMILLAN: They didn't know much about them, partly because when the revolution happened, communications were more or less cut because of the war, so there was very little back and forth. When William Bullet went to Moscow with Lincoln Steffens it was one of the first times that outsiders had actually got into Russia. The Allies did not know much about the Bolsheviks. What they did know, they didn't much like the sound of, because the Bolsheviks were broadcasting on shortwave radio, and they also were distributing statements which eventually made their way to Europe calling on the Europeans to rise up and overthrow capitalism. And so I think the feeling was that these are very dangerous people. The difficulty was, people tended to use language a bit loosely, and so when they talked about Bolshevism, they often meant every manifestation of a sort of strike or demonstration. Most people outside Russia didn't really know what Lenin's party was like. It was only later on that people understood that this was a very tightly knit revolutionary party with very dogmatic views. And so there was a tendency to call every upheaval Bolshevik or anarchy without really being fully clear what each was. The delegates would sit around the table at the Hotel Majestic, which was the British headquarters, saying, "Well we'll probably have a revolution here, too." But most don't seem to have really been seriously afraid of it. Lloyd George said to a British journalist when they were talking about this issue, "You know, the old Europe is pretty strong and it's withstood many storms before and I think it's not going to go the way of the Russians." And in fact, he was quite right. Again, with the benefit of hindsight, we can look back and see even what was going on in Germany with the revolutionary councils—these Soviets of workers and soldiers— in fact was very German and it was very bureaucratic and it wasn't really overthrowing the old society. In Vienna when locals inspired by the Bolsheviks tried to have a Communist Revolution—I've been told by an Austrian historian that they went to seize the main railway station and they all lined up to go through the turnstiles. And so . . .

AUDIENCE: Laughter.

MACMILLAN: Charles Maier has written about this, hasn't he? I mean bourgeois middle-class society and the structures were stronger than people might have thought at the time. And I think a lot of people really didn't know what the Bolsheviks were about because they couldn't. I mean Churchill talked about bloodstained hairy baboons, and he knew he didn't like them, but he wasn't all that sure what they stood for. Lots of rumors were coming out of Russia, that the Bolsheviks were abolishing human nature, or that they were getting rid of marriage and instituting free love, but there was little real knowledge about what they were up to. Certainly the middle classes were apprehensive that they were going to lose their property and the structures they felt important. But I think by the end of 1919, there was a sense that Europe was calming down a bit.

COOPER: A. J. P. Taylor, the great British historian, did not see the Versailles treaty as the beginning of the cold war. He said, "If they'd been that worried about Bolshevism, they would have been a lot easier on Germany." He was right. If they'd been that worried, it would have been a different treaty.

WINTER: The other minor point to make is that Lenin was the only successful antiwar leader in Europe. He got his country out of war, in March 1918, and he embarrassed the Allies by liberating German forces to kill British, French, Australian, Canadian, and all the others. So he was an enemy for having abandoned the cause, which is part of the reason why those Allied troops were there to guard Russian arms so they wouldn't get into the hands of Germans or their allies.

These are points we could continue to dispute for some considerable time. But for now it is entirely appropriate for me to ask you in the audience to join me in thanking our two speakers for sharing with you this conversation among historians of the Great War.

FIVE

The Great War
Midwife to Modern Memory?

Jay Winter, Yale University
Robert Wohl, University of California at Los Angeles

KEMPER: I'm Crosby Kemper, the director of the Kansas City Public Library, and it is my pleasure and my honor to welcome you to this symposium cosponsored by the Liberty Memorial and the National World War I Museum, the Truman Library and Truman Library Institute, and the Kansas City Public Library.

WINTER: Thank you, Crosby. I do want to say a word or two about the venue, where we are, and the proximity of the museum to it. Crosby's work and that of his colleagues in creating a space in which intellectual and cultural life can gravitate towards a major library is a remarkable achievement. As someone who lived and taught in Britain for thirty years—I know this kind of municipal library functions as an icon of urban pride. There is no such thing as a major city without a major library, and you've helped extend a long and distinguished tradition.

The second point that I'd like to draw to your attention is that when I first saw the memorial and the museum, it struck me as extraordinarily

British, probably unintentionally so, although cities—Kansas City and let's say, Birmingham or Liverpool or Leeds—these cities have very powerful memories of the Protestant voluntary tradition, where it is not the state, not the federal government or the regional authorities, that create institutions of significance, institutions which last; it is civil society. And it is for that reason that I have an answer when people ask me, as they have done many times, why is it that there's a museum and a great national memorial in Kansas City—why here? The answer to that question is that local and urban initiatives last. When things are done from on high, when Congress proposes or even disposes or provides money, which I gather they have not done in this case—what they've done is to legitimate a museum, to give it its seal of approval. But in the 1920s and yet again today, it was and remains the citizens of Kansas City who made it happen. It was the same in British cities, and it remains so today. The most powerful commemorative act in Britain is still the purchase of poppies—red poppies, which are sold by the millions in November every year. When they buy the poppies, people wear a little war memorial on their lapel. And the money goes to a charitable foundation which provides for the families of veterans, veterans of all the wars of the twentieth century and the twenty-first as well as for their families. This is an act not of the state, but of the people.

Now this notion that commemoration comes from below is a very powerful point to raise at the outset of our discussion. Today we are in the middle of what I call a memory boom. Everybody outside the academy and thousands in the academy are obsessed with memory. And one reason why I think this is so is that in war, family history and national history come together. Families know what war is. We have to distinguish between national narratives told and sold by those in power and the stories people remember about their kith and kin. The length of wars matter here. The First World War did not leave a deep trace on family histories since, fortunately for the United States, this country experienced only eighteen months of bloodshed. The Second World War was worse: four years of combat for American soldiers and sailors, less than the six most of Europe knew. The fighting in Vietnam lasted longer, though the surge in troop numbers came in 1967. This meant that the five years of combat until the administration recognized the war was lost roughly approximated the length of time American men spent in uniform in World War II. My father was drafted in 1942 and came home in 1947. American casualties were much lower in the Vietnam War than in the Second World War, but the bitterness of soldiers returning home after 1972 separated their and our experience of war from that of "the Great Generation" coming home after 1945.

For us, the Vietnam War was one of the great stimuli of First World War studies. Here was a war which in 1975 was ended on terms which varied emphatically from those American administrations and propagandists had framed in the previous decade. The United States left Vietnam, and no dominos fell. The Soviet empire or the Chinese empire were not enlarged. Puncturing the lies and illusions of a sequence of American military and civilian leaders was easy enough. The problem remained, if the official meaning of the war was nonsense, then what sense did it have? A war without sense, without logic, with huge casualties, albeit overwhelmingly on the side of the Vietnamese, drew the attention of scholars away from the Good War, the war against Hitler, the war to avenge Pearl Harbor, and turned it towards the 1914–18 conflict.

At the same time, by the 1970s and 1980s, there were audiocassette and videocassette recorders available to preserve the voices of those millions of people who went through war, whether or not in uniform. Now the Internet adds another gigantic repository to the ways we already had to keep hold of the voices and the stories of the survivors.

Some survivors wore uniforms; most did not. And here the slow but inexorable appearance of the survivors of the Holocaust as witnesses for our time made remembering a moral obligation. So to a degree, the memory boom is a product of twentieth-century warfare. It's been amplified and necessarily so, by the transformation of war from the clash of arms between those in uniform to what we now call asymmetric warfare, the clash of arms between armies and insurgents who rarely wear uniforms.

There is another element in the memory boom we should consider here and in the Liberty Memorial Museum. Anyone who visits such a museum, anyone who comes to a conversation like this one, is engaging in an act of commemoration. We are part of the story we are here to talk about. So in an extraordinary sense, you who have come here today are part of a conversation about what war is. That conversation is an act of commemoration, invoking fundamental questions of human values. That is true in all history, but it is much more so in a history of a set of events that took nine million lives and God knows how many arms and

legs and minds and dreams. The reason why the cultural history of the
Great War is such a popular and evocative subject is that it opened the
twentieth century.

In 1975, Paul Fussell famously said that the war produced a series of
novels, poems, plays which shared a very special outlook, a very special, ironic voice. He put these works under the umbrella of the word
"modern memory." Why did he write the book? Many years ago he
told me that he wrote it because he was fed up with cocktail parties
at Princeton where people were talking about body counts without
knowing a thing of what they were speaking. He knew. He still has, I
believe, some fragments of shrapnel in his leg from service during the
Battle of the Bulge in the Second World War. The Vietnam War was the
American First World War, a war which turned innocence into experience, naivete into irony, noble language into the visceral expressions of
disillusioned soldiers.

Reading poetry and fiction, or the memoirs that stand between fiction and fact is a critical way we know about war. Reading a novel about
war may be a commemorative act. Coming to a conversation between
scholars of war may be a commemorative act. It strikes me that one way
to understand why we're here together today is to think and feel the
force of this question: what is commemoration? And how do you honor,
glorify those who die in war, who need to be honored, without glorifying war itself? How do you do that? That question is a profound one,
and, to a degree, the cultural history of the First World War is a quest to
find that answer.

WOHL: Yes, one of the problems today will be, I tend to agree with
most of the things that Jay is saying, and so there may not be as much
contention up here as would be ideal, but I should really give it a little
bit of background here. He and I got into the cultural history business
at more or less the same time, I think. When both of us went to graduate
school to learn how to do history, we were not taught cultural history,
at least I wasn't. I had an embryonic interest in it, although I couldn't
have named it—I mean I had no word for it, exactly, because in those
days, there was more of a tendency to talk about intellectual history.
And when I think about the way that the writing of history has changed
during the decades when I have been a historian, beginning in the late
1950s and really in the early 1960s—when I think about the dramatic

way in which the writing of history has changed, I find it just extraordinary that this happened and, of course, this in itself requires an explanation. It's connected, probably, with the memory boom and I think that Jay is right about that, but it's connected to other things as well. When I first started studying the history of the First World War, it was common to claim that wars could not have any cultural dimension to them at all, that they destroyed culture. And I spent a lot of time arguing, beginning in the 1970s, that we may find it horrific, but whether we like it or not, the First World War was an extraordinarily important cultural event and its cultural impact took many, many different forms which people are studying today.

In the late 1960s, I set out seriously working on the generation of 1914, after finishing my first book on French Communism in the making. That was during the Vietnamese War, and I think that Jay is absolutely correct to establish a connection between what he calls the memory boom—I would call it the flowering of cultural history—and the beginnings of the American involvement in Vietnam. It coincided with the youth rebellion as well in this country. And that was really what convinced me to write a book organized around the concept of a "generation," because I discovered such a youth rebellion in late-nineteenth, early-twentieth-century Europe as well, and many of the people who later fought in the war of 1914–18 had been a part of it, or had been influenced by it in various ways. Now, it's no accident, as the Soviets used to love to say, that Paul Fussell's book appeared in 1975. It's no accident that it appeared at that time, and this is a book that has stood up very well, has stood the test of time very well. I can attest to that because I give it to my undergraduates, who are not slow to tell me about books that they don't like reading or that they find useless. They find Paul Fussell's book complex, demanding, but never boring.

Now, when I give classes on memory in the First World War—what I call Remembering the First World War—Paul Fussell's book is the first book that we read in that class. I use it as a kind of opening to the topic, and so I start out with my students in seminar situation—in good Socratic manner to have a discussion with them—and they start talking about chapter 1, naturally. And I always say, "Wait a moment, we're not going to start with chapter one." And I ask, "How many of you have read the dedication to this book?" And believe me, not many of them have. And the dedication to this book says everything about what's going to come. "To the memory of Technical Sergeant Edward Keith Hudson, ASN 36548772, Company F, 410th Infantry, killed beside me in France, March 15, 1945." And what that means is that this is a book about war and I've been to war, I know what it means, to see people dying next to me. And that was one of the things, I think, that made this book so moving. It has many different themes in it, many different arguments, some of which I disagree with—we should get into that issue. But it is a passionate book, and it is a book that is written out of personal experience. The connection is there, between the Great War and the Vietnamese War. The Vietnamese War triggers memories of the past, or of selected episodes of the past.

Now I'd just like to, before I give the floor back to Jay, I'd just like to add one thing to what he said about what cultural history means to him. I agree and maybe I'll put it in a slightly different way—cultural history is the study of meanings that people give to their experience. Now, this sounds like a fairly simple statement. But in fact, it isn't simple at all, because now we have to break this down and think seriously about how cultural memories come into existence. We would all agree, I think— most of us here would agree—that people have experiences, that we all think we have experiences, right? But we don't have access to all of the experiences that we've had. What we have is the memory of certain of those experiences that we've chosen to remember. Now, we all know this from our own lives, as a matter of fact. The way we choose to remember those experiences changes as the world around us changes, which further complicates the situation. The book Paul Fussell wrote in 1975 is not the book that he would have written in 1965 and it's not the book that he would have written in 1985 or 1995. It's a book that bears the marks of that period. Now, you have experience, you have the memory of experience, which is highly selective and undependable—we all know that—and of course, as we get older, it becomes even more undependable. My experience is also that young people's memory is pretty undependable—at least the memory of my son's is pretty undependable. We have the memory of that experience, which is highly selective, but how can we turn that into some kind of cultural phenomenon? That's yet another step. And it doesn't matter whether we're writing a novel, or we're writing a memoir, or we're writing a piece of music, or we're creating a war monument, we've got to choose a form through which the memory of that experience is going to be expressed, channeled, funneled.

And there are a finite number of those forms. And very few of us invent forms, cultural forms, maybe a few very unusual people, but most of us draw on forms that already exist. And then when you think of this process that I've been describing, you begin to realize why the use of memorial literature, let's say memoirs, the use of all types of memory in various forms is such a tricky thing for historians. All these operations have gone on and at the end, we have a cultural product which is very much a product of its time.

One of the best examples of this is Erich Maria Remarque's famous novel, *All Quiet on the Western Front*. This is often called the greatest war novel ever written. It certainly is often called the greatest novel of the First World War. But a funny thing about this book is, that it tells you more about what was going on in Europe in the late 1920s than it does about what was going on in the war—or at least it tells you as much. I don't know if you agree with that. I'm trying to find something that we will disagree on.

ALL: Laughter.

WINTER: I'll take that up. Interestingly, Paul Fussell's book that you've mentioned—and I share enormous admiration for it—was written by a professor of English literature, not a historian formerly or professionally. It is my view that that matters not at all. We historians have been forced to live with the neighbors, and doing so has created a new kind of cultural history full of anthropology, full of cognitive psychology, neuroscience, and perhaps above all, of insights drawn from literature and literary scholars. What's critical about Paul Fussell's book, entitled *The Great War and Modern Memory*, is that it is entirely based upon English letters, and it doesn't really tell us much about German or French writing. And the reason is, you need to live in England, I think, to really appreciate how fecund, how fruitful, and almost iridescent is the word "irony." It connotes not just a way of writing about war, but a way of living in a world that is full of absurdities. And one of the absurdities which never left Paul Fussell is embedded in the dedication you mentioned a few minutes ago. During his service in the Second World War, his sergeant led him around as a young twenty-year-old from Pasadena, near your hometown, Robert. Fussell had a heavy responsibility for the lives of his men and was understandably terrified of that responsibility.

Why did this sergeant, who was like a father to him or an uncle, certainly a benevolent spirit, who made sense of his—Paul Fussell's—life as a young officer in the Second World War—why was it that when the shell burst over their heads and they both hit the ground, why was the sergeant killed and he wasn't? That question lay at the heart of Fussell's understanding of a world which is absurd and dominated by mass death and arbitrary survival. Such a world is conveyed by one form of storytelling which is called ironic. And that is the form in which much Great War literature appeared.

Irony means many things. In the Greek, irony means that you say one thing and you mean another—"All Quiet on the Western Front": The hero dies on the day in which there is no news—his death is meaningless, it literally says that the war meant nothing because the message "All Quiet on the Western Front" savagely avoids denoting the extinction of the life of the one human being who is at the center of the novel. What is the appropriate form of writing to use to express the notion that war had no meaning? How do you write fiction which challenges the notion that a story has a beginning, a middle, and an end? How do you express the uncanniness of millions of people going to a war who wound up being confronted by Pandora's box and by opening it, having to fight another, much crueler, war entirely? Irony is one way to do it. Perhaps all wars are ironic in being worse than people think they will be. I think in fact, that's what happened in Iraq—whatever your political outlook. Iraq is an ironic war. It started off to remove certainly a cruel and sadistic dictator, but to get rid of weapons of mass destruction that weren't there. The anticipation and the outcome are radically different.

But irony means something else, too. It means an English way of looking at the world. The best example I know of this is an episode which recurred during two battles—the Battle of Loos in 1915 and the Battle of the Somme in 1916. In both there were British soldiers who kicked off the battle by kicking a football into no-man's land. One of these footballs survives in the National Army Museum in London, but none of the men who kicked off survived the first day of the Battle of the Somme.

Is it anything other than ironic to say that war is a sport? Usually people go home after a sporting match, but in 1914, someone changed the rules. Nine million men did not get to go home. This isn't war, this is bloody slaughter; this is what constantly comes up in the usage of the term, "modern memory" that Paul Fussell has given us. What he says is that this way of writing—this form, the creative cultural form—is the way we have come to look at the First World War, but not only that. Irony is embedded in the way we look at all war throughout the twentieth century. We stand on the shoulders of the poets of the First World War who created a new kind of ironic writing. We are not alone there. Think about Heller's *Catch 22*, in which someone says to Yossarian, I think when a Japanese attack is happening, "Don't worry, Yossarian, they're not trying to kill you, they're trying to kill everybody."

ALL: Laughter.

WINTER: Or the images of war in *MASH* where the only sane man is out of his mind. What does courage mean under such circumstances? Most soldiers who died in the First World War—80 percent—were killed by artillery; did it take courage to be blown up by a shell fired ten miles behind the lines? Did it take courage to fire it? Something has happened to language here. Words don't seem to fit experience. A courageous man, like the sergeant standing next to Paul Fussell, and a coward in his unit, had equal chances of getting blown to pieces. What Fussell has done is to tell us that noble language was blown up during the First World War. Meaning, like most soldiers' lives in the war, went underground. Meaning is to be found between the lines.

Let's go in another direction. What's wrong with the thesis of modern memory is as important as what's right with it. The first is, it doesn't belong to women. The cultural form we term irony is deeply gendered. It is a masculine point of view. Or is it? Here we need to go beyond Fussell. It has become ridiculous to say that war is boys with their toys. It isn't. And it never was.

WOHL: Let me add something to that, because the more I read and teach the *Great War and Modern Memory,* the more surprised I am that Fussell scarcely mentions the name of Vera Brittain, even though she's a very good example of the things that he's talking about. I mean that will give you an idea of how blind historians were to these issues. One of the most absurd notions about the First World War is that only men were deeply involved in it. Women were also deeply involved in the war. We don't have time to go into all the different ways that they were deeply involved, but they were deeply involved in the war—emotionally and practically and all kinds of ways. Now, when I wrote my book, *The Generation of 1914*—my book came out a few years after Paul Fussell's book—I was writing my book when his book came out, which almost caused me to abandon my book because my first reading was such that I thought, my God, he said it all. I mean there's nothing left for me to add to all that. But I somehow pulled myself together.

ALL: Laughter.

WOHL: Because I was a young professor and I didn't have any alternative.

ALL: Laughter.

WOHL: And Jay knows what I'm talking about. I had to publish something and because Paul Fussell was an English professor, I could always hope that nobody in my department . . .

ALL: Laughter.

WOHL: . . . would read him or know about him, which turned out not to be the case, by the way.

KEMPER: Robert, could I break in and ask you this question? Fussell says that the dominating form of modern understanding is that it is essentially ironic. And as Jay has said and you've said, essentially, that's an English view of the world. You write in *The Generation of 1914* about Ernst Jünger and many others in Germany, about Ortega in Spain, about Drieu La Rochelle or Malraux in France—all of whom, in writing in the twenties and thirties, were very un-ironic. How do you square this with Fussell's claim that the war set in motion a specific mode of writing dominating the interwar period and after?

WOHL: I would dispute that point about some of them. Take the French writer Drieu La Rochelle, who is a very well-known French writer, an intellectual in the 1920s and '30s and on into the Second World War when he got involved in collaboration with the Vichy regime. He wrote one book—well, he wrote several books that impinged on the

First World War, but he wrote one novel that could be considered to be a First World War novel that could be compared to *All Quiet on the Western Front*. It came out a few years later. There's a lot of irony in that book as well, I think. You know, Jünger's sense of humor has been vastly underestimated by people. I knew Ernst Jünger, even though my wife tells me that I shouldn't admit it because he was considered to be a fore-runner of Nazism (though there's a dispute about that). But I knew him, and one of the things that impressed me most about him was his irony, precisely. I asked him once if he had any occasion to change his mind about any of the things he'd written about the First World War in the 1920s, which is when he wrote most of his books about the First World War. He said, "No." He said that, "The only thing I regret . . ." then he moved to the present situation—he said, "The only thing I regret about the present situation is that we can't have any more wars in Europe, we'll have to fight them outside of Europe through surrogates." Was he being serious when he said this? I mean he said it with a twinkle in his eyes, certainly—his bright blue eyes. So, I think we should come back to this issue of irony—and this is an argument that Jay has made—and wheth-er irony is a specifically English characteristic, or a more generally Eu-ropean state of mind and form of writing. He may be right, although I would be more inclined to say that the English have a particular kind of irony; you see it in their movies and various forms of mass culture and so forth. To argue that the ironic voice didn't exist in other countries, I think, is a mistake. I don't believe this, and now maybe we can have a real argument, finally.

Let me be clear though. I think that in one sense the basic argument of the *Great War in Modern Memory* is mistaken. I cannot accept the no-tion that it was the Great War that shaped modern forms of life, how-ever we want to define those things after 1918. A thing that has always surprised me about Paul Fussell is that he was writing his book precisely at a moment when historians had begun to break with the notion that the First World War had changed everything in Europe; they started go-ing back to study the prewar period in depth. Precisely at a moment when they were finding the roots of modernism and of many, many other things—of political ideologies of various kinds, fascism, every-thing, Fussell said no, it was the war which formed the real rupture in history. And yet many scholars found that contemporaries discovered all those things in the late nineteenth century during the years before the war. There's scarcely a trace in Fussell's book of an awareness, an acknowledgment that this had been going on. Now, what makes it serious, from my point of view, is that he was writing precisely at the moment when there was a kind of renaissance in pre-1914 studies. I don't think that there are many historians around who would argue that the war experience of a very selective group of upper-middle-class English officers whose writings Fussell examines can lead us to conclude that the war transformed modern sensibility when lots of other things were transforming modern sensibility as well. It is always dangerous to say this year is the big break in cultural history, since someone is bound to say, what about the year before? But that's a very big issue.

WINTER: On that point, I think the critical choice is between a view that the Great War was revolutionary in cultural life and my perspective which is the exact opposite, that the Great War was a counterrevolutionary moment. The central reason I have come to this conclusion, counter to Fussell's point of view, was that the people during and after the war needed to find languages within which to express mourning and mass bereavement on a scale the world had never seen before. And what were the languages ordinary people or writers used? They're the ones that they used before the war—religious motifs, romantic motifs, classical ones, and Jünger, of course, goes back to the *Iliad* in a lot of his writings.

WOHL: Right.

WINTER: Now the point is, that a war as complicated as that and as global as that, is bound to have everything—is bound to have both movements forward and movements back. But if cultural history is the study of signifying practices, the practices that people develop—what they do, not just what they think—then the cultural history of the war must go beyond poets to look around at family practices and those in small villages and market towns as well as in the great intellectual centers. And if you do that, then you see not modern memory but older forms of remembrance when people do the work of mourning.

To some degree, we are still there, still at the moment, when the optimism of the nineteenth century came to an end, and we had to realize, as the great French writer Paul Valéry said of them and of us, we now know that our civilization is mortal. There is that wistful air, that sense that a world has been lost in all kinds of commemoration, including the site in Kansas City we honor today. Here we are still engaged in an act of commemoration, just as the war's survivors did nearly a century ago. Perhaps one of the things we mourn is the notion that war has meaning because good people die in it. Nine million men died; thirty million were wounded. These numbers are so vast that they challenge the notion that war or history has any meaning. This kind of skepticism appears to me to be very remote from Ernst Jünger, who loved studying insects, who viewed many people in the same way as he viewed the insects on his wall, and who used that kind of arrogance—he was too much of a snob to be a Nazi . . .

WOHL: That's true, to be sure.

WINTER: . . . and used that kind of arrogance to distance himself from a set of events that had very little meaning. We have to look at these writers over time to make sense of what they had to say. What Jünger did was to change the original text of *In Stahlgewittern (Storm of Steel)* because political organizations of veterans needed a book that could be sold at their meetings and signed after them. At the end of the sixth edition of the book—which is the one that got translated into English— there appears the phrase, "Germany lives and Germany will be great." That wasn't in the first edition, but it is there in the sixth; times change and so do editions. I don't see much irony there.

WOHL: Of course it wasn't.

WINTER: Yes, it wasn't there. So, the first thing I think we should do is to broaden the time period we examine and increase the kind and variety of texts we study. Perhaps we cultural historians need to go beyond the intellectuals. I think nowadays cultural history places intellectuals within much broader communities than they were located in the old German tradition of *Geistesgeschicte*—the history of ideas as the spirit of the age. That is where I began with Fritz Stern, my great teacher from Columbia. Cultural history moves out of the realm of the artists and intellectuals of the period to the public at large, and this is a real advance.

Cultural history has a very broad appeal, and cultural history of the Great War touches people in ways that make sense to them. Fussell wrote about writers, but he spoke to those outside of the academy, he said something that mattered to people who were not academics. That's why the book has sold so well for so many years, and through him and Sam Hynes and others, the cultural history of the First World War has become a matter of general knowledge, much more so in Europe than here, but even here this is more the case than it was thirty years ago. Cultural history is not only exponentially richer than it was thirty years ago, but it has become a way to bridge the gap between the academy and the educated public. And that's why, Crosby, you can't get off the hook by saying that you're not part of this conspiracy called the cultural history of the war—you're deeply implicated in our activities and through events like today's, in our achievements.

KEMPER: Let me take that as a cue to ask you a question from my experience of commemoration of World War I and war, generally. I remember—I went to Andover, the prep school, and there used to be a great Memorial Day parade—there may still be—and it always struck me as being very different in its purpose and its meaning than virtually anything I read about war. And people who were veterans of World War I, there were still in the mid-sixties veterans of World War I, they would march in the parade, Korean War veterans, World War II veterans, there were about to become Vietnam War veterans—I think there were a couple of Vietnam War veterans—and usually lining the streets in the late sixties, as I was about to graduate from Andover, there would be protesters of the Vietnam War; respectful protests—black armbands, that kind of thing—and it struck me that the purpose of the parade was very different than anything English literary figures or German literary figures were doing—the purpose of the parade was to bring the community together. It ended at the Bell Tower at Andover, which was much like the Cenotaph in London or maybe Liberty Memorial itself, the tower at Liberty Memorial—and it had—to use a word that you use—or a phrase that you use, Jay, in your book, the sense of a community of bereavement. If this wasn't quite bereavement, it touched on the same general idea: it was a way of bringing the community together to honor the dead and to honor the living who'd gone through the experience of war.

WINTER: And it was done at the local level. I think that's a critical point and why being here in Kansas City is so important to emphasize.

This is not something that happens at the centers of power alone. We don't need George Bush or Barack Obama or Hilary Clinton to tell us what war is. Democracies fight war in which every loss is equal to every other: that's what war memorials are all about: the names. That's what Maya Lin's Vietnam Veterans Memorial is all about—the names, and every name has the same value as every other one. She, by the way, took it directly from a war memorial done by the great English architect Sir Edward Lutyens, at Thiepval on the Somme. She conjured up her design in a paper she wrote at Yale, for which she got a B+, I might add.

ALL: Laughter.

WINTER: And one of her teachers, whose name I will not mention, also sent in a design for the Vietnam Veterans Memorial; he got nowhere, and she won it instead. I think the critical point is that what we're doing today and what people do every time anyone goes to the museum, is de-centering commemoration. It doesn't happen only on the Mall in Washington. It happens all over the place. The critical issue, in my view, is how to form an open conspiracy of academics, veterans, and the public to study a subject which won't go away.

I spent most of my academic life in Europe. Anyone who wants to understand the integration of Europe, this extraordinary creation of the last fifty years, has to understand the disintegration of Europe. That disintegration really did happen between 1914 and 1918. Here I would say that the prewar period is less significant than the shock of destruction in those years. What changed was not only the capacity for destruction, which expanded geometrically, but the extent to which, as Edmund Blunden, one of the great war novelists, put it in his *Undertones of War,* that whoever comes out on top in the war, the only winner was the war itself. That notion of 1914 as the opening of Pandora's box and the letting out a monster was in the minds of those who after 1945 created the new Europe.

Although there were lots of other reasons for doing it, the European vision of this story is, to a degree, different from the American vision. They have gone a different way after 1945, and kept war out of their lives, to be sure with the exception of Yugoslavia, but even that catastrophe has come to an end.

To understand Europe today, you need to feel the power of the cultural legacy of the Great War. That's why Jünger matters and why Paul

Fussell, I think, has to be praised and criticized. He lets us into the English version of that notion that something dreadful happened in 1914 and it must never happen again, a notion which made it necessary for the British, late and reluctantly, to join the European Union. They didn't want to get together or get in bed with the French and Germans, nothing of the kind. But the avoidance of war is so deep a cultural necessity, that when Tony Blair took his country to war over Iraq, he didn't take his countrymen with him. Whatever sources you cite, it is clear that 80 percent, 90 percent of the population felt the other way.

So to return to the question of whether 1914 was a caesura in European history, the answer must be yes and no. When we look at commemoration, the language and forms used come from the past. I think the critical point is that every nation creates its forms of commemoration and they frequently do so by going backward. Very rarely do we find really exciting breakthrough work. Picasso, so far as I know, in the First World War, didn't do much that had the war in it. He designed cubist masks for the first surrealist ballet *Parade* in 1917, but not much more about the world in which he lived than that. Twenty years later, he painted his *Guernica* in 1937; that's a different matter, that's later.

Picasso lived in Paris and survived a war in which the losses in human life mounted to a point no one had ever seen before. What the First World War created was a gigantic mountain of corpses and a question without an answer, which is, what meaning do you attach to it? What would you say, Robert, are the culturally explosive or creative facets of those men and women who went through war that would complicate and qualify this story, because no one interpretation of the First World War can be true, it's just too big.

WOHL: Absolutely. And there is no such thing as a narrative of the war, a story of the war. There are stories of the war, individual stories and then some stories which sometimes come together collectively. And that's why one historian has called the First World War a cubist war in part, because it's got all these jagged pieces that don't fit together. Now, I didn't mean to argue that the First World War didn't have a major impact on European life and European culture, European politics—far from it, as a matter of fact. I think it did, and if we wanted to restrict our discussion to culture alone for the moment, leaving aside the political issues and so forth, I think that one of the major results of the war—and

Jay may have to go along with me on this one—was to discredit the official culture that had existed before 1914 in various ways. This was not a
complete discrediting, but movements that had been tiny, un-influential
gatherings of intellectuals before 1914, after 1918 began to reach a larger
audience at that time.

And I've argued too that one of the impacts of the war was to acceler-
ate the diffusion of what we call modernism and modernist culture in
the 1920s and 1930s. The war seemed to support the modernists' claim
there was going to be a cultural break in Europe and that everything
was going to be different in the future than it had been in the past. The
war was a spectacular example of that. And there are many other ways,
I think, that the war affected culture, but surely one of the most important impacts that it had was that modernism and official culture, too,
high culture generally, which had tended to be optimistic before 1914,
became pessimistic. I think that was a very important change, if only
because it suggested the need for radical remedies of various kinds. And
both Communism and Fascism were the beneficiaries of that feeling
that there needed to be some kind of a radical change, particularly, if we
think of Fascism, as many historians have argued, not simply as a political movement, but as a cultural phenomenon as well and, of course,
that's the argument that Modris Eksteins makes in his book *Rites of
Spring*. Eksteins's book is full of outrageous statements, but it is very
exciting, very exhilarating to read, and very provocative, wouldn't you
agree with that?

WINTER: Absolutely.

KEMPER: The technology of remembrance changes dramatically in
the twentieth century. Film, for instance, becomes an important medium of interpretation. Jay, one of the most interesting passages in
your book *Sites of Memory, Sites of Mourning: The Great War in European Cultural History* is about Abel Gance's film, *J'accuse!* Could you
describe that?

WINTER: The one reason I think your use of the word medium, Crosby, is perfect, is that various forms of belief in the paranormal emerged
during the First World War. And at the same time, entirely independent-
ly, there was an enormous expansion of the size of movie houses, too. It

was an accident that the war happened at the very moment that film became the center of popular culture, mass entertainment, in Europe and beyond. So you have to imagine movie theaters holding four thousand to five thousand people—the big Gaumont theaters in Paris did that—and the lights going down, and you have a pianist at the front playing scary music. Then a film appears, and the audience goes through what we might describe as a collective séance. Imagine such a scene, and then it might be possible to understand why the cinema was a powerful vehicle for the dissemination of the idea that the dead might come back to ask a simple question of the living. What did we die for? Was it worth it, when I went off and got my mortal wound; did you, my neighbor, take advantage of my business, or you, who lived one street away from me and my wife, while I was away and maybe before I died, did you take advantage of my wife and her loneliness? Was our death something that contributed to anything that was worthwhile? Were the living worthy of this sacrifice?

The filmmaker Abel Gance asked these questions on film, by visualizing a moment in the vast cemeteries scattered on the battlefields of Verdun in northern France. That moment is a dream of a soldier who had gone mad; did it happen? Maybe; maybe not. But the dream takes on a life of its own. He calls the dead of Verdun to rise and go home, and see if their families had been worthy of their sacrifice. And one by one, they do. They rise, and join together, helping each other along, covered with bandages, and march through the country on their way home. Gance was not a man for modest statements. This is the apocalypse, the day of judgment he has filmed, using, by the way, hundreds of soldiers loaned to him by the French army to make his film for the propaganda effort of France. Many of those soldiers playing the dead on film became the dead in real life; they fell in combat in the last bloody months of the war. The madman tells this story to civilians in his village, and warns them to get ready; their dead are coming home. And what do they see when they reach their villages? The dead find the living, filled with remorse for the ordinary sins they committed—foreclosing mortgages; letting a business fall into debt; committing adultery. Just an ordinary town, like Kansas City. Then the dead return to their graves and the film ends.

Now this was so successful a film that Gance did it again in 1937, and this time, it was a talkie. This time the same man, poet, visionary, whatever, is a chemist who discovers the neutron bomb—it's not called that, but that's what it is, a weapon that can destroy people without destroying property. And this time, he goes to Verdun to call all of the dead of the First World War from all the armies, not just the French ones, to march home and tell their loved ones that there must never be war again. This was Gance's second attempt to imagine the dead of the Great War returning home, this time from everywhere, and to every land, saying that war is an abomination that can never be allowed to happen again.

That pacifist element in the interwar years is something that was carried by film and not only by film. Now let us leave the cinema and go to the homes of the bereaved. Nine million men died in the war, and God knows how many of their loved ones found conventional religious support useful. Many, many people did not. And thus they turned to the pagan perimeter of Christianity and sought the help of mediums and of the séances they led. These are people who believed that they really had to have a word with their son who died in the war. If you can imagine radio waves carrying messages across distances, why not say, maybe the electrical or chemical traces of the brain might be left, even after death and might facilitate communication with the living? And the form of this communication is a séance, led by a woman who is the medium, in which parents or relatives try to ask these questions of their departed: are you all right? Is it okay? And the answer almost always is "Yes, I'm here with my friends who were killed as well. You can go back to your lives again. It's all right. Life can go on. It doesn't have to stop in the shadow of our deaths." That extraordinary imagery of the magical, the mysterious, the otherworldly, in séances is also there in other kinds of images. It is there in spirit photography, which through double exposure, convinced the gullible that they could see the clouds of spirits above the living. It is there in experimental film, too, and I'm thinking of the great 1920 silent film *The Cabinet of Dr. Caligari*, with its madman's dream, and the invocation of insane asylums after the Great War.

WOHL: Yes indeed.

WINTER: Now, the reason why I think this is important to mention in answer to your question is it raises the issue of shell shock right away. The basic question in circulation at the time and beyond is whether anyone could say that the world is sane when it engages in a war of that kind. And if the word "sane" doesn't apply to a confrontation in which nine million people died and thirty million were wounded, then how did soldiers go through that unbelievable experience and retain their sanity?

The answer is, quite a few didn't. What are we going to call their condition? doctors asked each other. We're going to call it "shell shock," one British physician replied, because 80 percent of the men killed were killed by artillery. But soon enough he saw the error of his invention, since people went mad far away from the artillery. The term stuck even though its author disowned it. The term "shell shock" endured, but in part it became a metaphor for a revolution in warfare, for the war turned insane those men who before joining up had been perfectly normal.

Now, is it surprising that experimental film picked this up as much as popular film? Gance's *J'accuse!* was a romantic film, because it started out with a banal love triangle and then it turned into something entirely other when its director started to think about all those people coming back from war who not only had no arms and no legs, but no minds, or rather they had no minds that they could control. Their stories took over their lives.

Shell-shocked men had lives paralyzed by stories that kept coming back. The British novelist Virginia Woolf, who knew a thing or two about madness, wrote *Mrs. Dalloway* in 1923. Here is a fictionalized version of the true story of her husband's brother, her brother-in-law, who inspired her creation, Septimus Smith. In that novel, he jumps out a window because he was constantly being followed by the ghost of the man blown up next to him during the war.

So my point is simple. The media of the time dealt with issues of huge significance to contemporaries. I think it is true to this day. The mass media of the Great War period helped to break down the barrier between high art and low art or popular culture and high culture, so that what is experimental engages in what is popular and flows, as it were, into a stream that is enormously powerful in affecting us all. So what the Great War did was, to a degree, to democratize artistic expression and bring out lots of voices that spoke in different ways about the catastrophe of their time.

To be sure, art follows its own rules and rhythms. But even artists live in the world. Picasso himself was said to have told a friend in Paris, after watching a parade of camouflaged artillery go by, that artists invented the Great War because cubists invented camouflage. What would the naval war be without cubism? Because all the ships would have been sunk unless they looked like waves, or whatever, to avoid the U-Boats.

Here I touch on a puzzle I have never resolved. A great deal of commemorative art is allegorical in character. Yes, the fact of mass death is ubiquitous. No one could have missed it. But what do these different commemorative statements mean? Take the Liberty Memorial here in Kansas City. What do the sphinxes represent on either side of the tower? Maybe the sphinxes are there because they can't answer the question, how do you honor those who die in war without glorifying war itself? Maybe that's the question—the riddle within the sphinx within the war. Maybe that's it. But think about that. These are Egyptian forms, even the plinth—that is, an extended Roman form—but none of it is Christian, none of it. Maybe I've missed it, but so far as I can tell, the one thing that's extraordinary about that memorial and thousands of others is that they go back before Christianity to find the forms in which to express their views about a global disaster. This was a Christian world—it still is, to a degree, in this country, and it certainly was in Europe at the time. Then why not more Christian forms? The great cenotaph in the middle of London, Sir Edwin Lutyens's Cenotaph of 1919–20—it's not Christ's tomb, it's a Greek tomb, an empty tomb. Lutyens went back before Christ to express something about loss of life in war.

You can see my difficulty in fitting together these forms of remembrance with your argument, Robert, about the extraordinary assimilation and amplification of radical notions of change with this equal and maybe even more powerful movement culturally and intellectually towards an older, archaic, even counterrevolutionary direction. How would you put all that together?

WOHL: Yes. I'm prepared to answer that, although not perhaps to your satisfaction. I have been dissatisfied for a long time with the view of culture that sees one kind of culture replacing another kind of culture, so that you have a kind of succession of cultures over time. Now, maybe that makes sense if you're working on the middle ages or the renaissance, although I'd like to look at it carefully before I agree to that, but it certainly doesn't work in the twentieth century. I absolutely agree with Jay that there was a turning back to older forms in the 1920s and 1930s in the aftermath of the war. I don't think that there's any question about that, but I see a coexistence of various types of culture, or maybe you might want to call it a struggle that was going on between various types of culture, in which they were vying for hegemony, but none really exercised that hegemony. Now, Jay has talked about a popular culture and older cultural forms that I would tend to associate, maybe, with official culture as it existed in the late nineteenth century in Europe. I've talked about modernist culture which had an agenda of its own and which I would argue was much stronger after the war than it was before, although it changed its nature, also to a great extent, because of the war. That's another issue.

But there's another type of culture that further complicates the picture and that's mass culture. The entertainment industry, the culture industry, becomes very important in the postwar years. And there is a very strange relationship between modernism and that culture. Actually you just touched on it when you mentioned *The Cabinet of Dr. Caligari,* as a matter of fact. There was a lot of interaction between modernist culture and the new mass culture. And as a matter of fact, many people who had been involved in small literary cultural groups before 1914 moved over into the mass cultural realm in the years following the First World War. And there are many interesting examples of that. So I would simply try and complicate the picture. We don't have to choose between going back—culture looking backwards or culture looking forwards. However, one of the points that Jay made with which I would totally agree, and I don't think that there's any question about this, is the ways people dealt with the trauma of the war, which was a major issue after 1918 for all European countries that had been involved in the war, and Jay has written very eloquently about this. In dealing with the trauma over the war, it was much more effective to go backwards in terms of culture—to look backwards rather than to look forwards. I'll use the term that Jay uses in his book—you seldom saw effective mourning going on or even commemoration going on in highly experimental forms, and I think there was a reason for that. People have always been a bit mystified by the fact that the English writers of the First World War—especially the ones that Fussell talks about and others as well—people have been mystified by the fact that they seem to be quite conservative in their choice of forms in their work, and again, I think there was a reason for that. One reason, of course, is that they wanted to reach a larger audience, and the person who was most open about this was Robert Graves in explaining why he wrote *Goodbye to All That,* maybe to make money after a difficult divorce. He put a little bit of everything into it—everything he thought people would find interesting so that it would become a best seller.

Many people who have written on the connection between war and European culture in the 1920s and 1930s have been surprised by the conservatism of some of the writers who dealt with these issues. And I think that you've done a lot to explain why they were conservative. I mean why they did often look back to older forms. Although then, when you look more carefully, sometimes it becomes more complex, I mean even with the people that Fussell talks about. Siegfried Sassoon, the English poet, for instance: he did look backwards, but at the same time, he broke with his pre-1914 Edwardian style. It's a very complicated issue, but I think the central point here is that they and we cannot avoid the immense problem that bereavement and mourning presented for Europeans in the 1920s and 1930s. I don't think that we have even yet thoroughly understood the impact of the war refracted through this process. We haven't thoroughly understood how that process affected political decisions, for example, encouraged pacifism—we haven't talked about the various veterans' movements and so forth yet. We haven't talked about the atmosphere that made possible Neville Chamberlain's Appeasement Policy in 1938.

KEMPER: Can I ask—I think we want to go to questions from the audience and maybe get a summation from the two of you—but I want to ask one last question from my point of view about a figure that you disagree about a little bit in both your writings in getting to the idea of the impact on mass culture. This is an elite figure who became an icon of mass culture. I'm talking about T. E. Lawrence, Lawrence of Arabia, and Jay, you talked in *Remembering War* about Lawrence as a very alienated figure. You both use the same facts about his life—the illegitimacy, his involvement in languages in the Middle East, his disappointment with the Versailles settlement, et cetera, but your key word, Jay, is alienation—that he's an alienated figure. And Robert, the key thing you say about him is that he was always in search of a way to get out of inaction and in to action, I think is a phrase that you use—a search for commitment—and maybe it's opposite sides of the same coin, but you seem to have a different view of the meaning of Lawrence's experience in the war and after the war.

WOHL: I'd like to think that these two views could be reconciled because nobody could argue that Lawrence wasn't alienated after the war. People just disagree about the reasons for it. I mean there are psychological explanations and there are political explanations and cultural explanations, which is only to say that T. Lawrence was a very complex person and none of his friends really understood him. He was a man of a thousand faces. I think, if I did say that he was always looking for a chance to engage in action of various kinds—I didn't remember having said that, but if I did say that, I'm happy about it.

ALL: Laughter.

WOHL: It sounds like a promising line of argument. Let me just make a very simplistic argument in favor of that statement. After the war, Lawrence did not retire into an ivory tower, by any means. Since we've all seen the David Lean movie of his life, most of us think that his life was really over after Damascus was taken in 1918, but actually, he did a lot of things. He was very active in the attempt to refashion the Middle East, and he was very close to Churchill, who was British colonial secretary in the early 1920s. He joined the army and the air force and was thrown out of both, but he eventually was allowed to remain in the air force. And what he did when he was in the air force? He was testing various types of machinery. He loved fast machines. He of course was killed on a fast machine—he loved riding his motorcycle at high speeds, and it is true that he had a certain amount of political activity. At the end of his life, he was in very close contact with people who were involved or about to become involved in the British Fascist movement. So he was a very complex figure who cannot be encapsulated in a few sentences, even a few sentences written by me.

WINTER: The counterpoint to that argument is worth considering. I placed my reflections on T. E. Lawrence in a chapter of my book, *Remembering War,* on shell shock. It's not that he joined the army/air force, but he did so under two separate different names. He found different identities, which I think is extraordinary because the previous one or ones clearly were ones he could not bear, for whatever reason.

Here there is a story the full contours of which we will never know. Some say it didn't happen. I am not sure. It is the story that he was raped as a prisoner of the Turks during war. Some people say he made it up, some people don't. But isn't that what is always said about rape? I deliberately chose to put this matter in a discussion of Lawrence in a chapter on shell shock, because it struck me that forms of what we now call PTSD—post-traumatic stress disorder—are anticipated in the First World War, and many people were well aware of it at the time.

So, I use Lawrence for a different purpose—first of all, to open up the question as to what is shell shock? It's when memory and identity can't fit together. You have a story to tell yourself about your life, who you are, it's your story—it may not be completely accurate, but it's the story you use to tell other people who you are and what you've done. And then there are certain memories about war experiences, not only war experiences, but frequently about the war, which can't be interpolated. So what do you do? You forget about those memories, you lie about them, you say they never happened, or you interpolate the story—you say it's part of your life, the way Fussell did about his Second World War experiences.

But there's a third option; the third option is needed when you can't interpolate it and you can't forget it. That's what we call trauma or shell shock—that point when identities fragment under the stress of intolerable memories. Once we have the notion of fragmented identities, we have a framework within which to place the life of T. E. Lawrence and millions of other people, too. In such a framework, we might interpret differently some of his proto-Fascist activities, or his restless search for something that seemed to be eluding him all the time.

I know this is a tricky interpretation. I'm claiming something I will never be able to prove. It doesn't matter ultimately, whether we resolve the question was he raped or not by Turkish policemen after he was arrested as a spy. What mattered was the fragmentation of his identity and that of millions of other people who couldn't put their memories into their stories. Instead the stories seemed to take over their lives.

In 1980, the syndrome of post-traumatic stress disorder was recognized by the American medical profession, and, therefore, it became a pathway to pensions and entitlement, no question about it. It was a very important thing for Vietnam vets who couldn't get their lives together after the war to be recognized and legitimated. Doctors are people with white coats who legitimate conditions. They say that's what you have, it's true, and it's an illness. It's not malingering, it's not cowardice. So, I put Lawrence in that long tradition that has finally accepted that war is even crazier than the people who direct it, and that perfectly sane people go crazy in war. It's not because of family inheritance. It's not because of "Uncle Henry," whom we don't talk about, and the genes that get passed down or other biological explanations of insanity. It's because there are social and political practices which we call, collectively, warfare, which put people in places where they go mad.

I used that framework to try to understand what Lawrence of Arabia went through, and maybe my story is one in need of complication. I would agree with that entirely. But once we think of war as entirely a rational exercise, then we've lost any understanding of what it is. War is an experience that has so many facets, so many elements that the purely rational interpretation of tactics or strategy or operations or battles, has a certain insanity built into it. Therefore, I think it's utterly appropriate that we should invite our colleagues to consider whether commanders are sane or insane and whether the men who follow their orders are just as crazy as the ones who give them. In a way we are circling around the great question that John Keegan put in his classic work, *The Face of Battle*, published just one year after Fussell. The question is how is battle possible? How is war possible? Once we look at the Gorgon's face, how can we consider it to be something rational human beings do to each other? And yet they have.

WOHL: And just to tack a tiny coda on to what you've been saying, as well, is that the craziness of war and perhaps the craziness of some of the commanders raises the question of why so many men go ahead fighting when they realize that the whole thing is absurd. And there's a big debate now, and particularly in France, about this question. Obviously, Keegan addressed it in *The Face of Battle*, but it's always mystified me. A corollary of that is, why didn't statesmen negotiate an end to the war in 1915, 1916, or 1917, when they knew that no country would be the beneficiary of the war? Of course there's an answer to that, I suppose, in the sense that maybe some of them thought that, despite all of the terrible death and destruction, their country was going to benefit more than others. How wrong they were.

EPILOGUE

Hew Strachan, All Souls College, Oxford

It rained heavily in Glasgow on the morning of 2 August 1914. Despite that and despite the conventions of the Scottish Sabbath, after lunch Thomas Livingstone, a shipping clerk, walked from his home in the south side of the city, across the River Clyde, to the town center. He wanted to find out the latest news. As recent historians of the phenomenon known as "war enthusiasm" have pointed out, the crowds which gathered in the streets and public places of the cities of Europe at the end of July and the beginning of August 1914 did so less out of a desperation to fight than out of curiosity. Without radio or television, and certainly without CNN or Fox News, they relied on the latest editions of the newspapers to keep abreast of the unfolding crisis. Theirs was a literate generation, and the big press barons responded to their education with cheap papers, often publishing several editions a day.

Britain was not yet in the war, and not all the newspapers were clear that it should be. On the same day, C. P. Scott, the editor of the Liberal *Manchester Guardian*, sent a telegram to the Chancellor of the Exchequer, David Lloyd George, which began with a description and ended with a threat (at least for an ambitious politician): "Feeling of intense exasperation among leading Liberals here at prospect of Government embarking on war. No man who is responsible can lead us again."[1] At one level Scott's anxiety was well founded. Later that same day, Sunday or not, Lloyd George's friend in what proved to be Britain's last Liberal government, Winston Churchill, the First Lord of the Admiralty, met the French naval attaché to draw up the preliminary steps to coordinate the operations of their two navies, and shortly after 7 p.m. he signaled to the commander-in-chief of the British fleet in the Mediterranean that he should prepare for joint action with the French fleet. "Situation very critical," Churchill's message concluded; "Be prepared to meet surprise attacks."[2]

However, Scott might have been reassured if he had been able to read the letter which the prime minister, H. H. Asquith, then aged sixty-one, penned that night to his twenty-seven-year-old lover, Venetia Stanley. For Asquith the worst event of that Sunday was the absence of a letter from Venetia, but he conceded that it had been "pretty black" for other reasons as well. The prime minister had received the German ambassador to London over breakfast and assured the tearful emissary that Britain had no desire to intervene. Later in the morning, at a meeting of the cabinet, Asquith's dominant fear was that, if Britain were to enter the war, it would split the government and turn the bulk of his own party, the Liberals, against him. Britain, he told Venetia, had "no obligation of any kind either to France or Russia to give them military or naval help."[3]

From these internal divisions, and given the lack of resolution that they indicate, it can be easy to interpret the First World War, for Britain at any rate, as "a war of choice." Alone of the original belligerents, it did not confront an infringement of its territorial integrity. Even after Lloyd George made his name as the prime minister who had won the war, he remained sufficiently sensitive to Scott's warning to play down his own part in the British decision to enter the conflict. The crisis which had broken on 23 July 1914, when Austria-Hungary issued its ultimatum to Serbia, threatened hostilities only in the Balkans. This was the third Balkan war in fewer years, and neither of the first two had prompted anything more than saber rattling outside the region. By the time that Tommy Livingstone reached the center of Glasgow on the afternoon of Sunday, 2 August 1914, the third Balkan war had become the first general European war since 1815. The newspapers told him that Germany had declared war on Russia, that Russia had invaded Austria, and that Germany had crossed the French frontier. However, in the eyes of Liberals like Scott, not even war on this scale warranted British intervention.

Britain might lie adjacent to Europe, but in 1914, unlike 2008, it was not of Europe. Scott then, like Niall Ferguson today, saw Britain's task at this juncture as that of disinterested moderator, not of committed warrior. But by that Sunday Scott's position was becoming a minority view. Halfway round the world, Richard Meinertzhagen, a British army officer at the Staff College at Quetta, in what was then still India and is now Pakistan, had received a news update on 1 August, and had noted in his diary: "Europe is heading for disaster and there is going to be a most terrible catastrophe." What he envisaged was not just a European war, but—in his own words—"a world war," provoked by Germany and directed against Britain.[4] Tommy Livingstone, who in the event would leave neither his job nor Glasgow over the ensuing four and a half years, described it in the same terms. On the evening of 2 August, as he finished the diary entry reporting on his fact-finding mission into the city center, he added the single (ungrammatical) sentence: "The war of the world."[5]

At one level the title "world war," used particularly in Germany before the outbreak of the war, was metaphorical, a portent of how awful a major war involving the "great powers" would be. It was, after all, not genuinely global. Sir Ernest Shackleton led an expedition across the Antarctic which set out in the summer of 1914. Two years later, he arrived at the whaling station on South Georgia and said to its manager, "Tell me, when was the war over?" He was astonished to be told that it was not over, the manager adding: "Millions are being killed. Europe is mad. The world is mad."[6] For two years Shackleton had been in a part of the world that was not touched by the war. Nonetheless, when in 1914 the British used the term "world war" it was not just a figure of speech. The war that had broken out as Shackleton's expedition went south had grown in scale because it had become a concatenation of regional wars. The Balkan War between Austria-Hungary and Serbia was the first; the following month, on 23 August, Japan declared war on Germany to promote its ambitions in China and the Pacific; at the end of October, the Ottoman empire honored its alliance with Germany, not in order to pursue German ambitions across Asia but to fulfill its own security needs in the Aegean and southeast Europe; in 1915 the motivations of both Italy, when in May it sided with the Entente and attacked Austria-Hungary, and Bulgaria, when in September it joined with the Central Powers to overrun Serbia, were similarly local.

The aims of each of these later entrants to the war were also predominantly territorial. They set conditions for their entry and then held an auction between the opposing alliances. Although these terms massively complicated the making of the peace after the war, they were also inherently both definable and negotiable, and so were actually indicative of more limited and specific reasons for entering it in the first place. Britain's in 1914 were not—nor were any of those of the original belligerents, or not primarily. France did not go to war to recover Alsace-Lorraine, any more than Germany went to war to create a European economic bloc. Such war aims were adopted after the declarations of war, not before them. Instead they described this war in terms of values, of ideologies, and of big ideas. Richard Meinertzhagen, dreading the onset of hostilities for all that he was a professional soldier, responded to the news of 1 August by taking himself off to pray by the side of a gnarled old juniper tree. He asked that "if war there be, my country might prove victorious, as I believe in the righteousness of our cause and that it will be better for the world in general if we win."

For Britain, therefore, the war which it entered on 4 August 1914 was global for three reasons. First, it was not about territory, for all that the German invasion of Belgium was what eased the divisions that so threatened Britain's internal unity on 2 August. As Meinertzhagen's prayer hinted, most Britons were as persuaded as were most French and most Germans that what was at stake were ways of seeing the world that would shape the future evolution of civilization as surely as had the legacy of the French Revolution. The impact of the latter had been felt, of course, predominantly within Europe, and that was the second assumption which all three shared: that Europe was not an isolated continent, one of several, but the center of the civilized world. Each of them had good reason for believing that. The ideas which the revolutionaries of France had preached shaped the political discourse of the continent for the rest of the nineteenth century; Germany had become the home, indeed the founder, of academic research, and so the standard bearer in higher education; and Britain was the world's shipping, insurance, and financial center. These were the reasons why both Richard Meinertzhagen and Tommy Livingstone could slip so easily from describing this as a European war to seeing it as a global conflict.

Thirdly and finally, Britain, France, Russia, Belgium, and Germany were all colonial powers. Meinertzhagen was serving in India, the jewel in Britain's imperial crown, and Livingstone worked in the "second city of the empire" in a global business dominated by the shipyards of the Clyde. Britain possessed the greatest reach, but the other four powers also had reach in Africa or Asia or both. Britain's emigrant populations in Canada, South Africa, New Zealand, and Australia were quick to commit themselves both to serve "the old country" and, in due course, to develop their own territorial ambitions, as was made clear in the peace negotiations at Versailles in 1919. Overtly the colonies were a source of strength: Britain would turn to its "white dominions" and France to its African possessions for manpower for the Western front. But they were also a source of vulnerability: distant, scattered, and dependent on the fragile loyalties of subject peoples. On 14 November 1914, the Ottoman empire, in its role as the Caliphate, issued from Istanbul a summons to all Muslims to wage a Holy War against the Entente powers of Britain, France, and Russia. All three ruled over sizable Muslim populations, but the largest number, a third of the world's Muslims, lived under British government. The strategic threat to London was immediate: Jihad could cut the empire's communications at the Suez Canal, and split the Indian army along religious lines. The British Expeditionary Force would have to go, not to France, but to guard Egypt and the northwest frontier of India. Germany's scheme for revolution across North Africa, through Central Asia, and into Russia recognized the advantage of widening the war from Europe to the world.

In his introduction to this volume, Jay Winter recognizes the force of the argument that this was genuinely a global war, even if (as Margaret MacMillan reminds us) it was not as fully global as the Second World War was to prove. He then goes on to argue that therefore those who study its history today, the "fourth generation" of historians in his interpretation, are transnational historians. What is transnational history and how will its pursuit interact with a war which we now recognize to have been more genuinely global than narrowly European? How can it contribute to fresh understandings of a war which has already generated a literature of staggering range, complexity, variety, and scale?

Transnational history is not the history of international relations. That was where the history of the First World War began, almost as soon as the war itself began. The issue of responsibility for its outbreak, and the need to pin the blame on the enemy, became the departure point for propaganda, mostly directed at the world's neutrals and particularly at the United States. The publication of "white books," "black books," and "yellow books" was orchestrated by the foreign ministries of the belligerents, and the accusations and counteraccusations of responsibility meant that the controversies over the causes of the war, reflected in this volume by the exchange between Paul Kennedy and Niall Ferguson, found their roots in 1914 itself. It was revived in 1961 by Fritz Fischer's massive study of German war aims in 1914–1918. Although that book is focused on one country, its effect was to spawn studies of other countries, and for much of the next two decades this was where scholarly activity was focused. Most government archives in the Western world were at that time closed for fifty years, and the wartime negotiations and tergiversations of foreign ministries could not even begin to be explored until after 1964. Today diplomatic history has lost the preeminence in university history departments that it once had, but the debates generated by the war's origins and by its peace settlement have never forfeited their vitality.

To say that international history is not the same as transnational history does not mean that transnational history cannot contribute to our understanding of international relations in the First World War. Transnational history is comparative. The debates about the outbreak of the war and about the terms of the Versailles treaty pivoted on the issue of guilt and therefore on the roles of individuals. Did Germany cause the First World War? Was the refusal of the United States Senate to ratify the peace settlement the principal reason for its eventual failure? Transnational history has three contributions to make to such debates. First, it compares the views of the elites of the states, looking for similarities as well as for differences and discord: much united Europe in 1914, particularly for its bourgeoisie and particularly in terms of education and economic interest. Second, transnational history explores what a distinguished historian of the causes of the war, James Joll, called the "unspoken assumptions," pushing beyond the diplomatic exchanges to the views of the press and of other communities, not least that of big business. Third, it probes the responses of the lesser states, those that were not self-styled "great powers." The analyses of Paul Kennedy and Niall Ferguson pivot on the Anglo-German relationship (or antagonism), for all that the war began in the Balkans, and they tend to accord the allies of both sides, France and Russia, Austria-Hungary and Italy, only walk-on parts. Small powers, as Margaret MacMillan has shown in her study of the making of the peace, can tweak the tails of the big ones when they are locked in crisis.

What transnational history opens up is in the inner workings of a state at war, and so it provides the context within which a country's foreign policy is set. The consequences of the collapse of the Ottoman empire, the competing promises made during the war to Arabs and Zionists, and the growing significance of the oil stocks held within the region as the war ended, have meant that policy decisions made in the heat of the war, often driven by the immediate pressures of its conduct, both shaped the postwar Middle East and now generate passions which themselves continue to be sources of conflict. Treaties and agreements are the stuff of traditional international history. What they do not embrace is the views and reactions of the Arab peoples at the time, the social conditions in Jerusalem or Baghdad, the economic impact of the war in Syria, Palestine, or Iraq, and the effects of recruiting for the Ottoman army on the communities of those areas, and on the motivations of those who served and fought on the fronts in Palestine, Mesopotamia, and the Caucasus.

The research questions which we might ask in relation to such topics are very often shaped by the success in reaching answers to similar issues in states whose archives—and the languages in which they are written—are both more accessible and probably more revealing. In other words, transnational history prompts the asking of comparable questions across nations. Transnational history emerged early in relation to the soldiers who returned from the war, the survivors who in the 1920s formed a community of the trenches which transcended national boundaries and even the old fault lines of enmity. As a result historians have formed a view of the military which possesses a set of generic qualities, pivoting on morale, comradeship, and the experience of combat. As part of that package, they used to believe that soldiers at the front felt alienated from their home communities and found returning home on leave tense, fraught, and frustrating. This is the image propagated by many war memoirs, mostly written in the late 1920s. However, those books were reflective not so much of a mood prevalent in the war itself but of the loss of direction suffered after the war as the returning soldier experienced difficulty readjusting to civilian life. Erich Marie Remarque's *All Quiet on the Western Front* is a case in point, as Robert Wohl points out. Recent scholarship for the armies of the Western European powers, however, stresses the inter-dependence of home and front. Using letters and censors' reports rather than postwar memoirs, it stresses that during the war many conscript soldiers, citizens only temporarily in uniform, longed for news of home and to return to the embrace of domesticity. Did the same hold true for the soldiers of the Ottoman army? We don't know; we may never know, as the sources are probably no longer available, if they ever were. But a transnational approach to history alerts us to the question and may even one day provide at least a partial answer. Furthermore, until then we can argue that it is inherently probable that the Anatolian peasant serving in Iraq remained as worried about conditions on the land at home and about village life as did the peasants of France or Italy.

Two more of the four empires obliterated by the war, those of the Romanovs and the Habsburgs, are also ripe for revisiting along similar lines. The end of the Cold War promised a new dawn in the history of the First World War in central and eastern Europe. It became possible to study Russia's experience without the teleology of the Russian Revolution. The sufferings of the Russian soldier could be analyzed without the presumption that he was desperate to throw off the tsar in the name of Bolshevism. Some Western scholars did pioneering work in the archives in the 1990s, but sadly, having been opened, many of those are now closing again. More immediately promising are the possibilities in the former domains of the Austro-Hungarian empire, now made accessible by the collapse of Soviet rule. Moreover, in many of these countries, the end of the First World War, as much as the end of the cold war, marks the beginning of national independence. The impact of the war in states that did exist in 1914, Hungary, Serbia, Romania, and Bulgaria, remains relatively unknown. In many cases there is a reasonably significant body of literature, but it is written in languages that are not as readily accessible to a predominantly Anglophone community as are French and German, and it does not address the war with the sophisticated research tools of twenty-first-century academics. For the states that did not exist in 1914, those that were formed after the war like Poland and Czechoslovakia, and those that only achieved unambiguous statehood after the end of the cold war, like Slovenia, Croatia, Latvia, Lithuania, and Estonia, much of this history is being written for the first time. The editor of this volume, Jay Winter, together with Jean-Louis Robert, has pioneered the transnational history of the war in Western Europe with a comparative study of three capital cities at war—London, Paris, and Berlin. The contributors look at social, economic and cultural questions, at profiteering, housing, incomes, health, and food. In the future we can look forward to a comparison between Vienna and the other cities of the Habsburg empire, Prague, Trieste, Ljubljana, Budapest, or Graz, or between them and the cities of Russia.

Comparative history can set the agenda but it must not determine the outcome. The temptation when trying to write history that covers several countries is to embrace the familiar and the similar, but to ignore the exceptional and the particular. In a war that was fought so bitterly and at such cost, the postmodernist can too easily succumb to seeing national differences as variations on a related theme, however divisive they were at the time. There are many reasons for resisting this desire to "lump" experiences. The most important one is the most obvious: it was the differences that underpinned the hostilities between enemies and which the war aggravated. What very often created the points of comparison and similarity was not that the states were European or "modern," but that they were at war. War is a reciprocal act. Although its history is often written through the nationalist lens of one side only, its dynamic depends on the decision of the other side to resist, to fight back, so initiating a competitive relationship which includes imitation and emulation. The common experience was the war itself. It is that which provides the key transnational touchstone when comparing European with African, African with American, and American with Asiatic.

The big difference in tracing the transnational history of the war may therefore be the comparison between the belligerents of both sides and the neutrals who belonged to neither. In 1914, international finance depended on the gold standard; in other words, states tied the amount of paper currency in circulation to a ratio set by the amount of gold held in the nation's central bank. In order to lubricate the business of mobilizing the economy for war, most belligerents responded to the war's outbreak by effectively coming off the gold standard. They used government treasury bills, not gold, as the collateral for note issue, despite the fact that the government was now the principal purchaser of goods and services, so initiating an inflationary spiral that was one of the war's most obvious and immediately urgent legacies. Britain was an exception, essentially pegging sterling to the dollar in order to enable it to continue to pay for goods on international markets. The beneficiaries of the belligerents' demands for goods were the neutral powers, who frequently provided the loans required to buy them by taking gold as collateral. Thus, while the belligerents drained their gold stocks, the neutrals found themselves accumulating gold as a result of their pivotal role in maintaining the belligerents' trade and in providing the foreign loans to facilitate it. The influx of gold to countries like Switzerland, Sweden, Spain, and the Netherlands was so great that its ratio to the amount of paper notes in circulation soared. For the belligerents, relating note issue to gold still had the capacity to curb inflation, but for the neutrals the opposite now applied. Mounting gold stocks created an argument for increasing note issue, but if the money supply grew at a greater rate than did the goods available to purchase, inflation would be the result. By 1916 the neutrals too were rejecting the gold standard and were doing so for fear of inflation, but for reasons whose underlying causes were the opposite of those which applied in belligerent states. The United States was the exception, and by its own purchases in neutral countries and by enforcing an embargo on the export of gold sustained the exchange rate for the currencies of other neutrals. This is a transnational story that is richer and more complex than a facile use of comparative history reveals.

The experience of the neutrals in the war was self-evidently distinct from that of the belligerents in other ways too. Transnational history can again provide the insights for historiographical development. Given London's position as the center of global finance in 1914, but with Britain at war, neutrality became a relative term rather than an absolute one. In 1914 any state in the world which engaged in international commerce could not but be affected by what happened in the city of London. The war's effects on trade and finance were deepened with the British blockade, which extended to the interdiction of neutral trade with the Central Powers, and with Germany's response, the adoption of unrestricted U-boat warfare. Economic war did not spare the neutrals as more direct forms of fighting did, but little has been done to explore its impact on the neutrals' patterns of trade, on the consequences for their societies, and on the evolution of public opinion in those states.

So vast is the agenda in fields that historians have stubbornly refused to enter, and for which the archival resources are now available, that one is tempted to call time on some other debates that are in danger of becoming hackneyed and repetitive. Preeminent here is that on British generalship on the Western front, and to which Gary Sheffield has made a distinctive contribution. The agenda that Holger Afflerbach pursued in his study of Erich von Falkenhayn, the chief of the Prussian general staff between September 1914 and the end of August 1916, is very different from that of Sheffield in relation to Douglas Haig. Afflerbach's interest in operational matters extends only as far as they impinge on matters of strategy and politics; Sheffield's focus is almost exactly the opposite. In many respects that is a fair reflection of the preoccupations of both generals, but it is also a reflection of the different positions occupied in the national histories of Germany and Britain in the First World War by the armies of each.

The questions that transnational history puts to military historians are probably more direct and yet more often evaded than is the case for economic, social, or cultural historians. Armies (and navies) are symbols of national power, used in the national interest, and their achievements are then interpreted within the narrative of national history; they become part of a process of self-identification. Given the prevalence of conscription in 1914 (only Britain of the major powers did not have conscription and for many of the other powers, especially France, its burdens reached deep into the total adult male population), the armies that fought the First World War were genuinely representative of each nation's society as a whole. That was not true of the British army in Malakand in 1897, the French army in Morocco in 1911, the United States army in Mexico in 1916, or any of the European armies (including the German) that intervened in China to suppress the Boxer rising in 1900. Nationalism in 1914 had a military face, and yet once at war the armies were put to work in an international environment. Few, in fact almost certainly none, of the competitions between nations in the so-called age of nationalism rivaled the intensity of the First World War. The armed forces became the focus for every aspect of the nation's collective life, and the battlefield the payoff for its mobilization. Innovations in tactics by one side were either immediately imitated or countered by the other, or better still anticipated and preempted. Transnational history has an explanatory power in relation to the conduct of war, and of this war in particular, which exceeds most of its applications in other fields of inquiry.

Any yet the transnational history of the war's military operations has barely begun, not even for the Western front where its value is both self-evident and most closely related to the endeavors of those who bombed and patrolled, raided and defended, killed and maimed. This was a coalition war, and some good work has been done on the alliances at the strategic level, on the tensions generated for both the Austro-Hungarian and Ottoman armies by the Germans' assumption of military superiority, and—for the Entente—on the Anglo-Russian relationship in terms of strategy and supply, and on the military dimensions of the Anglo-French cooperation on the Western front. But much more remains: relations between Bulgaria and the other Central Powers, and between the original allies of the Entente and those who entered the war later. The attention to "total war" and its place in the twentieth century has demanded a comparative understanding of war, but it is one largely mediated by the interwar literature, itself reflective of the fact that the phrase "total war," rarely used in the First World War itself, was a retrospective description coined either as a warning to be conveyed to the future or a road map for the next great war.

Neither approach gets close enough to the texture of the war, to the tactical considerations which dominated the pattern of daily life for the units at the front, and which meant that this war was shaped from the bottom up rather more than from the top down. Commanders went to war in 1914 schooled in an operational vocabulary of advance guards and turning movements, of envelopments and lines of communication, which made them sensitive to a common heritage in the study of what they called strategy (by which they understood "the use of the battle for the purposes of the war").[7] This stretched back to Napoleon and was truly transnational. Before the war, each army read the works of theory published by the others. But as trench warfare gripped the fronts in the winter of 1914–1915, such phrases took second place to the technical demands of artillery and aircraft, to the demands of battlefield communication and intelligence on which those arms relied and which they supported or interdicted, and which left commanders struggling to reassert control of the environment that they saw as their professional obligation.

Attrition is the word that is now most often used to describe what happened. But it is a word without precision. It was first used in the winter of 1914–1915 to describe the conditions of trench warfare. It related to tactics: this was a long, wearing-out fight, dominated by artillery, in which casualty levels seemed to be the best way of calculating relative success. Before the war the destruction of the enemy's army had been held up as an objective of strategy. Insofar as destruction was defined (and for the most part it was not), what was at stake was an army's cohesion and discipline, the qualities that made it an effective fighting formation: breaking these would be the means to an end, the way in which the battle could best serve the purposes of the war. But as armies maintained their cohesion, sustained by the defensive strengths of the trenches and their effectiveness in blocking maneuver, destruction became more direct: annihilation, not exhaustion, became the object of attrition. Strategy therefore became subservient to tactics, not its master. The challenge was to think how attrition could best be yoked to strategy, and here ambiguity prevailed. The vocabulary of warfare lacked clarity. The Germans used three words, not one, all of them derived from verbs, *ermatten, reiben,* and *zermürben.* In France, Joffre used the word *grignotage,* or "nibbling." The latter was also derived from a verb, and the point about verbs was that they needed objects: attrition was a way of doing things, a means, not an aim. But in that case what was the aim? A war won through the physical exhaustion of the enemy was likely to produce a negotiated settlement, not the decisive victory that the losses and length of the war increasingly demanded. As the belligerents' war aims expanded, so policy demanded more than tactical realities could deliver. Strategy found itself unable to link tactical realities to political ambitions. The war and its conditions may have been a common denominator for all armies, but transnational approaches to the problem throw up differences. The British had no verb for attrition (the Americanism "to attrite" had yet to enter the vocabulary), and so in their case attrition, a noun, could be an object. But attrition was not a military objective. Douglas Haig aimed to convert the "wearing-out fight" into a breakthrough, and the issue he confronted was that of time: when would that moment come? Would it be in this battle or the next? Would it be this year or the year after? But attrition as an object could play when he went to the war cabinet, especially in the planning stages of the third battle of Ypres in the summer of 1917. For Britain, strategy was not just a matter for land forces, it was also—indeed in some peoples' eyes primarily—a matter of sea power. Maurice Hankey, the secretary of the cabinet, felt that the application of naval supremacy through the blockade would be decisive. Here attrition, when applied at the tactical level on land, dovetailed with a wider vision of how the war might be won. It may possibly be of significance that Britain's allies, the French, also had a phrase that incorporated the idea of attrition as an object, *guerre d'usure.* It would be interesting to know when it became current and in what contexts.

So far transnational history has tended to focus on the soldier's experience of the front at the existential level. Len Smith has linked the latter to battlefield outcomes for one element of the French army, but nobody has yet emulated him with a study for an army of another nation. What is at stake here is not just the negotiation between the soldiers of the French army and their commanders, but both their dealings with their opposites in the enemy army. This goes to the heart of the military historian's dilemma. War is one of the most written about of man's activities, and yet fighting itself, its intensity, its fear, its elation, its split-second decisions, can only be captured retrospectively. In action nobody has time to write, unless it is an order, reduced to a series of map references and a statement of intent, which may bear no relationship to the situation on the ground at the time or what then eventuated. Unit war diaries were inevitably written by the survivors after the event, and the more laconic they are, the more they may in fact reflect both the severity of the fighting and its importance. The words that participants in a battle use may convey specific meanings, and even smells and sounds, to those who have been there, but carry different connotations and can even be abstractions to those who have not. As Edmund Blunden wrote in Tokyo in 1924, in the "preliminary" to his war memoir, *Undertones of War* (which would in fact not be completed for another four years): "I know that the experience to be sketched in it is very local, limited, incoherent; that it is almost useless, in the sense that no one will read it who is not already aware of all the intimations and discoveries in it, and many more, by reason of having gone the same journey. No one? Some, I am sure; but not many. *Neither will they understand*—that will not be all my fault."

Blunden's sense of his own limitations pales alongside his implied criticism of the historian who has not experienced at first hand any war, let alone the First World War. And yet his statement is also a challenge, albeit one to which transnational history should respond with the humility of knowing that its answers are always likely to be partial and incomplete.

NOTES

INTRODUCTION

1. For a fuller discussion, see Jay Winter and Antoine Prost, *The Great War in History: Debates and Controversies, 1914 to the Present* (Cambridge: Cambridge University Press, 2005).

2. Daniel Todman, *The Great War: Myth and Memory* (London: Hambledon, 2005).

3. Paul Fussell, *The Great War and Modern Memory* (New York: Oxford University Press, 1975).

4. John Keegan, *The Face of Battle* (New York: Viking, 1976).

5. Eric Leed, *No Man's Land: Combat and Identity in World War I* (Cambridge: Cambridge University Press, 1979).

6. James Sheehan, *Where Have All the Soldiers Gone? The Transformation of Modern Europe* (Boston: Houghton Mifflin, 2008).

7. Erez Manela, *The Wilsonian Moment: Self-Determination and the International Origins of Anti-Colonial Nationalism* (New York: Oxford University Press, 2007).

8. Jay Winter and Jean-Louis Robert, *Capital Cities at War: Paris, London, Berlin, 1914–1919*, 2 vols. (Cambridge: Cambridge University Press, 1997 and 2007).

9. Jay Winter and Richard Wall, eds., *Family, Work and Welfare in Europe, 1914–1918* (Cambridge: Cambridge University Press, 1988).

10. Peter Gatrell, *A Whole Empire Walking: Refugees in Russia during World War I* (Bloomington: Indiana University Press, 1999); Nick Baron and Peter Gatrell, eds., *Homelands: War, Population and Statehood in Eastern Europe and Russia, 1918–1924* (London: Anthem Press, 2004).

11. Ernst Jünger, *Storm of Steel*, trans. Michael Hoffman (New York: Penguin Books, 2004).

12. On the Historial project, see Jay Winter, *Remembering War: The Great War between History and Memory in the Twentieth Century* (New Haven, Conn.: Yale University Press, 2006), ch. 10.

13. Among Paul Kennedy's works are the following: *The Rise and Fall of British Naval Mastery* (London: Allen Lane, 1978); *The Rise of the Anglo-German Antagonism, 1860–1914* (Boston: G. Allen and Unwin, 1980); *Rise and Fall of the Great Powers: Economic Change and Military Conflict from 1500 to 2000* (New York: Vintage Books, 1987).

14. Among Niall Ferguson's works are the following: *The Pity of War* (London: Penguin Press, 1998); *The War of the World: History's Age of Hatred* (London: Allen Lane, 2006); *Empire: How Britain Made the Modern World* (London: Allen Lane, 2003).

15. Among Holger Afflerbach's works are the following: *Falkenhayn: Politisches Denken und Handeln im Kaiserreich* (Munich: Oldenbourg, 2005); *Kaiser Wilhelm II. als Oberster Kriegsherr während des Ersten Weltkrieges—Quellen aus der Militärischen Umgebung des Kaisers, 1914–1918* (Munich: Oldenbourg, 2005); *An Improbable War: The Outbreak of World War I and European Political Culture before 1914*, ed. Holger Afflerbach and David Stevenson (New York: Berghahn Books, 2007).

16. Among Gary Sheffield's works are the following: *The Somme* (London: Cassell, 2003); *Leadership in the Trenches: Officer-Man Relations, Morale and Discipline in the British Army in the Era of the First World War* (Houndmills: Macmillan, 2000); *Douglas Haig: War Diaries and Letters, 1914–1918*, ed. Gary Sheffield and John Bourne (London: Weidenfeld and Nicolson, 2005).

17. Among John Horne's works are the following: *German Atrocities, 1914: A History of Denial* (with Alan Kramer) (New Haven, Conn.: Yale University Press, 2001); *Labour at War: France and Britain, 1914–1918* (New York: Oxford University Press, 1991); *State, Society, and Mobilization in Europe during the First World War*, ed. John Horne (Cambridge: Cambridge University Press, 1997).

18. Among Len Smith's works are *Between Mutiny and Obedience: The Case of the French Fifth Infantry Division during World War I* (Princeton, N.J.: Princeton University Press, 1994); *The Embattled Self: French Soldiers' Testimony of the Great War* (Ithaca, N.Y.: Cornell University Press, 2007); *France and the Great War, 1914–1918*, with Annette Becker and Stéphane Audoin-Rouzeau (Cambridge: Cambridge University Press, 2003).

19. Among Margaret MacMillan's works are the following: *Paris 1919: Six Months That Changed the World* (New York: Random House, 2002); *Nixon in China: The Week That Changed the World* (Toronto: Penguin Books Canada, 2006); *The Uses and Abuses of History* (Toronto: Viking Canada, 2008).

20. Among John Milton Cooper's works are the following: *Breaking the Heart of the World: Woodrow Wilson and the Fight for the League of Nations* (Cambridge: Cambridge University Press, 2001); *The Warrior and the Priest: Woodrow Wilson and Theodore Roosevelt* (Cambridge, Mass.: Harvard University Press, 1983); *Pivotal Decades: The United States, 1900–1920* (New York: Norton, 1990).

21. Among Robert Wohl's works are the following: *French Communism in the Making, 1914–1924* (Stanford, Calif.: Stanford University Press, 1966); *The Generation of 1914* (Cambridge, Mass.: Harvard University Press, 1979);

A Passion for Wings: Aviation and the Western Imagination, 1908–1918 (New Haven, Conn.: Yale University Press, 1994).

22. Among Jay Winter's works are the following: *The Great War and the British People* (London: Macmillan, 1985); *Sites of Memory, Sites of Mourning: The Great War in European Cultural History* (Cambridge: Cambridge University Press, 1995); *Remembering War: The Great War between History and Memory in the Twentieth Century* (New Haven, Conn.: Yale University Press, 2006).

WAR ORIGINS

1. Kenneth N. Waltz, *Realism and International Politics* (New York: Routledge, 2008); and his earlier *Man, the State, and War: A Theoretical Analysis* (New York: Columbia University Press, 1959).

2. John J. Mearsheimer, *The Tragedy of Great Power Politics* (New York: Norton, 2001).

3. Paul Kennedy, *The Rise and Fall of the Great Powers: Economic Change and Military Conflict from 1500 to 2000* (New York: Vintage Books, 1987).

4. Paul W. Schroeder, *The Transformation of European Politics, 1763–1848* (Oxford: Clarendon Press, 1994), and his *Systems, Stability, and Statecraft: Essays on the International History of Modern Europe,* edited and with an introduction by David Wetzel, Robert Jervis, and Jack S. Levy (New York: Palgrave Macmillan, 2004).

5. Barbara Tuchman, *The Guns of August* (New York: Macmillan, 1962).

6. Ivan Bloch, *La guerre future* (Paris: Plon, 1906).

7. Norman Angell, *Great Illusion: A Study of the Relation of Military Power in Nations to Their Economic and Social Advantage* (New York: G. P. Putnam's Sons, 1912).

8. Niall Ferguson, *The Pity of War* (New York: Basic Books, 1999).

9. James Joll, *1914: The Unspoken Assumptions* (London: London School of Economics, 1968).

10. Niall Ferguson, *The War of the World: History's Age of Hatred* (London: Allen Lane, 2006).

WAGING TOTAL WAR

1. See Hew Strachan, *The Politics of the British Army* (Oxford: Clarendon Press, 1996), ch. 6.

2. Robin Prior and Trevor Wilson, *Passchendaele: The Untold Story* (New Haven, Conn.: Yale University Press, 1996), ch. 14.

3. On this point, see Fabienne Bock, *Un parlementarisme de guerre 1914–1919* (Paris: Belin, 2002).

4. Quoted in Sheffield, *The Somme* (London: Cassell, 2003), 19.

5. Gary Sheffield, *Forgotten Victory, The First World War: Myths and Realities* (London: Headline, 2001), 156.

6. See Brock Millman, *Pessimism and British War Policy 1916–1918* (London: Frank Cass, 2001).

7. Holger Afflerbach, ed., *Kaiser Wilhelm II. als Oberster Kriegsherr während des Ersten Weltkrieges—Quellen aus der militärischen Umgebung des Kaisers 1914–1918* (Munich: Oldenbourg, 2005).

8. Barbara W. Tuchman, *The Zimmermann Telegram* (New York: Ballantine Books, 1958).

9. For a good and sharp analysis—as well as a good read: Sebastian Haffner, *Sieben Todsünden des Deutschen Reiches* (Hamburg: Nannen, 1965).

10. Michael Geyer, "Insurrectionary Warfare: The German Debate about a Levée en Masse in October 1918," *Journal of Modern History* 73 (September 2001): 459–527.

11. Wilhelm Deist, "The Military Collapse of the German Empire," *War in History* 3, no. 2 (April 1996): 186–207.

THE SOLDIERS' WAR

1. James Joll, *1914: The Unspoken Assumptions* (London: Weidenfeld and Nicolson, 1968).

2. Ernst Jünger, *Storm of Steel* (London: Bodley Head, 1929), 123.

3. Stéphane Audoin-Rouzeau and Annette Becker, *1914–1918: Understanding the Great War,* trans. Catherine Temerson (New York: Hill & Wang, 2000), 102–3.

4. Leonard V. Smith, *Between Mutiny and Obedience: The Case of the Fifth French Infantry Division during World War I* (Princeton, N.J.: Princeton University Press, 1994).

5. Jay Winter and Antoine Prost, *The Great War in History: Debates and Controversies, 1914 to the Present* (Cambridge: Cambridge University Press, 2005).

6. Niall Ferguson, *The Pity of War* (London: Penguin, 1998), 433–41.

7. See, for example, Trevor Wilson and Robin Prior, *The Somme* (New Haven, Conn.: Yale University Press, 2005).

8. "The Italian Experience of 'Total' Mobilization, 1915–1920," in John Horne, ed., *State, Society and Mobilization in Europe during the First World War* (Cambridge: Cambridge University Press, 1997), 223–40.

9. For the key work, which exemplifies and analyzes this "turn," see Jean Norton Cru, *Témoins* (1929; reprint edition, Nancy: Presses Universitaires de Nancy, 2006, with preface by Frédéric Rousseau).

10. For a recent example, see Brian Bond, *The Unquiet Western Front: Britain's Role in Literature and History* (Cambridge: Cambridge University Press, 2002).

11. Erich Maria Remarque, *All Quiet on the Western Front* (1929; English translation, London: Viking, 2007); Ernst Jünger, *Storm of Steel* (1920; English translation by Michael Hoffmann, London: Allen Lane, 2003). *All Quiet on the Western Front* rapidly became universal both as a novel (which had

sold three million copies in twenty-three languages by 1931) and in the form of the 1930 Hollywood film by Lewis Milestone, which appeared across the world in multiple adaptations.

12. Leonard V. Smith, *The Embattled Self: French Soldiers' Testimony of the Great War* (Ithaca, N.Y.: Cornell University Press, 2007).

13. Jay Winter, "'Witness to a Time': Authority, Experience, and the Two World Wars," *Remembering War: The Great War between Memory and History in the Twentieth Century* (New Haven, Conn.: Yale University Press, 2006), 238–71 (esp. 262–63).

14. For the concept of "war cultures," see Jean-Jacques Becker et al., eds., *Guerre et cultures 1914–1918* (Paris: Armand Colin, 1994), as well as Stéphane Audoin-Rouzeau and Annette Becker, *1914–1918: Understanding the Great War* (2000; English translation, London: Profile Books, 2002).

15. Jean Jacques Rousseau, *The Social Contract* (1762).

16. Marc Roudebush, "A Case of Shell Shock in the French Army," *Journal of Contemporary History,* special issue on shell shock, 30 (2000): 138–46.

17. Pat Barker, *Regeneration* (1991), *The Eye in the Door* (1993), *The Ghost Road* (1995), published as *The Regeneration Trilogy* (London: Viking, 1996). See also *Journal of Contemporary History* 30, no. 1 (January 2000), special issue on "Shell shock," edited by Jay Winter.

18. John Horne, "Entre expérience et mémoire: les soldats français de la Grande Guerre," *Annales: Histoire, Sciences Sociales* 60, no. 5 (September–October 2005): 903–19.

19. Ernest Hemingway, *A Farewell to Arms* (New York: Basic Books, 1929).

20. Jay Winter and Blaine Baggett, *The Great War and the Shaping of the Twentieth Century* (New York: Vintage Books, 1996), the book accompanying the eight-hour television documentary series on the Public Broadcasting System and the BBC.

ENDING THE GREAT WAR

1. As cited in MacMillan, *Paris 1919,* 15.

2. Erez Manela, *The Wilsonian Moment: Self-Determination and the International Origins of Anticolonial Nationalism* (New York: Oxford University Press, 2007).

3. The idea was first stated by Elie Halévy, in his 1929 Rhodes lectures, reprinted in *The Era of Tyrannies,* edited by Fritz Stern and R. K. Webb (New York: Oxford University Press, 1966).

4. John Dower, *Embracing Defeat: Japan in the Wake of World War II* (New York: Norton, 1999).

5. Edward Weinstein, *Woodrow Wilson: A Medical and Psychological Biography* (Princeton, N.J.: Princeton University Press, 1991).

6. John Milton Cooper, *Breaking the Heart of the World: Woodrow Wilson and the Fight for the League of Nations* (New York: Cambridge University Press, 2001).

EPILOGUE

1. Trevor Wilson, ed., *The Political Diaries of C. P. Scott 1911–28* (London: Collins, 1970), 94.

2. Martin Gilbert, *Winston S. Churchill,* Companion vol. 3, Part 1 (London: Heigemann, 1972), 12.

3. H. H. Asquith, *Letters to Venetia Stanley* (Oxford: Oxford University Press, 1985), ed. Michael and Eleanor Brock, 146.

4. Richard Meinertzhagen, *Army Diary 1899–1926* (Edinburgh: Oliver and Boyd, 1960), 77–78.

5. Thomas Livingstone, *Tommy's War: A First World War Diary 1913–1918,* ed. Ronnie Scott (London: Collins, 2008).

6. Ernest Shackleton, *South* (London: Heigemann, 1919).

7. The definition is Clausewitz's; the point is that "strategy" did not carry the connotations of a national security policy as it does today.

SELECT BIBLIOGRAPHY

GENERAL HISTORIES

Audoin-Rouzeau, Stéphane, and Annette Becker. *14–18, Understanding the Great War.* Trans. Catherine Temerson. New York: Hill and Wang, 2002.

Ferro, Marc. *The Great War, 1914–1918.* Trans. Nicole Stone. London: Routledge and K. Paul, 1973.

Gilbert, Martin. *The First World War.* London: Weidenfeld and Nicolson, 1994.

Howard, Michael. *The First World War.* Oxford: Oxford University Press, 2002.

Keegan, John. *The First World War.* New York: Knopf, 1994.

Prior, Robin, and Trevor Wilson. *The First World War.* London: Cassell, 1999.

Robbins, Keith. *The First World War.* New York: Oxford University Press, 1984.

Stevenson, David. *Cataclysm: The First World War as Political Tragedy.* New York: Basic Books, 2004.

Taylor, A. J. P. *Illustrated History of the First World War.* New York: Putnam, 1964.

Winter, Jay. *The Experience of World War I.* London: Macmillan, 1988.

———, and Blaine Baggett. *The Great War and the Shaping of the Twentieth Century.* New York: Vintage, 1996.

————, and Antoine Prost. *The Great War in History: Controversies and Debates 1914 to the Present.* Cambridge: Cambridge University Press, 2005.

WAR ORIGINS

Berghahn, Volker Rolf. *Germany and the Approach of War in 1914.* New York: St. Martin's Press, 1973.

Evans, Robert J. W., and Hartmut Pogge von Strandmann, eds. *The Coming of the First World War.* Oxford: Clarendon Press, 1988.

Ferguson, Niall. *The Pity of War.* New York: Basic Books, 1999.

Fischer, Fritz. *Germany's Aims in the First World War.* New York: Norton, 1967.

Joll, James. *1914: The Unspoken Assumptions.* London: Weidenfeld and Nicolson, 1968.

————. *The Origins of the First World War.* London: Longman, 1984.

Keiger, John F. V. *France and the Origins of the First World War.* Basingstoke: Macmillan, 1983.

Kennedy, Paul. *The War Plans of the Great Powers, 1880–1914.* Boston: G. Allen and Unwin, 1979.

Mombauer, Annika. *The Origins of the First World War: Controversies and Consensus.* London: Longman, 2002.

Renouvin, Pierre. *La crise européenne et la grande guerre (1914–1918).* Paris: Félix Alcan, 1969.

Steinberg, Jonathan. *Yesterday's Deterrent: Tirpitz and the Birth of the German Battle Fleet.* London: Macdonald, 1965.

Stevenson, David. *Armaments and the Coming of War: Europe 1904–1914.* Oxford: Clarendon Press, 1996.

————. *The Outbreak of the First World War: 1914 in Perspective.* London: Macmillan, 1997.

Williamson, Samuel R. *Austria-Hungary and the Origins of the First World War.* New York: St. Martin's Press, 1991.

STRATEGY AND TACTICS

Afflerbach, Holger. *Falkenhayn: Politisches Denken und Handeln im Kaiserreich.* Munich: Oldenbourg, 1994.

————, ed. *Kaiser Wilhelm II. als Oberster Kriegsherr während des Ersten Weltkrieges—Quellen aus der militärischen Umgebung des Kaisers, 1914–1918.* Munich: Oldenbourg, 2005.

Barnett, Corelli. *Swordbearers: Supreme Command in the First World War.* New York: Morrow, 1964.

Bock, Fabienne. *Un parlementarisme de guerre 1914–1919.* Paris: Belin, 2002.

Bond, Brian, and Nigel Cave, eds. *Haig: A Reappraisal Seventy Years On.* Barnsley: Pen and Sword, 1999.

Geyer, Michael. "Insurrectionary Warfare: The German Debate about a Levée en Masse in October 1918." *Journal of Modern History* 73 (September 2001): 459–527.

Griffith, Paddy. *Battle Tactics on the Western Front: The British Army's Art of Attack, 1916–1918.* New Haven, Conn.: Yale University Press, 1994.

King, Jere Clemens. *Generals and Politicians: Conflicts between France's High Command, Parliament and Government, 1914–1918.* Berkeley and Los Angeles: University of California Press, 1951.

Kitchen, Martin. *The Silent Dictatorship: The Politics of German High Command under Hindenburg and Ludendorff, 1916–1918.* London: Croom Helm, 1976.

Liddell Hart, Basil. *The Real War, 1914–1918.* London: Faber and Faber, 1930.

Murray, Williamson, and Allan Millett, eds. *Military Effectiveness.* Vol. 2: *The First World War.* London: Allen and Unwin, 1990.

Porch, Douglas. *The March to the Marne.* Cambridge: Cambridge University Press, 1991.

Prior, Robin, and Trevor Wilson. *Command on the Western Front: The Military Career of Sir Henry Rawlinson, 1914–18.* Oxford: Basil Blackwell, 1992.

————. *Passchendaele: The Untold Story.* New Haven, Conn.: Yale University Press, 1996.

Ritter, Gerhard. *The Schlieffen Plan: Critique of a Myth.* New York: Praeger, 1958.

Sheffield, Gary. *The Somme.* London: Cassell, 2003.

————, and Geoffrey Till, eds. *The Challenges of High Command: The British Experience.* Basingstoke: Palgrave Macmillan, 1999.

Strachan, Hew. *The First World War.* Vol. 1: *To Arms.* Oxford: Oxford University Press, 2000.

Terraine, John. *Douglas Haig, the Educated Soldier.* London: Hutchinson, 1963.

Travers, Timothy. *The Killing Ground: The British Army, the Western Front and the Emergence of Modern Warfare.* London: Allen and Unwin, 1987.

———. *How the War Was Won: Command and Technology in the British Army on the Western Front 1917–1918.* London: Routledge, 1992.

Tuchman, Barbara W. *The Zimmermann Telegram.* New York: Ballantine Books, 1958.

Van Creveld, Martin. *Command in War.* Cambridge, Mass.: Harvard University Press, 1985.

———. *Supplying War.* Cambridge: Cambridge University Press, 1977.

Wilson, Trevor. *The Myriad Faces of War: Britain and the Great War 1914–1918.* Cambridge: Polity Press, 1986.

Winter, Denis. *Haig's Command: A Reassessment.* London: Viking, 1991.

———. *25 April 1915: The Inevitable Tragedy.* St. Lucia: University of Queensland Press, 1994.

Woodward, David. *Lloyd George and the Generals.* London: Associated University Presses, 1983.

THE SOLDIERS' WAR

Ashworth, Tony. *Trench Warfare, 1914–1918: The Live-and-Let-Live System.* New York: Holmes and Meyer, 1980.

Audoin-Rouzeau, Stéphane. *Men at War, 1914–1918: National Sentiment and Trench Journalism in France during the First World War.* Trans. Helen McPhail. Providence: Berg, 1992.

Babington, Anthony. *For the Sake of Example: Capital Courts-Martial 1914–1920.* London: Lee Cooper, 1983.

Bean, Charles E. W. *The Story of Anzac.* Sydney: Angus and Robertson, 1934.

Bourke, Joanna. *An Intimate History of Killing: Face-to-Face Killing in Twentieth-Century Warfare.* London: Granta, 1999.

Cecil, Hugh, and Peter Liddle, eds. *Facing Armageddon: The First World War Experienced.* London: Cooper, 1996.

Dallas, Golden, and Gill Douglas. *The Unknown Army.* London: Verso, 1985.

Fuller, John G. *Troop Morale and Popular Culture in the British and Dominion Armies 1914–1918.* Oxford: Clarendon Press, 1990.

Gammage, Bill. *The Broken Years: Australian Soldiers in the Great War.* Canberra: Australian National University Press, 1974.

Horn, Daniel. *The German Naval Mutinies of World War I.* New Brunswick, N.J.: Rutgers University Press, 1969.

Horne, John, and Alan Kramer. *German Atrocities, 1914: A History of Denial.* New Haven, Conn.: Yale University Press, 2001.

Keegan, John. *The Face of Battle.* London: Jonathan Cape, 1976.

Keene, Jennifer D. *Doughboys, the Great War and the Remaking of America.* Baltimore: Johns Hopkins University Press, 2001.

Leed, Eric J. *No Man's Land: Combat and Identity in World War I.* London: Cambridge University Press, 1979.

Macdonald, Lyn. *1914–1918: Voices and Images of the Great War.* London: Joseph, 1988.

Middlebrook, Martin. *The First Day on the Somme, 1 July 1916.* London: A. Lane, 1971.

Rachamimov, Alon. *POWs and the Great War: Captivity on the Eastern Front.* Oxford: Berg, 2002.

Sheffield, Gary. *Forgotten Victory: The First World War—Myths and Realities.* London: Headline, 2001.

———. *Leadership in the Trenches: Officer-Man Relations, Morale and Discipline in the British Army in the Era of the First World War.* Houndmills: Macmillan, 2000.

Shepherd, Ben. *A War of Nerves.* London: Jonathan Cape, 2000.

Smith, Leonard V. *Between Mutiny and Obedience: The Case of the French Fifth Infantry Division during World War I.* Princeton, N.J.: Princeton University Press, 1994.

Winter, Denis. *Death's Men: Soldiers of the Great War.* London: Allen Lane, 1994.

PEACEMAKING

Boemeke, Manfred, ed. *The Treaty of Versailles: A Reassessment after 75 Years.* Cambridge: Cambridge University Press, 1998.

Cooper, John Milton Jr. *Breaking the Heart of the World: Woodrow Wilson and the Fight for the League of Nations.* New York: Cambridge University Press, 2001.

Keynes, John Maynard. *The Economic Consequences of the Peace.* London: Macmillan, 1919.

Krumeich, Gerd, ed. *Versailles 1919: Ziele-Wirkung-Wahrnehmung.* Essen: Klartext Verlag, 2001.

Luckau, Alma M. *The German Delegation at the Paris Peace Conference.* New York: Columbia University Press, 1941.

MacMillan, Margaret. *Peacemakers Paris 1919: Six Months That Changed the World.* Toronto: Random House, 2001.

Maier, Charles S. *Recasting Bourgeois Europe: Stabilization in France, Germany, and Italy in the Decade after World War I.* Princeton, N.J.: Princeton University Press, 1975.

Manela, Erez. *The Wilsonian Moment: Self-Determination and the International Origins of Anticolonial Nationalism.* Oxford: Oxford University Press, 2007.

Mayer, Arno J. *Political Origins of the New Diplomacy, 1917–1918.* New Haven, Conn.: Yale University Press, 1959.

———. *Politics and Diplomacy of Peacemaking, Containment and Counterrevolution at Versailles, 1918–1919.* New York: Knopf, 1967.

Renouvin, Pierre. *L'Armistice de Rethondes, 11 novembre 1918.* Paris: Gallimard, 1968.

Sharp, Alan. *The Versailles Settlement: Peacemaking in Paris, 1919.* Basingstoke: Macmillan, 1991.

Vincent, Charles Paul. *The Politics of Hunger: The Allied Blockade of Germany, 1915–1919.* Athens: Ohio University Press, 1985.

Winter, Jay M. *Dreams of Peace and Freedom: Utopian Moments in the Twentieth Century.* New Haven, Conn.: Yale University Press, 2006.

MODERN MEMORY

Connelly, Mark. *The Great War: Memory and Ritual. Commemoration in the City and East London 1916–1939.* Woodbridge: Royal Historical Society/Boydell Press, 2002.

Cork, Richard. *A Bitter Truth: Avant-Garde Art and the Great War.* New Haven, Conn.: Yale University Press, 1994.

Cru, Jean Norton. *Du témoignage*. Paris: Allia, 1989.

———. *Témoins*. Nancy: Presses Universitaires de Nancy, 1993.

Dagen, Philippe. *Le silence des peintres: Les artistes face à la Grande Guerre*. Paris: Fayard, 1996.

Eksteins, Modris. *Rites of Spring: The Great War and the Birth of the Modern Age*. Boston: Houghton Mifflin, 1989.

Field, Frank. *British and French Writers of the First World War*. Cambridge: Cambridge University Press, 1991.

Fussell, Paul. *The Great War and Modern Memory*. New York: Oxford University Press, 1975.

Gaffney, Angela. *Aftermath: Remembering the Great War in Wales*. Cardiff: University of Wales Press, 1998.

Gregory, Adrian. *The Silence of Memory: Armistice Day, 1919–1946*. Oxford: Berg, 1994.

Hynes, Samuel. *The Soldiers' Tale: Bearing Witness to Modern War*. New York: A. Lane, 1997.

———. *A War Imagined: The First World War and English Culture*. London: Pimlico, 1992.

Inglis, Kenneth S. *Sacred Places: War Memorials in the Australian Landscape*. Melbourne: Melbourne University Press, 1998.

King, Alex. *Memorials of the Great War in Britain*. Oxford: Berg, 1998.

Leese, Peter. *Shell Shock, Traumatic Neurosis and the British Soldiers of the First World War*. New York: Palgrave Macmillan, 2002.

Lloyd, David W. *Battlefield Tourism, Pilgrimage and the Commemoration of Great War in Britain, Australia and Canada, 1919–1939*. Providence/Oxford: Berg, 1998.

Mosse, George L. *Fallen Soldiers: Reshaping the Memory of the World Wars*. New York: Oxford University Press, 1990.

Natter, Wolfgang G. *Literature at War 1914–1940: Representing the "Time of Greatness" in Germany*. New Haven, Conn.: Yale University Press, 1999.

Panichas, George Andrew, ed. *Promise of Greatness: The War of 1914–1918*. New York: John Day Co., 1968.

Prost, Antoine. *In the Wake of War: "Les Anciens Combattants" and French Society 1914–1939*. Oxford: Berg, 1992.

Schivelbusch, Wolfgang. *The Culture of Defeat: On National Trauma, Mourning and Recovery*. New York: Metropolitan Books, 2003.

Sherman, Daniel J. *The Construction of Memory in Interwar France*. Chicago: University of Chicago Press, 1999.

Tippett, Maria. *Art at the Service of War: Canada, Art and the Great War.* Toronto: University of Toronto Press, 1984.

Vance, Jonathan F. *Death So Noble: Memory, Meaning and the First World War.* Vancouver: UBC Press, 1997.

Winter, Jay M. *Remembering War: The Great War between History and Memory in the Twentieth Century.* New Haven, Conn.: Yale University Press, 2006.

————. *Sites of Memory, Sites of Mourning: The Great War in European Cultural History.* Cambridge: Cambridge University Press, 1995.

Witkop, Philipp, ed. *German Student's War Letters.* London: Methuen, 1929.

Wohl, Robert. *The Generation of 1914.* London: Weidenfeld and Nicolson, 1980.

INDEX

Afflerbach, Holger, xii, 12, 13, 16, 61–90, 195
Agadir crisis (1911), 40
Agincourt, battle of, 5
Alanbrooke, Field Marshal, 83
Alexander, Brian, xiii
Allied intervention in Russia (1919–1921), 121, 133, 134
American entry into the war, German attitude toward, 87, 88
American Expeditionary Force, in Great War, 70, 71, 77, 78, 114, 124; and in occupation of Germany, 121, 122
Amiens, battle of (1918), 85
Angell, Norman, 45
Armenia, failure of United States to accept League of Nations Mandate for, 143, 144
Armistice Day, 41
Aron, Raymond, 5
Asquith, H. H., 47, 64, 65, 186
Ataturk, Mustafa Kemal, 7
Atrocities, German in 1914, 13, 92
Audoin-Rouzeau, Stéphane, 9
Australia, effect of Great War on, 59
Australian War Memorial, 3
Aviation, history of, 15

Balfour Declaration (1917), 144, 145
Balkan wars (1912–1913), 40, 187

Barker, Pat, 113
Barnett, Corelli, 116
Becker, Annette, 9
Becker, Jean-Jacques, 9
Belgium, vii, 13, 62
Berkheiser, Steve, xiii
Bethmann-Hollweg, Theobald, 11, 66, 87
Blair, Tony, 119, 174
Bloch, Ivan, 45
Blockade of Germany, after the Armistice of 1918, 79, 80
Blunden, Edmund, 173, 198
Borah, Senator William E., 143
Brandegee, Senator Frank Bosworth, 156
Brest-Litovsk, Treaty of (1918), 93, 150, 151
British Broadcasting Company (BBC), 2
British election of 1919, 81
Brittain, Vera, 167
Brockdorff-Rantzau, Ulrich Graf von, 80
Brooke, Rupert, 101
Bryce, James, 144

Cabinet of Dr. Caligari, The, 177, 180; reflection of shell shock in, 177
Cadorana, General Luigi, 106
Caen, battle of (1944), 71
Cambrai, battle of (1917), 65, 85
Caporetto, battle of (1917), 70, 94, 106, 109, 115

Carnegie Endowment for International Peace, 2
Cenotaph (London), 172, 179
Chamberlain, Joseph, 50
Chamberlain, Neville, 181; appeasement as response to Great War, 181
Charteris, General John, 68
Chemin des Dames, battle of (1917), 14, 67, 93, 94
China, disappointment over failure of Allies to return Shandong province to in 1919, 153
Chinese Communist party, 8, 133
Churchill, Sir Winston, 47, 48, 50, 51, 53, 67, 75, 76, 78, 85, 124, 133, 142, 186; and Bolshevism, 142, 157
Civil-military relations, in Great War, 62, 63, 64, 65, 66, 82, 83
Civil War (U.S.), vii, 44, 84, 103
Clausewitz, Carl von, 45
Clemenceau, Georges, 131, 133, 139, 140
Commemoration, vii, 7, 16, 160, 171, 172; as reflection of civil society, 160, 172, 173
Congress of Vienna, parallels to peace negotiations in 1919, 126, 154
Consent or coercion, debate on with respect to soldiers' morale, 96, 97, 98, 99, 100, 105, 109, 111, 112, 121
Cooper, John Milton, xii, 14, 15, 16, 123–58
Counterfactual history, 48, 49
Cowling, Maurice, 50
Currie, General Sir Arthur William, 84
Czech Legion, 116

Decolonization, effect of Great War on, 3, 7, 59
Defeat of Germany in 1918, causes of, 87
De Gaulle, Charles, 98
Devine, Michael, xiii
Dower, John, 131
Drieu La Rochelle, Pierre, 168, 169
Du Bois, W. E. B., 128, 129

Eksteins, Modris, 175
Endurance, determinants of among soldiers, 118

Etaples, British riot at in 1917, 94
European Union, 6
Executions, of soldiers on active service during the Great War, 119, 120

Falkenhayn, Erich von, 12, 63, 66, 82, 195
Ferguson, John, 41
Ferguson, Niall, xii, 11, 12, 14, 16, 33–60, 73, 89, 187, 190
"Fifty years' war," theory of, 57
Fischer, Fritz, 11, 190
Foch, Marshal Ferdinand, 79, 155
Franco-Prussian War (1870–1871), 92, 131; reparations paid by France after, 131
Franz Ferdinand, Archduke, 37
Freikorps, 6
French, Sir John, 83
French Communist party, 15, 163
Fussell, Paul, ix, 5, 6, 15, 16, 162, 163, 164, 165, 166, 168, 170, 171, 174, 181, 184; and interpretation of "modern memory," 164ff

Gallipoli, 4, 59, 67, 72, 76, 83
Gance, Abel, 175–76; J'accuse! (1919), 176, 178; J'accuse! (1937), 176–77
George V, 65
German revolution (1918), 100
Gettysburg, battle of, 68
Glasgow, 40, 185
Glasgow Academy, 41
Gorlice-Tarnow, battle of (1915), 69, 70
Graves, Robert, viii, 180, 181
Grey, Sir Edward, 47, 49, 52, 53
Groener, Erich, 82

Hackney, 8
Haig, Sir Douglas, viii, ix, 12, 64, 65, 66, 67, 68, 78, 83, 85, 89, 195
Haldane, R. B., 63
Hamburg, fire bombing of in Second World War, 80
Hankey, Maurice, 85, 197
Harris, Sir Arthur, 80
Harry S. Truman Presidential Library and Museum, xiii, xiv, 103, 122, 159
Heller, Joseph, 167

Hemingway, Ernest, 115
Higham, John, 124
Hindenburg, Paul von, 82
Historial de la grande guerre, Péronne, Somme, 9
History, official, viii; transnational, 189ff
Hitler, Adolf, 130
Ho Chi Minh, 128
Horne, John, xii, 13, 14, 16, 91–122
Hunter-Weston, General Sir Aylmer, 83, 84
Hynes, Samuel, 172

Imperial (Commonwealth) War Graves Commission, vii, viii
Imperial War Museum, 3, 139
Invasion of Germany (1918–1919), Allied decision against, 76, 124, 125, 142
Iraq War (2003–), 119
Italian front, in the Great War, 69, 70, 100, 106, 115

J'accuse! (1919), 176, 178
J'accuse! (1937), 176–77
Jacob, General Claude, 85
Japan, effect of Great War on great power status, 151, 152, 153
Jekyll, Gertrude, viii
Joffre, Marshal J. J. C., 197
Johnson, Senator Hiram, 143, 156
Joll, James, 52, 92
Jünger, Ernst, 93, 102, 168, 169, 171, 173

Kandinsky, Wassily, 16
Kansas City, Missouri, xii, 1, 34, 160, 172; Public Library, xiii, xiv, 159
Keegan, Sir John, vii–x, 5, 6, 184
Kemper, R. Crosby, xiii, 159, 172, 181
Kennedy, David, 148
Kennedy, Paul, xii, 10, 12, 14, 16, 33–60, 73, 190
Keynes, John Maynard, 151
Kipling, Rudyard, viii
Kitchener, Lord H. H., 65
Korean War, 42, 57
Kramer, Alan, 13, 92

Krumeich, Gerd, 9
Kun, Béla, 116

La Follette, Senator Robert, 143
Larkin, Philip, 4
"Last hundred days," British offensive during (1918), 70
Lawrence, T. E., 145, 181, 182, 183; multiple identities, 182; traumatic memories of war, 182, 183
League of Nations, 125, 129; Mandate system of, 129
Learning curve, theory of, ix, 12, 62, 69
Leed, Eric, 5, 6
Lenin, V. I., as only successful anti-war leader, 158
Liberal party (British), 47, 185
Liberty Memorial (Kansas City, Missouri), xiii, 172, 179; Liberty Memorial Association, xiii
Lin, Maya, 173; Vietnam Veterans' Memorial, 173
Lippmann, Walter, 125
Livingstone, Thomas, 185, 186, 187, 188
Lloyd George, David, 8, 14, 64, 65, 66, 67, 80, 85, 128, 133, 138, 139, 140, 144, 157, 185, 186
Lodge, Henry Cabot, 128, 144, 146
Loos, battle of (1915), 166
Ludendorff, Eric, 12, 13, 67, 81, 82, 86, 99
Lutyens, Sir Edwin, viii, 173, 179
Lyncker, General Moriz von, 73

MacArthur, General Douglas, 89
MacMillan, Margaret, xii, 14, 15, 16, 123–58, 189, 190, 191
Maier, Charles, 157
Malraux, André, 168
Manela, Erez, 7, 128
March 1918 offensive, by German army, 76, 86, 94
Marne, battle of (1914), 67, 72
Maurice, Sir Frederick, 64
Mearsheimer, John, 38
Meinertzhagen, Richard, 187, 188
Meuse-Argonne offensive (1918), 71
Modernism, impact of Great War on dissemination of, 175

Moltke, Helmut von, 54, 82
Monash, General Sir John, 84, 85, 86
Montgomery, Field Marshal B. L., 83
Morale, soldiers', 92, 111; and theory of
    consent, 95, 106, 107, 111
Mutiny, sources of, 92, 94, 95, 108;
    French (1917), 14, 92, 93, 94, 95, 108;
    German sailors' (1918), 94; Russian
    army mutinies (1917), 108, 115, 116;
    "silent mutiny" of German army in
    1918, 94, 109

National Army Museum (London), 166
National World War I Museum at Lib-
    erty Memorial, Kansas City, Missouri,
    xii, xiii, xiv, 17, 34, 40, 74, 103, 159,
    161
Nivelle, Robert, 14, 67, 93
Normandy, battle of (1944), 69, 70, 71

Orlando, Vittorio, 8, 136
Orpen, Sir William, 140
Ortega y Gasset, José, 168
Owen, Wilfred, 101

Pacific war (1941–1945), 69
Palestine, British breakthrough in (1918),
    70
Pan-African Congress (1919), 129
Pardon, posthumous, given to men ex-
    ecuted during Great War, 119, 120
Paris Commune (1871), 84
Passchendaele, battle of (1917), 65, 67, 85
Patton, General George, 113
Peace offers, made by Germany during
    Great War, 73, 74
Pershing, General J. J., 71, 77
Pétain, General Philippe, 94
Picasso, Pablo, 16, 174, 178, 179; camou-
    flage as cubism, 178, 179; cubist masks
    made for ballet Parade, 174; Guernica
    (1937), 174
Plumer, General Sir Herbert, 84, 85
Princip, Gavrilo, 37
Prior, Robin, 62
Proportionality, theory of soldiers' be-
    havior in battle, 92, 115
Public history, 35

Rawlinson, General Sir Henry, 85
Reed, Senator James A., 143
Refugees, 9
Remarque, Erich Maria, 102, 165, 191
Robert, Jean-Louis, 192
Robertson, General "Wully," 64, 65
Roosevelt, Theodore, 14, 150
Rumania, conquest of in 1916, 70
Rupprecht, Crown Prince of Bavaria, 82
Russian civil war (1918–1921), 116
Russian Revolution (1917), effect of on
    Great War, 75, 76, 93, 100, 116; Allied
    fear of spread of, 156, 157

Sachs, Jeffrey, 42
Salisbury, Lord (Robert Cecil), 50
Salonika, Allied breakthrough at (1918),
    70
Sassoon, Siegfried, viii, 181
Scheer, Admiral Reinhard, 81
Schlieffen plan, 45, 90
Schroeder, Paul, 39
Scott, C. P., 185, 186, 187
Seaforth Highlanders, 41
Second World War, vii, 4
Self-determination, 126, 127, 128, 132;
    commitment to of League of Nations,
    126; demand for during peace confer-
    ence of 1919, 127, 128
September program, statement of Ger-
    man war aims (1914), 49, 73
Serbia, conquest of in 1915, 70
Sergeant, John Singer, 139
Shackleton, Sir Ernest, 187
Shandong province, of China, 8
Sheehan, James, 6
Sheffield, Gary, ix, 12, 13, 16, 61–90, 195
Shell shock, in Great War, 110, 112, 113,
    119, 120, 177, 178, 182, 183; as form
    of refusal, 110; as reason for posthu-
    mous pardons of men executed, 119,
    120; treatment of, 112
Smith, Leonard, xii, 13, 14, 16, 91–126
Smuts, General Jan Christiaan, 85
Soldiers' memoirs, 100, 101, 103, 114,
    115, 116, 117, 164, 165
Somme, battle of (1916), 5, 50, 62, 67,
    68, 72, 104, 166

Spiritualism, efflorescence of during and after the Great War, 177
"Stab in the back" legend, 76
Stalingrad, battle of, 5, 104
Stanley, Venetia, 186
Stern, Fritz, 171
Strachan, Hew, 185–98
Stresemann, Gustav, 143
Submarine warfare, 76, 88

Tactics, on the Western front, ix
Taylor, A. J. P., 157
Terraine, John, viii
"Thirty Years' War," second, theory of, 124
Thompson, George, xiii
Total war, 1914–1918 conflict as, 66, 79, 80, 97, 196
Treaties of Peace (1919–1923), 7, 10, 77, 129, 130ff, 131; and Middle East, 131, 132; war guilt clause, 231; in Treaty of Versailles, 10, 15
Truman, Harry S., 58, 89, 110
Tuchman, Barbara, 45
Turner, Victor, 6

United States Senate, rejection of Versailles Treaty by, 137–38

Valéry, Paul, 170
Verdun, battle of, 5, 62, 68, 72

Vietnam Veterans Memorial, Washington, 173
Vietnam War, 4, 42, 173; as stimulus to Great War scholarship, 161, 164

Waltz, Kenneth, 38
War cemeteries, vii, viii
"War culture," theory of, 95, 109
War films, as misleading introduction to Great War, 117
War museums, 9, 34, 40
War origins, xii, 10, 33–60
Warburg, Max, 54
Waterloo, battle of, 5, 68
Weber, Max, 82
Weizmann, Chaim, 144–45
Wilhelm II, 54, 73, 80, 94
Wilson, Sir Henry, 64, 85
Wilson, Woodrow, 8, 14, 15, 80, 82, 121, 125, 127, 128, 129, 134, 135, 138, 140, 141, 146, 147, 148, 153, 155, 156; and Bolshevism, 140, 141; medical condition of in 1919, 135–37
Wohl, Robert, xii, 15, 159–85, 191
Woolf, Virginia, 178; presentation of shell shock in Mrs. Dalloway, 178

Zimmermann telegram (1917), 74, 75

ABOUT THE EDITOR

JAY WINTER is Professor of History at Yale University and author or editor of many books, the most recent being *Remembering War: The Great War Between Memory and History in the Twentieth Century.* He lives in Guilford, Connecticut.